Japanese women working

Japanese women working

Edited by
Janet Hunter

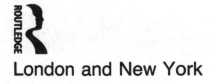

London and New York

First published 1993
by Routledge
11 New Fetter Lane, London EC4P 4EE

Simultaneously published in the USA and Canada
by Routledge
29 West 35th Street, New York, NY 10001

© 1993 J. Hunter

Phototypeset by Intype, London
Printed and bound in Great Britain by Mackays of Chatham PLC,
Chatham, Kent.

British Library Cataloguing in Publication Data
A catalogue record for this book is available from the British Library

ISBN 0–415–06188–1

Library of Congress Cataloging in Publication Data
Japanese women working / edited by Janet Hunter.
    p.   cm.
    Includes bibliographical references and index.
    ISBN 0–415–06188–1
    1. Women—Employment—Japan—History—20th century.
I. Hunter, Janet.
    HD6197.J355   1993
    331.4'0952—dc20   92—26228
                                                          CIP

Contents

Figures

Tables

Contributors

Joy Hendry is Reader at the Scottish Centre for Japanese Studies, University of Stirling, and Principal Lecturer in Social Anthropology at Oxford Polytechnic. Based on research in rural, provincial and urban areas of Japan, she has published *Marriage in Changing Japan* (1981), *Becoming Japanese* (1986) and *Understanding Japanese Society* (1987).

Janet Hunter is Senior Lecturer and Saji Research Lecturer in Japanese Economic and Social History at the London School of Economics and Political Science. She is the author of *Concise Dictionary of Modern Japanese History* (1984), *The Emergence of Modern Japan: an Introductory History since 1853* (1989), and a number of articles on the economic and social development of modern Japan. She is currently working on a book on female textile workers and the labour market in the pre-war years.

Alice Lam took her doctorate at the London School of Economics and is currently Lecturer in Organizational Behaviour and Management at Manchester Business School, University of Manchester. She is the author of *Women and Japanese Management: Discrimination and Reform* (1992), and has written on various aspects of human resource management.

D. P. Martinez did her first degree at the University of Chicago and her postgraduate work in social anthropology at Oxford University. Her thesis on the *ama* was completed in 1988. She is currently Lecturer in Anthropology with special reference to Japan at the School of Oriental and African Studies, University of London. Among her recent publications are 'Tourism and the *ama*:

the search for a real Japan', in E. Ben-Ari *et al.* (eds) *Unwrapping Japan* (1990), and 'The dead: Shinto aspects of Buddhist ritual', *Journal of the Anthropological Society of Oxford* (1991).

Regine Mathias studied at Bochum, Fukuoka and Vienna universities, and has taught at Bonn University. She is now Professor of Modern History and Culture of Japan at the University-Gesamthochschule Duisburg. She has published widely on the development of coal-mining in Japan, and is currently working on the rise of the new middle class in Japan, especially the appearance of white-collar women workers.

Barbara Molony is Associate Professor of History at Santa Clara University, California. She is author of several scholarly articles on economic, business and work history, the 'Introduction' and 'Afterword' to *Facing Two Ways: The Story of My Life* by Baroness Shidzue Ishimoto (1984), *Technology and Investment: The Prewar Japanese Chemical Industry* (1990), and, with Kathleen Molony, *Ichikawa Fusae: A Political Biography* (forthcoming).

Kōnosuke Odaka is Professor of Economics at the Institute of Economic Research, Hitotsubashi University. He has written extensively in both Japanese and English on various aspects of the development of the Japanese economy, and contributed to the recent Iwanami Shoten series, *Nihon Keizai Shi*.

Eiko Shinotsuka is Associate Professor of Economics at Ochanomizu University, Tokyo, and currently serves as a member of government advisory committees on national life and employment policy. She has written widely in both Japanese and English on various aspects of labour economics, econometrics and gender issues. Her publications include *Nihon no Joshi Rōdō* (1982), 'Employment adjustment in Japanese manufacturing' (1987) and *Nihon no Koyō Chōei – Oil Shock ikō no Rōdō Ijō* (1989).

Kathleen Uno, Assistant Professor of History at Temple University, Philadelphia, has previously published works on the history of women and child care in modern and post-war Japan, including 'Women and changes in the household division of labour', in G. L. Bernstein (ed.) *Recreating Japanese Women, 1600–1945* (1991) and 'The death of "good wife, wise mother"?', in A. Gordon (ed.)

Postwar Japan as History (1992). At present she is completing *Childhood, Motherhood and State in Early Twentieth Century Japan*, and doing research for a new work on the history of child care in Japan.

Preface

Editing and producing a volume of essays of this kind invariably takes more time and effort than the editor initially anticipates. I would like to express my gratitude to Peter Sowden of Routledge, who in the first place broached the possibility of a book of papers on Japanese women workers, and who has shown considerable encouragement and patience in waiting for the manuscript. Thanks are also due to the participating scholars, who agreed to submit papers for a volume which is not associated with any conference or symposium, and who had little opportunity for mutual exchange of information or ideas. In the light of this, they are all to be thanked for their hard work in producing a set of papers which have so many issues in common, and, in some cases, for showing confidence in an editor they had yet to meet.

Janet Hunter
London School of Economics

Please note that Japanese words are transcribed according to the standard modified Hepburn romanization. Japanese names are given in the normal Japanese order, with the family name preceding the given name.

Chapter 1

Introduction

Janet Hunter

In Japan, as elsewhere, patterns and conditions of work in both the pre-industrial and industrial economies have become differentiated by gender. The reasons for this are ideological, political, economic and social, or, more accurately, a complex interaction of all of these. For much of the twentieth century, in almost all countries, this differentiation was taken for granted. That women invariably earned lower wages than men, had less bargaining power in the labour market and only ventured outside the domestic sphere because of economic necessity, tended to be taken as axiomatic. Few asked why. In the early twentieth century a small, very exceptional group of writers began to question these assumptions by looking in more detail at the past and contemporary experiences of working women. In the case of England, for example, there are the pioneering works of writers such as Clementina Black (1915), Alice Clarke (1919), Vera Brittain (1928) and Ivy Pinchbeck (1930), but many aspects of women's work remained unstudied. Following the appearance of pioneering theoretical and empirical works in the 1960s and 1970s, more attention began to be paid to contemporary issues of women's work. Some of its neglected history began to be resurrected as scholars started to look further back, in an attempt to see how women's economic position had changed over time, especially in response to the industrialization process. A partial integration of gender issues into theories of development followed, though there is still a long way to go. Sadly, gender studies – too often, but understandably, identified with women's studies – remains a largely female area of research. It is regrettable, though unsurprising, that this volume has only one male contributor, while another recent compilation, *Recreating Japanese Women*, edited by Gail Lee Bernstein, can also boast only one out of a total of thirteen. This has not, however, totally prevented a wider recognition of the importance of women in the economy, which has led in turn to substantial reappraisal of how economies operated in the past, and how they may develop in the future.

In Japan, too, women's work has moved away from being considered exclusively as a women's issue. It is now widely recognized that an understanding of the factors influencing female labour force participation and the way in which women's involvement in economic activity has evolved is a crucial element in understanding the dramatic transformation of Japanese economy and society in general. Female labour force participation is a crucial question for contemporary Japanese economic policy makers, and will remain so into the twenty-first century, particularly in the light of labour shortages and the rapidly ageing population. The role of women in Japan, and their position in the work-force, is thus a key issue for all those concerned with the past and future development of a country which is now one of the world's economic superpowers.

In some ways Japan's working women have been neglected less than those in some other countries, particularly as far as the modern period covered in this book is concerned. Almost any Japanese of the twentieth century is likely to be aware that Japan's early industrialization was spearheaded by textile industries worked overwhelmingly by young female workers. With agriculture of continuing significance, and with more women than men working in the sector from the 1930s, the work of agricultural women has been often highlighted in surveys and in government policy. Some particular groups, such as divers and geisha, gained some attention for their reputedly high status, religious significance or notorious behaviour, or because for some reason they attracted the attention of westerners. Female labour assumed considerable importance in the Japanese capitalism debate, as shown, for example, in the writings of Yamada Moritarō (1934). By categorizing the earnings of the young female workers in the early textile mills as *kakei hojoteki* (supplementary to the household income), Yamada identified the 'premodern' agricultural household as a basis of Japanese capitalism, and at the same time called attention to one of the most critical issues of all discussions relating to women's position in the workplace.

Yet the attention given to these women workers has been extremely patchy. Moreover, it has often been of a kind to distort any broader, more balanced picture. Female textile workers, for example, have been constantly cited as examples of the iniquitous exploitation resulting from the capitalist system. Women workers on family farms, performing what was essentially considered part of their domestic duties, were only doing what was expected of them. If the state was concerned about them, it was often because it feared that they were unable to bear healthy children, or were less able to contribute to the national good through efficient use of labour. For protagonists in the Japanese capitalism debate, women were important in the production and reproduction processes, but these writers' perspectives were far from revising the understanding of Japanese development in the direction of more 'woman-centred' historical interpretations. The study of women's work in Japan, therefore, has suffered from a different kind of neglect. It is all the more disadvantaged, perhaps, because of the strong ideology of domesticity which has prevailed in the country for much of the twentieth century, and continues to prevail. The works of pioneering writers like Takamure (1954–8), Sanpei (1936; 1948; 1957; 1961) and Shimazu (1953) – again, all of them women – broke new ground but were slow to find successors among the next generation of scholars.

To explore further the position of women in the Japanese economy has not been easy for Japanese academics. Some disciplines have proved more encouraging than others to a move in this direction, which has been strongly dependent on the committed lone scholar to lead the way. In general, entrenched academic attitudes and social conservatism have contributed to the subject's being categorized as 'peripheral'. Nevertheless, over the past two decades major theoretical and empirical works have appeared in economics, history, political theory, sociology and other fields. In history, for example, major compilations of source material, such as *Nihon Fujin Mondai Shiryō Shūsei* (Collected Materials on the Women's Problem in Japan) (Domesu Shuppan 1976–81), have made it easier to study the position of Japanese women without engaging in primary research. Bibliographical guides such as *Nihon Joseishi Kenkyū Bunken Mokuroku* (Bibliography of Research on the History of Japanese Women) (Joseishi Sōgō Kenkyūkai 1988) have revealed the wealth of materials which can be used by researchers wanting to explore the subject further. Substantial compilations of authoritative articles include the multi-volume *Nihon Joseishi* (History of Japanese Women) (Joseishi Sōgō Kenkyūkai 1982) and

Nihon Josei Seikatsu-shi (History of the Life of Japanese Women)
(Joseishi Sōgō Kenkyūkai 1990). The compilations have sought to
remedy the long-standing gender bias in historical interpretation,
and arouse interest in the activities and lives of Japanese women,
many of which have not been the subject of conventional historiography.

While there is evidence that in studies of both the past and the
present scholars are moving away from the study exclusively of
women's work to look at the totality of women's lives, the study
of work has continued to play a pivotal part in studies of women.
As in many other economies, it has been widely assumed in Japan
that achievement of equality in the workplace is essential if women
are individually and collectively to attain to economic independence and self-respect. It is not possible here to discuss in any
detail the various lines of argument which Japanese scholars have
taken on this subject. The substantial literature on the Tokugawa
period (1600–1867) alone raises complex issues and fierce debate,
and the situation is multiplied for the post-Meiji years. Nevertheless, two particular strands in the debate are worthy of mention
here. One is the locating of the study of women's work in the
context of the patriarchal *ie* (family) system of Japan, which has
led many writers to argue that any change in women's earnings,
or in women's position in the workplace or labour force, requires
a fundamental change in that patriarchal family system (for
example, Takenaka 1989, 1991; Ueno 1985, 1990). The other is
the contribution of economists, whose analysis of women's work
ascribes current features to factors such as segmentation of the
labour market (for example, Shinotsuka 1982). These perspectives,
and many others, have been expressed in a considerable literature
of books and articles, scholarly and popular.

So far little of this Japanese writing on women's work has
made its way into English. These important contributions are
therefore largely inaccessible to non-Japanese speakers. Their non-
availability makes it proportionately more difficult to incorporate
Japan as an element in comparative history, economics or gender
studies – a major gap, given the importance of modern Japan.
The lacuna is being filled, at least in part, by works in English
by western scholars, particularly those from the United States.
The scholarship of many of these writers not only draws on
Japanese language materials, but is increasingly informed by a
knowledge of western theoretical and empirical studies on gender

issues. Not all, of course, concern the position of women in the economy, but many have some bearing on it. Earlier works such as those of Lebra, Paulson and Powers (1976), T. S. Lebra (1984) and Sievers (1983) have much which concerns women's work. The papers in the above-mentioned *Recreating Japanese Women* (Bernstein 1991) contain major contributions to this area of research. Important monographs in which the working life plays a focal part have been published by writers such as Kidd (1978); Cook and Hayashi (1980); R. J. Smith and Wiswell (1982); Bernstein (1983); Tsurumi (1990); Saso (1990); Kondo (1990); and Lo (1990). Works in other western languages include that by Lenz (1984). Several of the contributors to this volume have books in press, and others are in preparation. A succession of important articles have appeared. The high quality of many of these books and articles, as well as their number, are making it easier to bring a critical area of Japanese economic development and activity to the attention of non-specialists.

It remains the case, though, that the sum contribution is inadequate. An important aim of the present collection is therefore to add to the literature, making it easier for more people to study and know about the past and present of women working in Japan. The papers are not limited to a single disciplinary approach. Women's work is a topic of shared interest for economists, historians, sociologists, anthropologists and others, and this volume includes contributions from a variety of disciplinary perspectives as well as from a range of academic and geographical backgrounds. The inclusion of two historical papers by Japanese economists will, it is hoped, help to give some flavour of the research being undertaken there. The contributors are brought together in a search to understand some aspect of the interrelationship between women's role and position in the work-force, the growth and industrialization of the Japanese economy and the influence of state policy and social attitudes towards women. The volume is not, of course, an attempt to provide a comprehensive picture of the past and present of women's work in Japan, although it should give some pointers in that direction.

An understanding of the way in which women's involvement in economic activity has evolved over the last century is of enormous importance if we are to understand women's current position in the Japanese labour market, and their domestic role as housewives and mothers. For these reasons, and in order to emphasize the importance of longer-term historical perspectives, the papers in this volume appear in a broadly chronological order. In this context one factor in particular is of major significance in trying to understand what has happened to women's roles in the Japanese economy over the past century. Japan has moved within a relatively short space of time from being a non-developed, agrarian economy, to being a highly-developed, industrial one. Both before and since the Pacific War dramatic changes have taken place in the economy as a whole and in its discrete sectors. The rapid transformation of the Japanese economy over this period means that Japan has combined features of both developing and industrial economies, and that the experiences of women in the Japanese economy at least up to the 1960s may have important implications for the study for women in development.

The multidisciplinary approach contained in this volume has, if anything, highlighted the existence of common issues, notwithstanding the wide range of subject matter covered in the contributions. These themes are by no means new. Many of the issues which confront Japanese women operating in the labour market transcend national and cultural boundaries. The locational and institutional manifestations may be different, but the underlying issues suggest that when it comes to their position in the economy, Japanese women have much in common with women elsewhere.

In pre-industrial economies the distinction between 'work' and domestic responsibilities was rarely clear cut. In the predominantly agricultural Tokugawa Japan (1600–1867) the majority of women not only discharged domestic duties, but worked in the fields or performed other tasks associated with the family economy. The pursuit of by-employment (subsidiary or secondary occupation) by both women and men increased with the move away from subsistence, but only with the onset of industrialization in the late nineteenth century were increasing numbers of women compelled to consider work (in agriculture or elsewhere) and domestic duties as alternatives, rather than as parts of an integrated whole. Nor did this happen overnight. The papers here which deal with the pre-war period demonstrate that in various ways traditional forms of economic activity continued to influence women's work. Regine Mathias shows that, in Kyushu coal-mining, women's work in the industry only gradually lost its character of family/by-employment operation, a process which eventually undermined women's position in this particular occupation. This was accompanied by a shift away from indirect to direct forms of labour management, though in the case of the care assistants studied by Eiko Shinotsuka this intermediary activity has persisted. In another area, home-working, the apparent coexistence of paid work and domestic activities persisted, though Kathleen Uno's paper mounts a power-ful challenge to the idea that such homeworking was necessarily easier to combine with child care and other home responsibilities.

In the decision to enter the labour market, too, earlier modes of economic activity continued to play a major role. Kōnosuke Odaka's paper clarifies how in one major occupation, domestic service, working girls made choices based on labour supply con-ditions in the agricultural sector from which most of them came. The rural connection remained of the utmost importance not only in determining the decision of many women to enter the labour market, but their choice of employment within it, their duration of service and the conditions which they experienced there. The underlying importance of this connection, shown not only in Odaka's paper, but in those by Mathias, Shinotsuka and myself as well, serves to characterize the nature of Japan as a developing economy. Even where industrialization takes place rapidly, there is no instant appearance of a fully-fledged industrial or 'modern' labour force, and the economy must find means of accommodation between modern methods of production and management and distinctly 'unmodern' human capital and social practices. This is not to deny the arguments of historians such as T. C. Smith (1988), who has suggested convincingly that many Japanese men and women were better prepared for industrial values and methods than their counterparts in other countries, only to note that the transition to industrial society is never instant nor easy.

Once women have made a decision to enter the emerging labour market they have to cope with a quite different set of conditions from those encountered by men. As many of the papers in this volume show, the labour market itself is highly gendered, with sharp distinctions between 'men's jobs' and 'women's jobs', between male and female wage rates and working conditions. The maids, care assistants and textile workers who figure in this volume were pursuing what were widely thought of as 'women's work', while the formalization of such categories which accompanied the industrialization process helped to encourage a decline in women's participation in mining, considered by many as socially unsuitable work for women. Mathias notes that gender-related wage

differentials in mining increased with the progress of industrialization. Alice Lam's paper shows that such job segregation has
persisted, with women finding themselves predominantly outside
the formal job hierarchy and organizational structure. For much
of Japan's recent development, there have effectively existed two
separate labour markets, the rationale for whose existence is gender.
In post-war Japan the degree of labour market segmentation has,
if anything, become even greater, and Alice Lam's study of the
effectiveness of the 1985 Equal Employment Opportunity legislation shows just how difficult it is in the Japanese case to make
headway against such entrenched labour market segmentation.

Perceiving accurately the disadvantages which they face in
attempting to break down this gendered situation in the labour
market and compete with men, many Japanese women, economic
circumstances permitting, pursue an entirely rational course of
action and opt out of the unequal struggle altogether. The 'professional housewives' studied by Joy Hendry accept the logic of
their situation and maximize the advantages of it. For these
women, Hendry shows, domestic responsibilities are a genuine
labour market choice, entailing duties and rewards. Rewards may
be pecuniary. Having such a wife will liberate the husband to
maximize his career prospects and family earnings. They may be
less tangible returns; the work of the professional housewife serves
to enhance the present and future welfare of the household unit
concerned, a practice which Hendry sees as analogous to the
traditional Japanese concern with the welfare of the *ie* (house).
The result of this choice is that, in a society where social role is
a key determinant in individual or family status, these women
enjoy through their husband a high status, while working women,
particularly those needing to earn for financial reasons, may not
be so fortunate. The social cachet awarded by the possession of a
wife who does not go out to work is a familiar one. 'Idle' women
have long been an indicator of prosperity.

Despite the disadvantages women in general face in the labour
market, some groups in particular have been perceived as enjoying
a relatively high social status. Among these are the diving women
(*ama*) considered in D. P. Martinez's paper. Martinez finds that
in this case, however, the gulf between perceptions and reality is
considerable. *Ama* experience no higher status within their families
or in society than other Japanese women, while the work itself is
regarded as of low status, with only the most profitable tasks ever

undertaken by men. Both Martinez's paper and that of Hendry, show that the relationship between occupation, social status and economic well-being is neither clear cut nor universal. For Japanese women, moreover, it is invariably mediated by marital circumstances, rather than by occupation. Martinez also suggests that any assumption of congruence between modes of production and forms of social organization is often ill founded, and always difficult to prove.

While some women may respond to an inequitable position in the workplace by opting out, for many women labour force participation is either necessary or desirable, or both. As a result, very large numbers of women have been working in Japan throughout the modern period. In 1930 around 49 per cent of the female population aged fifteen or more was in work, and between the wars women comprised 35–40 per cent of the total labour force. The figures for 1990 are very similar: just over half of all adult women were working, and women comprised around 40 per cent of the Japanese work-force. In 1990 26 million women were working in Japan. In simple numerical terms, therefore, women workers would appear as a group to have long possessed the kind of economic power needed to bring about some change in their situation. In fact, activism and agitation figure rarely in this volume. Writers such as Tsurumi (1984; 1990), Molony (1991) and Gordon (1991) have shown that, even in the early stages of industrialization, women workers were far from being totally passive creatures. However, a combination of official suppression, economic weakness at the workplace, lack of organization and absence of male support and leadership, made it more difficult for them to oppose and change the gendered system. Conservative views of what was 'appropriate' were held by both women and men, while the economic imperatives of family survival invariably took precedence over fighting to the end against inequality at the workplace or in the labour market. Well into the post-war period, despite greater legal rights, Japanese working women failed to come together to fight for substantive change in the system, and Lam's comment on the 1980s is that there has continued to exist a low consciousness of issues of equality among Japanese women workers.

This is not to say there have not been movements for change. Both before the war, and since 1945, there have been pressures to modify the conditions of women workers, and legislative moves have resulted. The protective labour legislation of the first half of the twentieth century contained many provisions specifically targeted at women and minors. In modern Japan attitudes towards the physiology of reproduction served to emphasize women's inability to act in the labour market in an identical fashion to men. The physical involvement of women in pregnancy and childbirth affected the manner in which women were willing or able to discharge work responsibilities on a par with men, while the state, particularly in the pre-war period, placed a strong emphasis on concepts of motherhood and female domesticity. Together these factors raised even in the most conservative minds fears that physical damage inflicted on working women by inferior wages and working conditions could have major repercussions for Japanese economy and society as a whole. This is shown in my own paper on the tuberculosis question among Japanese textile workers. Under such circumstances, pressure for legislation, particularly from the state, could follow. Although positive, in terms of protecting women from some extreme forms of exploitation, such legislation also tended to reinforce the gendered character of work.

After the war the new constitution (1947) and new legislation such as the Labour Standards Law allotted women nominal equality in the workplace, and the equal opportunity legislation of 1985 discussed by Lam has already been referred to. Legal reform has not, however, achieved everything it has promised. Mathias comments how protective legislation relating to female coal-miners led to their being driven out of the industry or into its unprotected parts. Lam notes that the effectiveness of the 1985 legislation has been undermined by the widely-held concept in Japan of the law as a hortatory moral concept, rather than a set of rules to be imposed and enforced. Above all, the question of legislation aimed at enhancing women's working conditions, particularly protective legislation aimed specifically at women, raises a fundamental issue relating to the position of women in the workplace; that is, the question of the relationship between production and reproduction.

The availability, or absence of gendered provisions to protect women at work, is closely tied to the whole question of labour market segmentation. In Japan, those who have argued that the physical health of women should be protected, if only for the sake of their roles as mothers or future mothers, have frequently been those who have also contended that women are temporary, peripheral, uncommitted participants in the labour market; that they should be the first to be discharged at times of recession and rationalization; that their earnings are supplementary to the income of the main (male) breadwinner; and that they therefore merit less protection of their interests and less representation by organizations such as labour unions. That such views of women's work have been widespread in twentieth-century Japan is demonstrated in many of the papers in this volume. Some of the theoretical issues relating to the production-reproduction axis are discussed by Barbara Molony in her essay on *bosei hogo* (motherhood protection). This nebulous concept, which could be used on the one hand to deny workplace equality and on the other to facilitate mothers' employment, epitomizes the crucial tension between equality and difference in the case of early twentieth-century Japan. Molony's use of menstruation leave as a case study shows how very important physiological factors are in determining women's position in the workplace, and how factors associated with the reproduction function can assume a greater or lesser importance according to specific historical circumstances.

For most Japanese working women, consideration of such fundamental questions has been a luxury they have been unable or unwilling to afford. How working women attempt to achieve a balance between their domestic and work responsibilities, and how they allocate their time and their energies, are thus core features in many studies of women's work. These considerations figure not only in Molony's paper, but prominently in those by Mathias and Martinez, and by Uno, who shows how important it is to explore women's domestic experiences if their work situations are to be properly understood. A critical factor in this balancing, it becomes apparent, is time allocation. Women, like men, have at their disposal only twenty-four hours a day, and, likewise, need to undertake certain bodily functions such as sleeping and eating. Unlike men, though, they have in modern Japan invariably been expected to undertake women's 'two roles'. As Uno's paper shows, how they allocate their time between these two roles is critical to the degree of success with which they can discharge them. Contrary to expectations, she shows that this was not necessarily any less true of women engaged in homeworking than those working outside the home. Even where women were engaged in production at home, it was often dependent on the saving of time through the delegation of domestic responsibilities either to other family members, or by practices such as the purchase of pre-prepared foods

from outside. Time allocation has continued to be of major importance in the study of women's work. Hendry shows that by enabling
a husband to devote himself unstintingly to his work, the full-time
housewife subscribes to a gender-based role and time allocation.
This in turn helps to perpetuate a workplace system in which she
herself is even less willing to be involved. Hendry and Lam's
papers both confirm that a critical factor in women's advancement
in the workplace in Japan now and in the future is the degree to
which current *male* work practices are likely to change, particularly
where the length of working hours is concerned.

The worsening labour shortage of the Japanese economy of the
1990s would appear of itself to be a cogent argument for improving
Japanese women's working conditions, and for recognizing them
as long-term and committed members of the work-force. Many
women already fall into this category – length of service among
Shinotsuka's care assistants is growing, and research shows the
same is true of many part-time workers – but they rarely receive
the remuneration, training and rewards granted to their male
counterparts. Conservative attitudes towards women's work
remain strong in Japan among both men and women, and the
power of ideology and social convention is immense. State policy
towards women since the Meiji period (1868–1912) has sought to
promote a 'domestic' image of women; and while this dominant
theme has appeared in a variety of forms, it has never been
abandoned. If anything, contemporary concern over falling birth-
rates and population decline, combined with concerns over changes
taking place in social attitudes, threaten to stimulate a raft of
programmes to encourage women to become more, rather than
less focused on the domestic function. The success of any such
programme is, of course, a matter of debate. In this very contemporary question, though, economic rationale (the need for more
women in the labour force) would appear to be in direct conflict
with what many Japanese consider to be socially desirable. It
highlights a final crucial question relating to women's work,
namely, the interrelationship between ideological and economic
factors in determining women's position in the labour market and
in the workplace.

The cause and effect relationship of economic and ideological
forces in women's work cannot be explored here. The best theoretical work on women in the economy takes account of both perspectives, and the strong Marxist influence in much Japanese scholar-

ship, particularly in history, tends to ensure that this is so in the Japanese case. There is no doubt that participants in any labour market hold a range of views and prejudices which, together with economic imperatives, help to determine policies and structures. It is also the case that the same actors utilize widely-accepted ideological and social attitudes to justify policies which may have a specifically economic rationale. However, that economic motivations are of great significance can never be denied. Several of the papers here, notably those by Lam and Hendry, demonstrate the importance of economic imperatives in stimulating or impeding change in practices relating to women workers. That national economic imperatives have been significant in the past in determining the fate of women workers is suggested by the emphasis placed by contemporaries on the concept of national efficiency, discussed in Molony's paper, and in my own. What is clear is that in all three of state, business and individual considerations, a major role is played both by economic reasoning and by attitudes and prejudices. Where these coincide or are mutually supportive, they tend not to cause debate. Where they do not, compromising action has to be taken or change engineered. Odaka shows, for example, that higher wages had to be paid to women working in factories than to those in domestic service to compensate for what were generall·· considered to be less desirable working conditions. Acknowledgement of this interaction reinforces the fact that the monocausal explanation, and the monodisciplinary approach, are likely to be less than helpful if they fail to take into account other explanations and the approaches of other disciplines. It underlines the fact that the study of women working needs a multidisciplinary, indeed an interdisciplinary perspective, if it is to be genuinely advanced. Recent writing on Japanese women working has, for the most part, learnt this lesson well. It is to be hoped that the present volume will constitute a useful addition to this tradition.

NOTE

I would like to express my gratitude to Kaoru Sugihara of the School of Oriental and African Studies, University of London, for sharing with me some of his ideas on the Japanese literature relating to women and work. Being able to draw on his considerable knowledge helped to expand the scope of this introduction.

REFERENCES

Bernstein, Gail Lee (1983) *Haruko's World: a Japanese Farm Woman and her Community*, Stanford, CA, Stanford University Press.

Bernstein, Gail Lee (ed.) (1991) *Recreating Japanese Women, 1600–1945* Berkeley, CA, University of California Press.

Black, Clementina (1915, repr. 1983) *Married Women's Work*, London, Virago.

Brittain, Vera (1928) *Women's Work in Modern England*, London, Noel Douglas.

Clark, Alice (1919) *Working Life of Women in the Seventeenth Century*, London, Routledge.

Cook, Alice H. and Hayashi, Hiroko (1980) *Working Women in Japan: Discrimination, Resistance and Reform*, Ithaca, NY, New York State School of Labor and Industrial Relations, Cornell University.

Domesu Shuppan (various editors) (1976–81) *Nihon Fujin Mondai Shiryō Shūsei* 10 vols, Tokyo, Domesu Shuppan.

Gordon, Andrew (1991) *Labour and Imperial Democracy in Prewar Japan*, Berkeley, CA, University of California Press.

Joseishi Sōgō Kenkyūkai (ed.) (1982) *Nihon Joseishi* 5 vols, Tokyo, University of Tokyo Press.

Joseishi Sōgō Kenkyūkai (ed.) (1988) *Nihon Joseishi Kenkyū Bunken Mokuroku* 2 vols, Tokyo, University of Tokyo Press.

Joseishi Sōgō Kenkyūkai (ed.) (1990) *Nihon Josei Seikatsushi* 5 vols, Tokyo, University of Tokyo Press.

Kidd, Y. Aoki (1978) *Women Workers in the Japanese Cotton Mills: 1880–1920*, Ithaca, NY, Cornell University East Asia Papers 20.

Kondo, Dorinne K. (1990) *Crafting Selves: Power, Gender and Discourses of Identity in a Japanese Workforce*, Chicago and London, University of Chicago Press.

Lebra, J., Paulson, J. and Powers, E. (eds) (1976) *Women in Changing Japan*, Stanford, CA, Stanford University Press.

Lebra, T. S. (1984) *Japanese Women: Constraint and Fulfilment*, Honolulu, University of Hawaii Press.

Lenz, Ilse (1984) *Kapitalistische Entwicklung, Subsistenzproduktion und Frauenarbeit: der Fall Japan*, Frankfurt and New York, Campus Verlag.

Lo, Jeannie (1990) *Office Ladies, Factory Women: Life and Work at a Japanese Company*, Armonk, New York and London, Sharpe.

Molony, Barbara (1991) 'Activism among women in the Taishō cotton textile industry', in Bernstein (ed.) *Recreating Japanese Women, 1600–1945*, Berkeley, CA, Univeristy of California Press.

Pinchbeck, Ivy (1930) *Women Workers and the Industrial Revolution*, London, Routledge.

Sanpei, Kōko (1936) 'Meiji zenki ni okeru fujin oyobi yōnen rōdōsha no jōtai', *Rekishi Kagaku* 5 (11): 55–78.

Sanpei, Kōko (1948) 'Fujin rōdō ni kansuru shiryō kaisetsu', *Fujin no Seiki* 7 (October).

Sanpei, Kōko (1957) *Nihon no Josei*, Tokyo, Mainichi Library.

Sanpei, Kōko (1961) *Hataraku Josei no Rekishi*, Tokyo, Nihon Hyōronsha.

Saso, Mary (1990) *Women in the Japanese Workplace*, London, Hilary Shipman.

Shimazu, Chitose (1953) *Joshi Rōdōsha*, Tokyo, Iwanami Shoten.

Shinotsuka, Eiko (1982) *Nihon no Joshi Rōdō*, Tokyo, Tōyō Keizai Shinpōsha.

Sievers, Sharon (1983) *Flowers in Salt: the Beginnings of Feminist Consciousness in Modern Japan*, Stanford, CA, Stanford University Press.

Smith, R. J. and Wiswell, E. L. (1982) *The Women of Suye Mura*, Chicago, University of Chicago Press.

Smith, T. C. (1988) *Native Sources of Japanese Industrialization*, Berkeley, CA, University of California Press.

Takamure, Itsue (1954–8) *Josei no Rekishi* 3 vols, Tokyo, Kōdansha.

Takenaka, Emiko (1989) *Sengo Joshi Rōdō Shiron*, Tokyo, Yūhikaku.

Takenaka, Emiko (ed.) (1991) *Shin – Joshi Rōdō Ron*, Tokyo, Yūhikaku.

Tsurumi, E. Patricia (1984) 'Female textile workers and the failure of early trade unionism in Japan', *History Workshop Journal* 18 (autumn), 3–27.

Tsurumi, E. Patricia (1990) *Factory Girls: Women in the Thread Mills of Meiji Japan*, Princeton, NJ, Princeton University Press.

Ueno, Chizuko (1985) *Shihonsei to Kaji Rōdō*, Tokyo, Kaichōsha.

Ueno, Chizuko (1990) *Kafuchōsei to Shihonsei*, Tokyo, Iwanami Shoten.

Yamada, Moritarō (1934) *Nihon Shihonshugi Bunseki*, Tokyo, Iwanami Shoten.

Chapter 2

Redundancy utilized: the economics of female domestic servants in pre-war Japan[1]

Kōnosuke Odaka

I

The purpose of the present essay is to suggest an interpretation of the working of the female labour market in the early phases of Japanese industrialization (1880–1940), by focusing attention on the determination of wages and employment of female domestic servants.

As the principal vehicle of analysis I shall rely on historical statistics, such as population census figures, government wage statistics, private survey returns, and so on, as described in the Statistical Appendix at the end of the essay. Whereas this methodology provides one with hard materials with which to form an image of the female working life of the day, it obviously has certain limitations. Among other things, the 1880s are the earliest date one can possibly go back to with the help of such statistics.

In the following pages the term 'maid' will be used interchangeably with 'female domestic servant'. Strictly speaking, these two terms should be differentiated, the former referring to a person whose major responsibility is looking after the personal needs of her mistress, the latter to female domestic helpers in general. In the Japanese language, the term *jochū* signifies both meanings.

One notes in this context that in the Meiji era (1868–1912) the term *gejo* was commoner than *jochū*. The latter replaced the former during the Taisho period (1912–26), as *gejo* had the distinct connotation of being a subclass person. On the other hand, *kaseifu*, a variation of *jochū*, came to be used during the same period to represent a commuting household helper (charwoman), who carried out simple routine tasks such as cleaning and laundry.

In the present essay, all these titles, that is, *jochū*, *gejo* and *kaseifu*, are grouped together and referred to simply as maid, or female domestic servant.

II

It is well-documented knowledge that the textile industry formed a leading sector in the early phases of Japanese industrialization, and that its work-force was dominated by the female gender. This is evidenced by a 1909 central government survey of factories employing five or more operatives, which reported that the proportion of female operatives comprised no less than 85.2 per cent of production workers in the industry. By contrast, female production workers accounted for 34.5 per cent in food, 33.5 per cent in chemicals, 32.9 per cent in miscellaneous, and a tiny 2.0 per cent in machinery and metal manufacturing industries (Nōshōmushō 1910: 11–23).

The female textile workers, most of whom had been recruited from the rural sector, were characteristically young in age. According to a 1900 survey of eight large cotton-spinning mills in Osaka Prefecture, for instance, as much as 71.3 per cent of the total of 4,627 female operatives fell in the age bracket of 14 to 24 (Nōshō-mushō 1911/1947: 7). The percentage was even higher (77.2) in the case of weaving factories, which employed 63,701 female production workers in the same year (ibid.: 220–4).

Quite as striking as textile operatives in terms of their sheer absolute number, however, were female domestic servants, the majority of whom were also of rural origin. The 1920 and 1930 national population censuses report that the number of maids was 584,000 in 1920, comprising 1.04 per cent of the population (or one maid per nineteen households), and that the figure went up to 710,000 in 1930, embracing 1.10 per cent of the population (or one maid per seventeen households).[2] Not only did 'domestic servant' constitute one of the top four non-agricultural occupations which lured large numbers of women from the early 1900s to the late 1930s, but its size exceeded that of the female textile workers at the beginning of the twentieth century (see Table 2.1). In the 1910s and in the 1930s, on the other hand, the growth of textile employment overwhelmed all the other categories of non-agricultural occupations, although the relative share of textile employment was reduced somewhat in the 1930s with the growing importance of entertaining and/or personal services.

Table 2.1 The distribution of gainfully employed women, 1906–36 (%)

Industry	1906	1916	1926	1936
1. Agriculture and forestry	65.5	63.2	60.5	57.4
2. Fisheries and salt making	0.8	0.6	0.5	0.5
3. Mining and quarrying	0.4	0.6	0.5	0.2
4. Construction	0.1	0.1	0.1	0.2
5. Textile industry	6.4	7.8	8.8	8.9
6. Clothing industry	1.7	1.8	1.9	1.9
7. Wood and bamboo products	2.0	1.3	1.1	0.6
8. Food and beverage industry	1.2	1.4	1.8	0.9
9. Other mfg and utilities[a]	1.5	1.3	1.5	1.6
10. Commerce	9.9	10.5	7.5	7.3
11. Domestic service	7.7	7.9	5.2	8.0
12. Hotel, restaurant and others[b]	–	–	6.3	8.1
13. Other tertiary industry and nowhere else classified	2.8	3.5	4.4	4.2
14. Totals (actual figures in thousands)	100.0 (9,920)	100.0 (9,988)	100.1 (10,436)	99.8 (11,691)

Source: Adopted from Umemura et al. (1988): 201–14

Notes: (a) 'Utilities' refer to the supplies of gas, electricity and water.
(b) In 1906 and in 1916, hotel and restaurant employees were included in general commerce

Maids were also dominated by young girls. According to a questionnaire survey of maids in the metropolitan district of Tokyo in March-July 1930, 686 of the total of 834 respondents (or 82 per cent) were 24 years old or younger. The number went up to 738 (or 88 per cent) if one allowed for those aged between 25 and 29 (Shakai Rippō Kyōkai 1931: 15).[3] Turning to the corresponding national figure, the majority (86.5 per cent) of female domestic servants in the same year were aged 29 or below and their average age was 21.3 (Naikaku Tōkei Kyoku 1935: 174–5).[4]

Incidentally, the ratio of female to male domestic servants declined markedly in the 1910s and the 1920s: 15.1 in 1910, 8.3 in 1920, and 7.7 in 1930. Maids' wage rates correspondingly skyrocketed against their male counterparts' in the 1920s (Umemura et al. 1988: 207, 213; and Ohkawa et al. 1967: 245).

Figure 2.1 depicts changes over time in the relative size of the

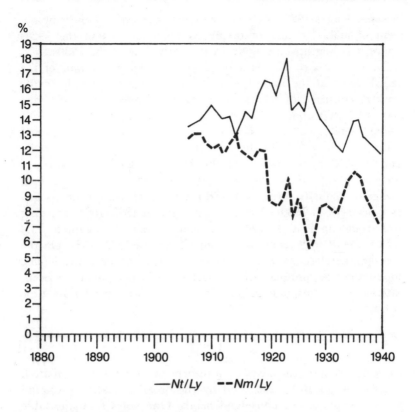

Figure 2.1 Employment ratios, 1906–40

two groups of non-primary female workers, maids (*Nm*) *and* female textile workers (*Nt*), both being measured against the young female population of ages 15 to 29 (*Ly*). The averages of the ratios in the years 1906 to 1940 are 0.099 and 0.142 respectively.

One notes in Figure 2.1 that the two ratios move in opposite directions until around 1930, after which they fall in a similar pattern. During those times when the Japanese textile industry, particularly cotton-spinning, was growing fast in its scale while its average labour productivity was more or less stagnant (say, 1894–1925), its employment expanded markedly *vis-à-vis* that of maids.[5] On the other hand, female employment in the textile mills displayed sizeable dips in the late 1920s and the early 1930s, corresponding to timely, upward shifts in their labour productivity, whereas the absolute number of female domestic servants began

to expand after 1927. As a consequence, the ratio of the employment of maids to that of textile workers declined in the 1920s
before it swung upward again in the early part of the 1930s.

On the basis of the data displayed in Figure 2.1 and of the
knowledge that the majority of the maids *and* the female textile
workers consisted of relatively young girls (aged 15 to 29), one
may infer that about a quarter $(0.099 + 0.142 = 0.241)$ of the
young, female population flowed into cities throughout the period
under consideration. On the other hand, the proportion of young
women in the age bracket in the entire female population was
fairly constant (about 25 per cent), although it displayed long
swings of about twenty years of duration, increasing from its low
23.4 per cent in 1880–89 to 25.7 per cent in 1895–1904, receding
to a trough in 1910–19 (24.5 per cent), and rising again to 25.8
per cent in 1930–9 (computed from Umemura 1988: 168). On the
average, therefore, as much as 6 to 7 per cent of the entire female
population was continuously earmarked, as it were, for these occupations, while their allocation between the two varied from time
to time.

III

Table 2.2 reports the average numbers of maids per population
(maid ratio, or B/A), classified by the broad industrial grouping
of the occupations of household heads. One notes from the table
that (a) families engaged either in trading or in professional services were more inclined to hire female domestic servants, and
that (b) a metropolitan district such as Tokyo had an understandably higher dependency on maid services even in the early days
of industry's coming of age.

The case of mining in this table deserves special attention for
its remarkably high maid ratio in 1908–10. One recalls that the
mining industry was the leading, prosperous sector of the economy
then, and that its head offices were located mostly in the city of
Tokyo. In 1910 mining recorded the highest net value-added per
employment (681 yen) of all the two-digit industrial groups,
whereas the corresponding figures for manufacturing and the
national average were 286 and 278 yen, respectively. The mining
industry's supremacy over manufacturing in this sense was not
overtaken by the latter until as late as 1939, when their respective
per capita net products were 1,076 yen and 1,112 yen.[6]

Table 2.2 Total number of household members (A) and number of female domestic servants (B)
(A and B in thousands, and B/A in permillage)

Industry code	1908/10 Greater Tokyo			1920 Whole nation			1930 Whole nation		
	A	B	B/A	A	B	B/A	A	B	B/A
Agr	379.6	2.6	6.8	28,416.5	147.1	5.2	28,012	101	3.6
Mng	20.0	1.1	55.0	867.4	6.3	7.3	659	1	1.5
Mfg	650.6	10.2	15.7	8,673.7	89.2	10.3	7,670	98	12.8
Cst	143.9	1.5	10.4	1,798.9	8.8	4.9	1,881	14	7.4
Fct	210.1	2.1	10.0	2,753.2	18.5	6.7	2,580	20	7.8
Cmc	597.0	27.3	45.7	7,141.6	163.5	22.9	8,993	226	25.1
Svc	259.6	16.4	63.2	4,238.5	88.3	20.8	3,941	134	34.0
Oth	133.1	8.5	63.9	1,438.3	51.6	35.9	2,566	74	28.8
Total	2,393.9	69.7	29.1	55,328.2	573.3	10.4	56,302	668	11.9

Sources: Umemura (1988), Tables 25, 26 and 29, and Naikaku Tōkei Kyoku (1932), Table 25

Notes: 1 Servants and house tenants are not counted in 'household members'.
2 The total numbers of maids in 1920 and in 1930 reported in this table differ from those referred to in the text and also data at the end of the essay. The discrepancy in the case of the 1920 census was probably due to yet unidentified technical reasons in occupational classification. The statistics for 1930 in this table, on the other hand, are based on a randomly-selected sample.
3 Industry codes:
   Agr = agriculture, dairy, forestry and fishery
   Mng = mining
   Mfg = manufacturing
   Cst = construction
   Fct = facilitating (i.e., gas, electricity, water supply, transportation and communication)
   Cmc = commerce
   Svc = government and professional services
   Oth = others, rentiers, and those with no occupation

One can uncover little, in terms of hard statistics, concerning the social and working conditions of female domestic servants. However, according to the aforementioned, private survey return on maids in Tokyo in 1930, not only had 776 of its respondents (93 per cent) completed primary school education, but as many as ninety of them (12 per cent) had been exposed to education at junior-high school level or above. Surprisingly, the median duration of their service was as short as 1.1 years. As many as 391 of the maids replied that they had no holiday privileges, although this may be due partly to their relatively short length of service. The median size of the maid's quarter was 2.41 *jō*, or approximately four square metres per person. Finally, the median size of the household where the respondents were employed was considerably larger (7.7 persons) than the corresponding national average in 1930 (5.2 persons), and the median number of maids per household was 1.5 (Shakai Rippō Kyōkai 1931: 15–20).

IV

The pecuniary compensation of domestic servants was by no means great, even after adding to the reported wages the estimated costs of room and board.[7] Whereas their money wage (Wm) increased, at first slowly and quite rapidly in the 1910s until it reached its pre-Second World War peak in 1924 (as reported in the Statistical Appendix), its level was below that in agriculture (Wa) and in the textile industry (Wt) except for the 1890s and the first half of the 1930s (see Figure 2.2).

In 1885–1900 maids enjoyed stronger earning power compared to female agricultural labourers, either because the former were in excess demand, or employment opportunities in the primary sector were relatively scarce, or both. But the relative value of domestic servants against that of agricultural labour kept deteriorating until the very end of the 1920s: a phenomenon which must have reflected, at least partially, improvements in the physical labour productivity of farming (Yamada and Hayami 1979). The technological advance in agriculture finally reached a plateau in 1930, by which time the growth of demand for agricultural products had become retarded due to the post-First World War depressions and the importation of rice from Korea. On the other hand, the intensified pace of urbanization raised the demand for maids' services,

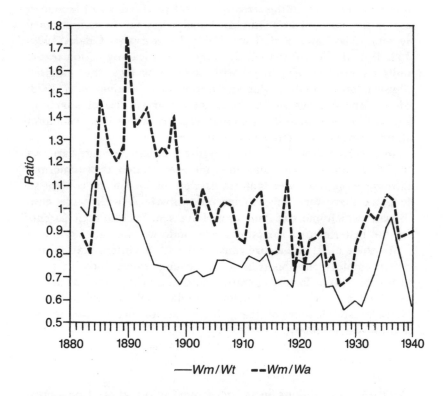

Figure 2.2 Female wage ratios, 1880–1940

resulting in a phenomenal upward shift of the maid-to-textile wage ratio (Wm/Wt) in the early 1930s.

Factory labour in the textile industry offered a well-paid employment opportunity for young women in the countryside; it offered much higher wages (Wt) throughout the period under study (Figure 2.2), and successfully drew those who met the stricter standard of qualification. An alternative, possible interpretation of the positive margin of the textile workers' wage over the maids' (that is, $Wt - Wm$) could be that it was necessary to compensate for the extra disutility of factory labour. Reportedly, the occupation of maid was preferred to factory work in textile mills, particularly in the Kansai district.[8]

Regarding the wage levels during the period of 1906–40, it has been shown in the past that (a) the market wage of farm labour was roughly equal to the *average* physical productivity of labour in agriculture as well as to the unskilled wage in the non-primary sectors (Nishikawa and Torii 1967: 14; see also Odaka 1989: 152–3), and that (b) the hourly wage in the leading cotton textile mills followed closely, albeit with some time lags, the marginal physical productivity of labour in the same (Fujino *et al* 1979: 31–3). The findings suggest that there was surplus of labour in agriculture and that the farming wage constituted a minimum standard of labour compensation in the society.

In any event, the discovery in Figure 2.2 that the wage earnings of female domestic servants did not even match the subnormal farming wage, indicates that maids were obliged to be content so long as they were fed, clothed and provided with some cash income, which many of them must have sent back to their parents for the betterment of the latter's economic well-being.

All these observations are consistent with an interpretation that urban employment opportunities for young women, notably those at textile mills as factory operatives and at private homes as maids, provided a vent for surplus for abundant labour, which was a characteristic feature of the primary sector of the pre-Second World War economy.

V

With the above discussion as background information, I now present a hypothetical model of employment and wage determination of female domestic servants in pre-Second World War Japan.

During the early phases of Japanese industrialization (1883–1939), major occupational choices for a young woman in the primary sector were largely confined to the following three: (1) remaining in her parents' household and serving as an occasional helper in family production (farming, principally), (2) working at a factory in a town, notably in the textile industry, or (3) making herself available as a domestic servant. From the girl's point of view choice (1) yielded the highest comfort and the least anxiety, but had little prospect of making a positive economic contribution, since her marginal productivity in farming, in all likelihood, would be less than the market agricultural wages (*Wa*).

On the other hand, not every young girl met the quality requirements for an industrial worker, that is, diligence, obedience, physical alertness, power of concentration, and the like. The factories would exploit personal information such as school attendance, transcription of records, and teachers' evaluation as signals with which they could identify the most qualified personnel, as there was believed to be a close empirical relationship between school performance and high proficiency on the shop-floor. Big, well-known textile factories could exert their monopsony power in the labour market and skim the top of the cream. Applicants who were second or below in the ranking might then qualify as domestic servants.

It is envisaged here that a young woman made up her mind in two steps: first, whether or not to seek an employment opportunity outside her household, and, second, given the decision to partici-pate in the urban labour market, where to seek employment, if any. Her selection among (1), (2) and (3) was made in the light of their relative pecuniary positions plus latent non-pecuniary con-siderations, such as socio-cultural inhibitions against factory labour, whose influence gradually waned with the spread of industrialization. For empirical purposes, however, non-economic factors are assumed to be constant from one occupation to another.

In view of the above discussion, I postulate that the ratio of maid employment (Nm) to the young female population of aged 15 to 29 (Ly), or employment ratio for short, is a positive function of relative wages between maid and textile labour: the two trades which compete for the young, female labour. In other words, the employment ratio goes up when the daily earning of a maid (Wm) increases relative to that of a female textile worker (Wt), and vice versa. It is appropriate in this setting to use as the explanatory variable the wage ratio which prevailed in the *previous* year, since it would take some time before job-market information could be transmitted from one place to another, and be absorbed in the minds of prospective suppliers and their families.[9]

By the same token, the employment ratio must be negatively associated with a rise in average, real income of agricultural house-holds in the past year (Ya_{-1}), because improved agricultural con-ditions would, other things being equal, lessen the need for the country girls to seek outside employment. Whereas a rise in the maid-to-textile wage ratio represents a 'pull' from the labour market external to agriculture, a decline in average agricultural income works as a 'push' from the primary sector.

Similarly, the prospect of future growth in agricultural earnings, as judged by the latter's record in the immediate past, would discourage the supply of female domestic servants. For this reason, the rate of change in the annual real income of farming households has been added as an independent variable of the supply behaviour.[10]

The statistical fitting of the relation, as applied to the historical data covering the period 1906–39, has yielded the following result with the use of maximum-likelihood, iterative procedure assuming the first-order auto correlation of the error term:[11]

$$ln(Nm/Ly) = \underset{(0.444)}{0.940} + \underset{(2.853)}{0.521}\ ln(Wm/Wt)_{-1} - \underset{(-1.485)}{0.534}\ lnYa_{-1}$$

$$- \underset{(1.468)}{0.377}\ ln(Ya/Ya_{-1}), \tag{2.1}$$

$$R^2 = 0.559,\ d = 1.74,$$

where ln denotes natural logarithm. Figures in parentheses report student's t statistics, and R^2 and d are the coefficient of determination adjusted for the degrees of freedom and Durbin-Watson statistic, respectively. All the estimated parameters have the expected signs, and are significantly different from zero at the 10 per cent level of significance except for the intercept.

One observes from the estimated equation that the supply of maids was by no means price elastic, as the estimated parametric values of Wm/Wt and of Ya_{-1} were less than unity (in absolute terms). Moreover, the power of 'pull' was roughly matched by that of 'push', for the respective parameters (again in absolute terms) were approximately of the same magnitude.

A portion of the young female population having thus been allocated to maid services (Nm), the latter's wage was determined next in such a way that excess demand for maids was cleared in the market. Put another way, it is postulated here that the wage of the female domestic servants was supply-determined. At the same time, however, the wage could also be raised (or lowered) by favourable (or depressed) business conditions, as reflected in larger (or smaller) values of the diffusion index (D), or an indicator of business conditions: that is to say, the whole demand curve would be shifted up (or down) according to higher (or lower) values of D.

Taking the real wages of maids, that is, the maids' nominal wages divided by the consumer price index (Wm/P), as the dependent variable and both the employment ratio (Nm/Ly) and Fujino's cumulative diffusion index with one year's lag (D_{-1}) as the independent variables, the demand curve for maids has been estimated as:[12]

$$ln(Wm/P) = \begin{array}{cc} -0.0659 & - & 0.237 & ln(Nm/Ly) \\ (-0.0463) & & (-2.137) \end{array}$$

$$\begin{array}{cc} + & 0.426 & ln\ D_{-1} \\ & (2.387) \end{array} \qquad (2.2)$$

$$R^2 = 0.923,\ d = 1.65.$$

According to the result of the computation, the wage elasticity of demand for maids was as high as 4.2, suggesting that their services were indeed a highly luxurious commodity even in those times.

These regression analyses suggest that economic calculation as well as market forces had a solid place in the determination of employment and wages of female domestic servants.[13]

As an alternative way of describing the transactions in the labour market, one may experiment with a reduced-form, Phillips-type formulation, where the rate of change in money wage (Wm/Wm_{-1}) is associated with the degree of excess demand in the market (Phillips 1958). For this purpose I have taken as independent variables (i) the excess-demand index of maids in the previous year (V_{-1}), as indicated by the ratio of two figures registered at the public labour exchange bureaux, number of job openings/number of job applicants, (ii) the rate of change in the excess demand index (V/V_{-1}), and (iii) the rate of change in consumers' price index (P/P_{-1}). Statistical fitting of the data for the period covering 1923–38 has yielded:

$$Wm/Wm_{-1} = \begin{array}{ccc} 0.0952 + & 0.0174\ V_{-1} + & 0.433\quad V/V_{-1} \\ (0.769) & (1.602) & (5.118) \end{array}$$

$$\begin{array}{cc} + & 0.435\ P/P_{-1} \\ & (2.575) \end{array} \qquad (2.3)$$

$$R^2 = 0.973,\ d = 2.65.$$

The greater the excess demand for maids, as indicated by larger values of V_{-1}, (V/V_{-1}) and (P/P_{-1}), the higher was the growth rate of their money wage.

The explanatory power of equation 2.3 is surprisingly good, and this confirms the view that market clearing forces as described by the demand-supply relations were highly relevant in explaining the behaviour of the wage of female domestic servants.

It is notable here that (1) the rate of change of V was, if anything, more relevant statistically than V itself, pointing to the important role played by expectation in the determination of money wages, and that (2) the parametric value of the rate of change in prices is significantly smaller than unity, indicating that there was a lag of adjustment between inflation and any corresponding rise in pecuniary compensation.

VI

Finally, using the estimated parameters of the labour allocation function (2.1), I have estimated the number of maids in the earlier decades, 1883–1905, as depicted in Figure 2.3. According to the diagram, the opportunity to work as domestic servants loomed just as large in the earlier days, particularly in the 1890s.

This finding comes as no surprise, because being a female domestic servant had been established as a socially accepted, popular employment opportunity for women long before the age of modern economic growth. This was especially the case in a big commercial town such as Osaka, but was by no means confined to urban places. Contemporary village documents of a central Honshū area in the period 1775–1870 reveal that it was quite customary for young girls (especially in the western parts of the country) to seek employment as household servants, either in the same or a neighbouring village, or sometimes even in far distant places (Hayami 1988: 78–91, 111–35).[14] On the demand side of the picture, historical documents from two downtown districts of the city of Osaka show that the proportion of female servants to the total number of the residents increased from a low of 6.5 per cent in 1700 (or thereabouts) to a high of 16.7 per cent in 1860! Whereas in 1700 a maid was found in every 3.03 households on average, the ratio went down to 1 to 1.05 in 1860.[15]

If anything, it was factory labour in textile mills that was quite foreign to the traditional pattern of labour transaction. No wonder it faced all kinds of resistance both from the factory girls themselves and from social critics. Herein lies, perhaps, a part of the reason why the textile wage (Wt) needed some edge over the earnings of maids (Wm).

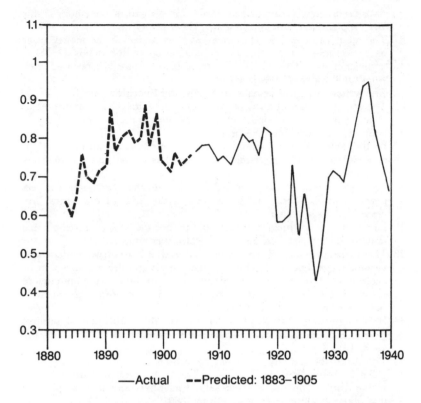

—Actual   ==Predicted: 1883–1905

Figure 2.3 Number of maids

NOTES

1 Discussions with Professors Takenori Inoki, Kyoji Fukao and Osamu Saito on an earlier version of this paper have been highly profitable. However, I take sole responsibility for any remaining errors.
2 The numbers of maids have been taken from Umemura *et al* (1988: 213), and population and household figures from Naikaku Tōkei Kyoku (1929 and 1935).
3 The total number of questionnaire sheets distributed was about 6,000 (see Shakai Rippō Kyōkai 1931:1).
4 The figures become 89.2 per cent and 20.3 per cent respectively, if one counts only the living-in maids who formed as large as 96 per cent of the maid population. Understandably, older maids opted to commute.
   5 The data relating to the cotton textile industry in this paragraph were drawn from Fujino *et al.* (1979) especially its diagrams on pages 5 and 28.
6 Value added figures in this paragraph have been computed from the

data available in Ohkawa *et al.* (1974: 226–9) and in Umemura (1988: 204–15), and are all expressed in 1934–6 prices.

7 The retail value of 0.9 *shō* of rice has been added to the money wage as an estimate of non-pecuniary compensation for maids (1 *shō* is equivalent to 1.8039 litres). The retail price of rice has been adopted from Ohkawa *et al.* (1967: 153–4).

8 The writer owes this remark to Professor Minoru Sawai.

9 The speed of transmission of the information may have improved as time went on. This aspect of changes over time, however, has not been incorporated into the present study.

10 By the same reasoning, the rate of change in the wage ratio (Wm/Wt) is a candidate for an explanatory factor, but has proved to be statistically insignificant.

11 The same method has been adopted in all the regression analyses reported in this essay, with the help of the TSP (Time Series Processor) package, version 4.0.

12 I have tacitly assumed here that the proportion of servant-employing households did not change dramatically over time.

13 The present model of equations 2.1 and 2.2 has two endogenous variables, Nm and Wm, while all the other variables are taken to be exogenous. The model is recursive in construction. A simultaneous system of demand and supply equations has also been experimented, but has proved to be unsuccessful.

14 It is interesting that Hayami reports the short duration of services (one or two years) of male and female servants in those days (Hayami 1988: 131).

15 The ratios for the city of Osaka have been computed from the data given by Inui (1980: 14–15, 26–7). The total number of the residents in the districts, inclusive of household members and their employees, was about 1,600 in 1700 and 996 in 1860.

STATISTICAL APPENDIX

A note on statistical data

Most of the data in this paper have been either taken directly or adopted from the LTES (*Estimates of Long-term Statistics of Japan since 1868*) series.

In particular, the wage statistics of the maids (Wm) have been taken from p. 245 of volume 8 of the series, entitled *Bukka* (Prices), and are based on the regional surveys supervised and collected for publication by the Ministry of Commerce (*Shōkō Shō*). The series extends back to as early as 1883, but lacks the figures for 1933–40, which have been estimated as weighted averages of maid wages in the cities of Osaka and Nagoya with the use of *Osaka-fu Tōkei Sho* (Statistical Yearbook of Osaka Prefecture) and of *Aichi-ken Tōkei Sho* (Statistical Yearbook of Aichi Prefecture), the 1930 census counting of maids in the cities serving as weights.

Note in this context that maids were in principle hired on yearly contracts and that they received a pecuniary monthly stipend as well as payments in goods (room and board, in particular). In view of this, the

Table 2A.1 Source data for female domestic servants in Japan, 1880–1940

Year	Wm (sen)	Wt (sen)	P (1934–6 = 1)	Ya (yen)	Nm (000)	Ly (000)	v	D
1880	17.6		0.2456	193		4,319		
1881	16.8		0.2695	189		4,331		
1882	14.2	16	0.2440	194		4,344		
1883	11.5	14	0.2042	198	632.5	4,406		
1884	10.9	11	0.1934	199	605.8	4,427		
1885	11.5	8	0.2234	211	652.4	4,431		
1886	9.5	7	0.2033	234	756.9	4,431		
1887	8.8	7	0.1987	253	703.5	4,439		
1888	8.9	7	0.1996	245	683.3	4,486		
1889	9.8	8	0.2089	216	723.5	4,609		236,670
1890	14.0	8	0.2429	256	732.4	4,727		353.330
1891	12.0	9	0.2320	246	870.0	4,835		253.330
1892	12.5	9	0.2317	255	766.7	4,950		350.950
1893	13.0	9	0.2350	247	809.7	5,069		527.740
1894	13.4	10	0.2488	270	818.1	5,166		882.000
1895	13.4	11	0.2713	272	790.3	5,275		1,187.890
1896	14.9	12	0.2961	241	802.1	5,382		1,546.710
1897	18.0	15	0.3474	224	866.9	5,494		1,870.240
1898	21.4	16	0.3818	298	780.9	5,547		2,082.000
1899	17.2	17	0.3685	261	836.9	5,602		2,205.530
1900	19.3	19	0.4065	278	732.0	5,676		2,526.890
1901	20.0	20	0.3966	300	711.5	5,724		2,432.160
1902	20.8	22	0.4121	245	767.8	5,836		2,435.710
1903	22.6	21	0.4344	292	729.3	5,916		2,600.590

Table 2A.1 continued

Year	Wm (sen)	Wt (sen)	P (1934-6 = 1)	Ya (yen)	Nm (000)	Ly (000)	v	D
1904	21.4	22	0.4395	323	739.9	5,985		2,720.680
1905	21.4	24	0.4716	261	758.1	6,056		3,064.680
1906	24.6	25	0.4953	307	763.9	6,021		3,256.620
1907	27.5	27	0.5239	328	778.1	6,038		3,537.750
1908	27.5	27	0.5368	333	779.8	6,044		3,447.430
1909	25.1	29	0.5219	330	751.8	6,061		3,413.990
1910	24.7	29	0.5157	310	736.0	6,110		3,598.390
1911	30.0	30	0.5789	336	751.7	6,141		3,794.880
1912	33.2	32	0.6221	330	726.4	6,191		4,061.550
1913	34.7	32	0.6456	332	762.7	6,276		4,231.720
1914	28.6	33	0.5669	378	814.8	6,344		4,229.630
1915	25.1	32	0.5383	376	787.5	6,462		4,184.470
1916	26.0	33	0.5849	413	790.0	6,617		4,574.540
1917	34.4	37	0.7280	391	757.8	6,731		4,937.820
1918	50.4	47	0.9846	369	825.1	6,790		5,220.430
1919	71.4	97	1.3104	400	808.7	6,797		5,429.120
1920	102.9	131	1.3356	399	584.3	6,876		5,624.780
1921	88.8	117	1.2355	353	583.5	6,958		5,416.080
1922	98.9	130	1.2076	369	606.8	7,074	4.042	5,603.040
1923	98.4	126	1.2105	344	730.9	7,213	3.535	5,618.980
1924	102.3	129	1.2190	364	556.1	7,376	3.420	5,711.730
1925	83.6	130	1.2514	401	659.8	7,520	2.505	5,813.180
1926	84.2	130	1.1977	362	540.1	7,672	1.990	5,823.330
1927	79.4	133	1.1444	394	420.9	7,847	1.971	5,769.700
1928	73.7	135	1.1186	389	491.3	7,994	1.625	5,747.960
1929	73.5	129	1.0861	394	690.7	8,158	1.796	5,729.120

Year	Wm	Wt	P	Ya	Nm	Ly	v	D
1930	69.0	116	0.9962	418	709.9	8,292	1.635	5,410.280
1931	54.9	99	0.8757	353	700.8	8,409	1.210	5,161.010
1932	55.2	85	0.8868	405	672.7	8,505	1.327	5,189.990
1933	56.2	79	0.9179	451	749.8	8,591	1.189	5,411.730
1934	61.9	77	0.9623	353	860.9	8,679	1.539	5,540.720
1935	68.2	74	1.0067	384	934.6	8,894	1.865	5,634.920
1936	69.7	73	1.0290	421	937.4	9,063	1.853	5,730.570
1937	72.8	84	1.1119	432	815.3	9,194	1.917	6,066.060
1938	76.2	88	1.2293	416	766.9	9,316	2.042	6,144.690
1939	87.9	101	1.3182	454	718.1	9,411		6,387.240
1940	90.2		1.4969	422	670.2	9,556		6,660.300

Key: Wm = daily wage of female domestic servant, payment in goods inclusive;
Wt = daily wage of female textile worker;
P = price index of consumer goods;
Ya = real value added per farming household, net of depreciation (in 1934–6 prices);
Nm = number of female domestic servants, estimated figures to 1905;
Ly = female population aged 15–29;
v = job opening-applicant ratio for female domestic servants, as registered at public labour exchange bureaux; and
D = Fujino and Igarashi's cumulative diffusion index, as of October each year.

Notes: Blank space indicates data deficiency
100 sen = 1 yen

wages of maids in the original monthly figures were, first, converted to a daily basis by dividing the original figures by 30, and, second, modified by adding imputed boarding cost, which was assumed to be equivalent to 0.9 *shō* of polished rice.

The textile wage series (*Wt*) comes from p. 274 of *Sen'i Kōgyō* (Textiles), volume 11 of the series, except for the period 1938–9, for which the data from volume 8 of the LTES series (p. 243) have been utilized.

The consumer price index (*P*) adopted herein is the implicit deflator of the personal consumption expenditures, as reported in M. Shinohara, *Kojin Shōhi Shishutsu* (Personal Consumption), LTES volume 6, 1967: 106.

The real annual income of agricultural household refers to net value added (forestry excluded) divided by the number of farming households, as reported in Umemura *et al.*, *Nōringyō* (Agriculture and Forestry), LTES volume 9, 1966: 182 and 218–19 respectively.

The numbers of maids (*Nm*), textile workers as well as young female population (aged 15–29) have been taken from Umemura *et al.*, *Rōdōryoku* (Manpower) volume 2 of the LTES series: 168 and 207–15. The employment figures are available only from 1906.

The original sources of the excess demand index for maids (*v*) are: Chūō Shokugyō Shōkai Jimu Kyoku (The Central Labour Exchange Bureau), *Shokugyō Shōkai Nenpō* (Yearbook of Labour Exchange) (up to 1935), and Kōsei Shō (Ministry of Welfare), *Shokugyō Shōkai Tōkei* (Statistics on Labour Exchange) (for years 1936–8).

Finally, the diffusion index (*D*) is a monthly time-series showing the percentage of rising items in a set of statistics with a close bearing on the state of the economy, for example, construction starts, imports, production indices, and so on. The annual October figures have been utilized here in order to avoid seasonal disturbances. I have also adopted the cumulative version of the diffusion index (Fujino and Igarashi 1973: 328–9), since I wish it to reflect the progress of industrialization rather than the mere ups and downs of business cycles.

REFERENCES

Fujino, Shōzaburō and Igarashi, Fukuo (1973) *Keiki Shisū: 1888–1940 nen* (Diffusion index: 1888–1940), processed, Tokyo, Documentation Centre on Japanese Statistics, Institute of Economic Research, Hitotsubashi University.

Fujino, Shōzaburō *et al.* (1979) *Sen'i Kōgyō* (Textiles), vol. 11 of *Estimates of Long-term Economic Statistics on Japan since 1868* series, Tokyo, Tōyō Keizai Shinpō Sha.

Hayami, Akira (1988) *Edo no Nōmin Seikatsu Shi, Shūmon Kaichō ni Miru Nōbi no Ichi Nōson* (A History of Farmers' Life in the Edo Period, The Case of a Village in the Nōbi Area as Recorded in the 'Registry of Religions'), Tokyo, Nihon Hōsō Shuppan Kyōkai.

Inui, Hiromi (1980) 'Osaka chōnin shakai no kōzō, jinkō dōtai ni okeru' (The structure of Osaka merchants' society, as viewed from their population dynamics), in H. Tsuda (ed.) *Kinsei Kokka no Tenkai* (The Evolution of the Modern State), Tokyo, Hanawa Shobō: 11–64.

Naikaku Tōkei Kyoku (Statistical Bureau, Prime Minister's Office) (1929) *Taishō 9-nen Kokusei Chōsa Hōkoku* (The Report on the 1920 Population Census), vols 2 and 3, Tokyo.

Naikaku Tōkei Kyoku (1932) *Chūshutsu Chōsa ni yoru Shōwa 5-nen Kokusei Chōsa Kekka no Gaikan* (An Overview of the 1930 Population Census: Results of Sample Tabulations), Tokyo.

Naikaku Tōkei Kyoku (1935) *Shōwa 5-nen Kokusei Chōsa Hōkoku* (The Report on the 1930 Population Census), vol. 2 (Occupation and Industry), Tokyo.

Nishikawa, Shunsaku and Torii, Yasuhiko (1967) 'Nōgyō genkai seisanryoku no jōshō to hi-nōgyō chingin e no hakyū' (The rising marginal productive capacity of agriculture and its spread to non-agricultural wages), *Nihon Rōdō Kyōkai Zasshi* (The Monthly Journal of the Japan Institute of Labour) 9 (12), 13–24.

Nōshōmushō, Kōmukyoku (Bureau of Factories, Ministry of Agriculture and Commerce) (1910) *Kōjō oyobi Shokkō* (Factories and Production Operatives), Tokyo.

Nōshōmushō, Shōkōkyoku (Bureau of Commerce and Manufacturing, Ministry of Agriculture and Commerce) (1911/1947) *Menshi Shokkō Jijō* (Field Surveys on the State of Factory Operatives: Report on the Cotton Textile Industry) and *Orimono Shokkō Jijō* (Field Surveys on the State of Factory Operatives: Report on the Weaving Industry). Originally released in 1911, edited with commentary by T. Tsuchiya and reprinted by Seikatsu Sha, Tokyo in 1947.

Odaka, Kōnosuke (1989) 'Nijū Kōzō' (The Dual Structure), in T. Nakamura and K. Odaka (eds) *Nijū Kōzō* (The Dual Structure), ch. 3, Tokyo, Iwanami Shoten.

Ohkawa, Kazushi *et al.* (1967) *Bukka* (Prices), vol. 8 of *Estimates of Long-term Economic Statistics on Japan since 1868* series, Tokyo, Tōyō Keizai Shinpō Sha.

Ohkawa, Kazushi *et al.* (1974) *Kokumin Shotoku* (National Income), vol. 1 of *Estimates of Long-term Economic Statistics on Japan since 1868* series, Tokyo, Tōyō Keizai Shinpō Sha.

Phillips, A. W. (1958) 'The relation between unemployment and the rate of change of money wage rates in the United Kingdom', *Economica*, new series, 25 (100), 283–99.

Shakai Rippō Kyōkai (Association for Social Enactment) (1931) *Jochū ni Kansuru Chōsa* (A Survey on Maids), Tokyo.

Shinohara, M. (ed.) (1967) *Kojin Shōhi Shishutsu* (Personal Consumption), vol. 6 of *Estimates of Long-term Economic Statistics on Japan since 1868* series, Tokyo, Tōyō Keizai Shinpō Sha.

Umemura, Mataji *et al.* (eds) (1966) *Nōringyō* (Agriculture and Forestry), vol. 9 of *Estimates of Long-term Economic Statistics on Japan since 1868* series, Tokyo, Tōyō Keizai Shinpō Sha.

Umemura, Mataji *et al.* (1988) *Rōdōryoku* (Manpower), vol. 2 of *Estimates of Long-term Economic Statistics on Japan since 1868* series Tokyo, Tōyō Keizai Shinpō Sha.

Yamada, Saburō and Hayami, Yūjirō (1979) 'Agricultural growth in Japan, 1880–1979', in Y. Hayami, V. W. Ruttan and H. M. Southworth (eds) *Agricultural Growth in Japan, Taiwan, Korea, and the Philippines*, Honolulu, the University Press of Hawaii, 33–58.

Chapter 3

One day at a time: work and domestic activities of urban lower-class women in early twentieth-century Japan

Kathleen Uno

This chapter explores the question: How did modern[1] pieceworkers and other urban lower-class women balance paid employment with domestic responsibilities during the early stages of Japanese industrialization? Framing my question in this way establishes a dichotomy between work and domestic life for the analytic purposes of this essay. Although it can be argued that emphasizing polarization between women's work and home lives has a social basis in the increasingly visible separation of workplace and home which emerged during the industrialization of the modern period, developing an approach to women's history grounded in this opposition is not my primary aim. Rather, in this essay I wish to probe the lives of working women of the urban lower classes – female pieceworkers, entrepreneurs, family workers and employees, especially the former, in a more unified fashion, in an attempt to bridge our current rather dichotomized understandings of modern Japanese women. While earlier western works have focused on the domestic life and concomitant public activities of modern Japanese middle-class women, including feminists,[2] studies of urban lower-class women have largely treated their recruitment to, and participation in, the public world of the economy as workers and labour activists.[3] Yet it is surely important to begin to recover the domestic experiences of lower-class working women and to consider the lives of married women workers in cities, which differed in some respects from those of younger single textile operatives.[4] Probing both the domestic and work activities of urban lower-class women and the relationship between the two enriches our visions of little-known aspects of their lives and the continuous reconstructions of womanhood and gender which took place in modern Japan.

The boundaries of the group 'early twentieth-century urban lower-class women' are somewhat vague and shifted over time. Much of the amorphousness of lower-class women as a social group stems from the social classifications employed in contemporary sources. Late nineteenth and early twentieth-century observers referred to male and female members of the poor (or underclass) and the nascent working class as the *toshi kasō*, the 'urban lower-classes', or 'urban lower class' (Chubachi and Taira 1976: 395–7; Nakagawa 1987: 31). Instability of employment and income made the daily subsistence of these urban groups insecure, especially before the First World War.[5] Popular and official writers of that era applied another amorphous term, *saimin* (literally 'thin people') to the lower ranks of society. As neither the 'urban lower class' nor the 'thin people' were defined precisely by income level or occupation, their ranks included self-employed artisans and petty retailers, factory workers, and homeworkers. Below them were the *hinmin* (the poor, or paupers), those enduring severer hardships, and the *kyūmin* (the destitute), those facing terrible deprivation. However, during and after the First World War, improvements in the real wages and standard of living of factory operatives and the revival of labour and social movements encouraged social observers more carefully to distinguish between the working class and the poor. New terms – worker (*rōdōsha*) and proletariat (*musan kaikyū* or *puroretaria*) were applied to factory operatives, while *saimin*, *hinmin*, and *kyūmin* were generally attached to those with less stable livelihoods (Chubachi and Taira 1976). Some degree of overlap remained, since the incomes of those in the lower ranks of the working class did not differ greatly from the incomes of the richest poor. Reflecting the shifting terminology in the sources, this study treats city women of both the poor and working classes *before* the end of the First World War and *thereafter* mainly those of the underclass.

The first section of the chapter explores the income-earning activities of urban lower-class women, especially those of pieceworkers. What types of work did they do? Under what conditions did they labour? Why did they engage in income-earning activities? It also touches on some of the implications of paid work for home responsibilities. The second section considers how urban lower-class women tackled their domestic chores. Paid employment as well as housing and overall conditions in lower-class districts shaped the home life of urban lower-class women. Whether they worked as pieceworkers, petty entrepreneurs, unpaid family workers or factory operatives, the need to bring in income affected their performance of domestic tasks. Long hours of toil for meagre wages prevented urban lower-class women from dedicating themselves exclusively to housework and childrearing; however, their economic contributions were crucial to their households. Moreover, unfavourable living conditions in urban lower-class districts, especially poor housing, also hampered a wife's handling all aspects of domestic work by herself within the confines of a private household unit.

Although I have divided the body of the chapter into sections on paid and domestic work for the analytical purposes of this essay, the sections are not intended to be discrete entities. To some extent, discussions of domestic work intrude in the section on paid employment, and material on paid work appears in the domestic section, in order to blur the dichotomy of work and domestic life, which might not have clearly existed in the minds of pre-war urban lower-class women themselves. Domesticity – responsibility for housework and child care – as opposed to participation in economic and political activities in the world beyond the home – came to figure very prominently in state and elite conceptions of Japanese womanhood from the end of the nineteenth century (Uno 1988, 1991b, 1992a). However, early modern prescriptions for womanhood which emerged before widespread diffusion of the separation between home and workplace probably had greater influence on urban lower-class woman. In early modern enterprise households in city and countryside, women as well as men and children could and did participate with relative ease in what later came to be called domestic work – cleaning, cooking, and child care – and what later came to be called productive work – activities contributing to the household livelihood. Although young wives residing with their in-laws generally lacked authority over household affairs, including their own participation in income-earning activities, they laboured at productive and domestic tasks in order to assist, directly or indirectly, the household enterprise. Thus nineteenth-century and twentieth-century farm women helped earn household income through hard physical labour at cultivating wet and dry fields, through less strenuous work at by-employments such as silkworm raising, spinning, weaving, and straw sandal-making, and through domestic tasks such as cooking, laundry, cleaning, preparing the bath, and child care.[6]

The great majority of rural women laboured from dawn into the night at agriculture and handicrafts in the peak seasons at the expense of domestic chores such as childrearing and housekeeping. For this reason, standards of cleanliness, child care, personal hygiene and nutrition were low in ordinary village households.[7]

This study is a preliminary venture – a foray into a relatively new historical terrain. It surveys the types of work, the working conditions, and the home life of urban lower-class women and begins to consider how urban lower-class women themselves regarded their work and domestic activities. Their actions, recorded by middle-class observers, hint at their values, priorities and identities; however, studies based on materials that reveal more clearly the multiple, shifting voices of urban lower-class women are needed. In particular, further investigation of how they acted in ways reflecting their sense of self and how they formulated goals and strategies to achieve their aims is needed. The limitations of this work will, I hope, invite further research into the little-known, diverse world of lower-class city women – married and single pieceworkers, petty entrepreneurs, unpaid family workers, and employees outside the home.

The significance of this study is twofold. First, it sheds new light on the social consequences of industrialization in modern Japan by considering the work experiences of pieceworkers, employees who engaged in production for low pay outside Japan's burgeoning factories. The labours of this underprivileged group of workers also constitute part of the economic and social history of industrial capitalism in Japan since the Meiji Restoration (1868). However, this study also explores married women workers' home lives, including the effects of wage labour on their domestic activities. Ideally, the impact of industrialization on male wage workers' participation in home life also deserves attention, however, detailed consideration of this subject lies beyond the scope of this study.

Second, this discussion of work and domestic activities in the lives of urban lower-class women in modern Japan contributes to comparative study of the relationship between changes in conceptions of gender and early industrialization. Rendall (1990) argues convincingly that the following are crucial questions for such study: (1) What was the meaning of 'work'? (2) How did the family and work lives of women interact? (3) To what extent were all forms of domestic labour, paid and unpaid, important in middle-class and working-class households? (4) To what extent did new definitions of manhood and womanhood sharpen divisions between the worlds of women and men which varied by class? Her work treats modern England, but these issues merit consideration in other industrializing societies as well. Rendall's questions are particularly useful because, except in the second, she avoids embracing fully the conventional dichotomy of work and home. This brief study cannot treat thoroughly all of these issues, but it explores the meaning of work for lower-class women (which I argue was intimately related to the interaction of their work and domestic activities); discusses their efforts to manage unpaid domestic labour in lower-class households despite the constraints of work and environment; and considers shifting boundaries between men's and women's worlds in modern Japan.

PAID EMPLOYMENT

Many urban lower-class wives engaged in piecework (*naishoku*) – the manufacturing, assembly, or finishing of goods at home rather than in a workshop or factory.[8] To poor women piecework was an attractive form of employment, for it required neither vocational skills, education, capital, nor the time, effort and expense of commuting;[9] however, as we shall see, outwork had disadvantages for women as well.[10]

Underclass women undertook varied types of piecework. In 1893, during the initial stage of Japan's industrial takeoff, a magazine article mentioned several types: finishing knitted goods, labelling and packing cartons, and tinting lithographs (Ogi *et al.* 1990: 386–91). In 1896 an observer of lower-class life listed nine types – 'matchbox assembly, shaving toothpicks, sewing sandal straps, painting blackboards, making Japanese-style socks, stretching tobacco, carving fan spokes, polishing metal wares, and sorting scrap paper' (Matsubara 1896: 35; see also Yokoyama 1898: 51–2). The proximity of factories to poor neighbourhoods fostered occupational specialization by district. For example, around 1900 matchbox assembly was a common form of piecework among the poor women of Nago-chō in Osaka, Tachibana-chō in Kobe, and Samegahashi in Tokyo; in the latter district there were also numerous cigarette-rolling outworkers (Futaba Yōchien 1900: 1; 1908: 10; Yokoyama 1898: 52, 158; also Taiga 1893: 110–11).

Three decades later, a Tokyo City Social Bureau survey[11] reported 41,000 pieceworkers, nearly 90 per cent of them married women, engaging in over 300 types of homework. It listed Japanese sewing (6,280), sandal-thong stitching (4,524), toy assembling and finishing (4,050), paper-bag pasting (3,258), knitwear finishing (2,750), machine sewing (2,638), and attaching footwear soles (2,549) as the seven most common forms of outwork in Tokyo in 1925 (Tōkyō-shi Shakaikyoku 1926: 8–9).[12] For the 3,280 out-workers surveyed in greater detail,[13] the average wage of 9 yen per month constituted 12.6 per cent of the 71.8 yen average monthly household income. Other family members provided an additional 8.5 yen (11.8 per cent) of the average monthly income (ibid.: 15). The age distribution was 8 per cent aged 15 to 25, 75 per cent aged 25 to 50, and 9 per cent aged 50 to 60 (ibid.: 77).[14] The outworkers' marital statuses were: single, 9 per cent; married, 78 per cent; widowed, 10 per cent; and divorced 1 per cent, while 87 per cent of them had children (ibid.: 77). On the average, their households contained 5.3 members, compared to national and Tokyo averages of 4.6 and 4.5, respectively (Tōkyō Shōkō Kaigisho 1928: 19). Clearly, most pieceworkers of the 1920s were low-income, middle-aged women with a husband and children who made less than a living wage.

While one might imagine that pieceworkers were able to balance paid work and domestic tasks more easily than employees such as factory operatives who worked outside their homes, in fact their work regimes obstructed smooth fulfilment of household responsi-bilities. Although pieceworkers laboured at home, subcontractors typically brought them large quantities of work to be done on short notice.[15] Despite the inconvenience, women who needed additional income rushed to meet jobbers' tight deadlines. When they toiled day and night to complete their consignments on time, their paid employment interfered with household chores such as shopping, cooking, cleaning and child care. Not only did female outworkers labour long hours and face domestic disruptions, but, as the follow-ing examples show, wages were so low that they had to work many days a month just to earn a pittance.

In 1893, matchbox assemblers in Nago-chō, Osaka, earned 3.5 sen[16] for 750 boxes; their workday was 12 hours long (Taiga 1893: 110). An 1898 observer reported somewhat better wages in Tokyo where matchbox homeworkers could earn 12 sen for assembling a case of 1,200 boxes. 'While a skilled worker who works with all her might into the night can finish a case in one day, the ordinary outworker who does child care and cooking finishes a case in two days', earning an average of 6 sen per day (Yokoyama 1898: 52). In Kobe, the rate was lower, 8.5 sen per 1,000 boxes (ibid.: 52). For cigarette-rolling the piece rate in one Tokyo district was 1.5 sen per 100. A skilful worker could earn 18 to 22.5 sen per day by rolling 1,200 to 1,500 cigarettes per day; a top worker, 30 sen, by completing 2,000 (Futaba Yōchien 1900: 1). For attaching hemp sandal soles, an outworker earned nine sen for 10 pairs in 1910. Since the thread cost her two yen, her net pay rate was seven sen. Fast workers could complete 15–20 pairs a day (Futaba Yōchien 1908: 9–10), earning 11 to 14 sen, but estimating from Budget no. 2 in Table 3.1 below, a poor family of 3.5 members spent three to four times that amount just on food and shelter (33 sen per day on food and 8 sen for rent in 1910). Clearly, even the fastest, most diligent of turn-of-the-century matchbox, cigarette, and hemp sandal outworkers did not earn enough to provide for the daily needs of their families. In the 1920s pieceworkers still did not make a living wage. The average daily income of the 1926 pieceworkers mentioned above would have been 36 sen per day if they worked 25 days per month; however, daily expenses for food and shelter alone for a poor family of 4.5 persons averaged 1 yen 45 sen.[17]

Urban poor women of the pre-war era engaged in a wide variety of occupations besides piecework. Some were self-employed as scavengers of Japanese or western paper, scrap metal, old socks and underwear, or ashes; street vendors of fermented beans, baked sweet potatoes, sweets or noodles; petty retailers of candy, crackers, cookies or sundries; hairdressers; laundresses; or proprietors of boarding houses, noodle shops and tea stores. Others worked as factory operatives, servants, waitresses or even day labourers (Suzuki 1888: 145; Taiga 1893: 110–14; Matsubara 1896: 84–7; Kikumura 1981: 14–15; Naimushō Chihōkyoku 1912: 31–2; Tōkyō-shi Shakaikyoku 1921: 15). The wives of petty entrepreneurs, for example, greengrocers, fish sellers, candymakers, innkeepers and leftover rice vendors often helped with the household business (Matsubara 1896: 23–4, 39–40; Yokoyama 1898: 122). Another group of women who worked hard on behalf of their families of procreation were married factory operatives. A 1926 Tokyo Social Bureau survey stated that 31 per cent of female factory workers (jokō) were married and 38.1 per cent were between the ages of 25 and 50 (Tōkyō-shi Shakaikyoku 1926: 77), in contrast to the higher proportion of young, single girls one to two decades earlier.[18]

However, like piecework, all of these occupations were characterized by long hours, poor working conditions, and low wages.[19]
Like pieceworkers, self-employed women who worked at home had
to juggle paid employment and domestic tasks day and night. On
the other hand, women who worked outside the home confronted
household chores before and after a long, tiring day outside the
home. Certainly, full-time women workers could earn more than
pieceworkers,[20] but they earned far less than full-time male operatives (Hazama 1976: 35; Tsurumi 1990: 105, 150), and had considerably less flexibility in handling domestic chores than homeworkers, self-employed women, or unpaid family workers, for
female machine-weavers and spinners worked twelve to eighteen
hours per shift during the Meiji era (Tsurumi 1984: 7).

Women's work and family budgets

Scrutiny of household budgets from 1890 to the late 1920s suggests
that economic need strongly informed lower-class women's motivation for employment, although not all wives engaged in income-
earning activities. In families with an adult male earner, wives'
earnings constituted a small but vital part of household income,
for husbands' income was unstable and at best barely covered
household expenses.[21] When bad weather, illness, injury, layoffs,
or unwillingness to go to work, decreased male earnings, the wife's
income (and possibly that of older children) became the mainstay
of the household economy. Women's contributions to household
income were difficult to calculate precisely, especially for the late
nineteenth century, but seem to have been smaller than those of
male earners. None the less, particularly before the First World
War, women's earnings were essential to precarious urban lower-
class household economies.

Two turn-of-the-century household budgets hint at a substantial
contribution by working wives, but other examples suggest that
they earned a smaller share of earned income. While daily expenses
in one meagre 1896 budget – rent in a back alley tenement room,
food including white rice, and firewood – cost 20 sen per day, the
wife made 4 sen per day hemming shirts, sock or handkerchief
edges (Matsubara 1896: 159). If she worked full-time, her earnings
would have provided 25 per cent of basic living expenses.[22] The
earnings of the hemp sandal-solers discussed above would have
contributed 20.6 to 26.2 per cent of the income of Budget no. 2

in Table 3.1. On the other hand, the wife did not work in Budget
no. 1's poor household in 1896 (see Table 3.1), although the male
head's earnings failed to provide even the bare necessities of food,
shelter, and fuel. Since members other than the head contributed
only 13 to 19 per cent of the 3,000 household incomes averaged
in Budget no. 2 in 1898, obviously many wives' earnings fell well
under a quarter of total income. And by the late Meiji period
(1912), an Interior Ministry survey of workers' (*shokkō*) budgets
found that of the 17 yen earned monthly by those who could at
best be considered the lowest ranks of the working class (*saimin*)
– janitors, errand boys and coolies (*ninsoku*) – 82.4 per cent was
earned by the head. Yet despite multiple earners, Budgets no. 2
and no. 3 (in Table 3.1), still ended up with net monthly deficits.
Based on these examples, it seems unlikely that turn-of-the century
wives routinely provided one-fourth of household income. None
the less, given the tendency of lower-class household budgets to
run a monthly deficit or at best a tiny monthly surplus, wives
made signficant economic contributions to their households even
though they earned far less than did their husbands.

Table 3.1 Meiji period urban lower-class (*toshi kasō*) household
budgets

Budget no.	Year	Monthly income (yen) (% earned by head)	Monthly expenses (% for food, rent, miscellaneous items)	Persons per household (no. of cases)
1	1896	25 (100)	26.5 (72, 8, none)[1]	5 (1)
2	1911	16 (81–7)[3]	15.43 (65, 16, 17)[2]	3.5 (3,000)
3	1912	17 (82.4)	19.28 (68, 13, 18)	5 (1)

Notes
1 11 per cent for rental of bedding and 9 per cent for fuel.
2 This apparently includes 1 yen spent on food and drink as entertainment.
   If the 1 yen is shifted to the food category, monthly expenditures on food
   rises to 75 per cent and those for miscellaneous items fall to 10 per cent.
3 Calculated from an estimate in the source of 2 to 3 yen per month for
   earnings by members other than the household.

Source: Budgets 1, 2, 3 are from Nakagawa 1982: 146–8.

Although it is unlikely that the proportion of income earned by
married women increased by the 1920s, none the less, the finances
of households in the lower ranks of urban society, especially the
working class, improved somewhat. The budgets of the poor still
tended to run a monthly deficit (Table 3.2), but those of late

Table 3.2 Taisho era lower-class (toshi kasō) household budgets

Budget no.	Year	Monthly income (yen) (% earned by head)	Monthly expenses (% for food, rent,[1] miscellaneous items)	Persons per household (no. of cases)
4	1921	61.8 (84.1)	59.8 (58, 8,[1] 19)	4.3 (497)
5	1921	under 30, average 25.6 (72.9)	26.3 (66, 12,[1] 13)	3.7 (3)
6	1921	60–70, average 57.9 (70.3)	56.7 (62, 8,[1] 17)	4.3 (111)
7	1921	120–50,[2] average 98.56 (73.1)	96.83 (41, 8,[1] 35)	4.5 (14)
8	1926–7	82.01 (72.4)	80.38 (45, 14, 24)	4.5 (58)
9	1926–7	less than 60, average 50.64 (85.2)	51.35 (58, 9, 20)	4.0 (20)
10	1926–7	60–80, average 70.27 (75.5)	72.26 (46, 16, 22)	4.6 (13)
11	1926–7	below 60 and 60–80, average 58.37 (80.6)	59.98 (52, 12, 21)	4.2 (33)
12	1926–7	100–120,[3] average 108.09 (61.1)	106.6 (41, 15, 26)	5.1 (7)

1 This figure denotes housing expenses, including rent.
2 For comparison with 1921 working class budgets.
3 For comparison with 1926–7 working-class budgets.

Sources: Budgets 4–7 from Saimin tōkei hyō, 1921, cited in Nakagawa 1982: 181–2; budgets 8–12 from Naikaku tōkei chōsa, 1926–7, cited in Nakagawa 1982: 183)

Taisho workers routinely showed a surplus (Table 3.3). Among the poor, the proportion of income earned by household members other than the head increased slightly on the whole, ranging from 15 to 30 per cent (Table 3.2). Among the working class, their contribution was smaller, roughly 10 to 20 per cent (Table 3.3). Unfortunately, as these budgets lump together the earnings of all family members other than the head, the income of wives cannot be distinguished from that of daughters, sons, parents or in-laws. As mentioned above, the 1926 Tokyo Social Bureau piecework

Table 3.3 Taisho era working-class (*rōdōsha*) household budgets

Budget no.	Year	Monthly income (yen) (% earned by head)	Monthly expenses (% for food, rent, miscellaneous items)	Persons per household (no. of cases)
13	1921	115.1 (83.7)	110.4 (37, 11, 29)[1]	4.3 (74)
14	1921	100–150, average 109.1 (81.8)	106.3 (39, 11, 30)[2]	4.4 (35)
15	1926–7	119.4 (79.6)	107.6 (37, 15, 27)[3]	4.4 (383)
16	1926–7	100–120 average 111.4 (81.2)	102.9 (38, 15, 26)[4]	4.1 (81)

Notes:
1 Including rent, total housing expenditures were 14 per cent; clothing constituted 14 per cent of miscellaneous items.
2 Including rent, total housing expenditures were 14 per cent; clothing constituted 13 per cent of miscellaneous items.
3 Including rent, total housing expenditures were 18 per cent; clothing constituted 12 per cent of miscellaneous items.
4 Including rent, total housing expenditures were 19 per cent; clothing constituted 12 per cent of miscellaneous items.

Sources: Budgets 1 and 2 from *Hōkyū seikatsusha shokkō seikei chōsa hōkoku*, 1925, cited in Nakagawa 1982: 174–5.
Budgets 3 and 4 from *Naikaku tōkei chōsa*, 1926–7, cited in Nakagawa 1982: 178–9.

survey indicated that outworking wives furnished on the average 12.6 per cent of household income in 3,280 households (Tōkyō-shi Shakaikyoku 1926: 15). As in the decades before, wives' meagre incomes helped to keep household finances solvent.

Women as paid workers

While previous sections discuss urban lower-class woman's diverse occupations and the contributions of working wives to the household economy, this section provides concrete examples of married women's paid work suggesting its relationship to the employment and income of other earners in the household over three decades. These examples reveal not only the employment of young adult working wives who were also mothers, the focal point of this chapter, but the wage-earning activities of girls, single mothers, and widows as well. Older women, whether married or widowed, found piecework and self-employment, especially petty retailing, attractive, for they could earn income at home. Single mothers and wives of ill or disabled male workers, even those with young children, often engaged in wage labour outside the home, out of a desperate need for income, even though they faced child care problems and did not necessarily earn a living wage. And self-employment as a boarding house proprietor seems to have been popular with married women of all ages, as a supplement to wage labour, piecework or petty entrepreneurship.

One journalist recorded the diverse occupations of the female as well as the male members of a poor family in the Nago-chō district of Osaka in 1891:

> At the entrance to a tenement room four and a half mats [about 3 by 3 metres] in size, wearing only a loincloth, slept the 24- or 25-year-old son, who occasionally worked as a toilet cleaner or transporter of cholera victims. In a dark corner, a 70-year-old woman was making matchboxes while shooing away a grandchild of about age 4 who was spitting into the boxes. She sometimes hit the toddler on the head with her fists . . . The wife of the house, who was generally sick and unable to engage in an occupation, lay holding an infant on the ragged straw mat floor without any bedding . . . As for the 15- and 12-year-old sisters, the older clutched a samisen and the younger leaned against a *katsura* tree holding a tattered fan in her hand as they quarrelled over where to work. The older favoured the red light district while the younger wanted to stay near Nago-chō. Their father had left home early to scavenge for waste paper, and their grandfather had . . . gone out to beg near Tennōji Temple . . . One or two male boarders resided with them as well . . . This astonishing scene was an everyday condition in this grotto of the poor.
>
> (Taiga 1893: 110–11)

The occupations of the grandmother as a pieceworker, the daughters as street entertainers, the grandfather as beggar, the father as paper scavenger, and the grown son as the lowest of casual labourers were outside the formal economy. Consequently, all made marginal wages. Every able-bodied member of the household, six out of nine household members, engaged in income-earning activities, yet the household remained desperately poor. Only the infant, toddler, and bedridden mother did not seek renumerative work.

A Tokyo City Social Bureau survey suggests patterns of lower-class married women's employment in the early 1920s, including the occupations and wages of single mothers and widows. One elderly wife, 79-year-old Mrs Masuda, earned 3 yen per month making tags at home as a homeworker, while her 76-year-old husband made 12 yen per month as a street vendor of grilled chicken when he was healthy enough to go to work. Their combined incomes barely paid for their food and a three-by-three metre longhouse room costing 3 yen 50 sen per month. The wages of female household heads were no higher than those of married women, which caused extreme hardships for deserted, divorced and widowed women, especially those supporting young children. Forty-seven-year-old Mrs Asada, a single mother with three school-aged children, earned 20 yen per month as a day labourer. None the less, her income from full-time work could not support her family, so she earned an additional 30 yen by subletting part of her four-by-five metre rented house to seven boarders – five men and two women. Mrs Uchida, a 69-year-old widow, also engaged in two forms of paid work in order to support herself and her 54-year-old daughter. After her husband dissipated the family fortune left to Mrs Uchida, she set up shop as a petty retailer of sweets. In addition, she also took four male and female boarders into their tiny three-by-four metre rented house (Tōkyō-shi Shakai-kyoku 1921: 144–5).

Low wages were the striking feature of the work of lower-class women – whether pieceworker, self-employed or wage labourer. Although Mrs Asada the day labourer earned more than Mrs Masuda the pieceworker and Mrs Uchida the petty retailer, she still could not support a household on the income from full-time employment. Throughout the period under study, urban lower-class households relying on the women's earnings or the income of male casual labourers required more than one income to survive. Thus lower-class women not infrequently worked at more than one job.

DOMESTIC ACTIVITIES

What were the implications of long hours and low wages for urban lower-class women's involvement in home life? Living in households enmeshed in a money economy, they sought employment that produced cash income sufficient to meet minimum needs – food, shelter and fuel. But whether they held jobs inside or outside the home, the long hours over many days that lower-class women devoted to paid work reduced the time they could spend on domestic tasks. By the late 1920s, middle-class observers criticized homeworkers' management of women's domestic responsibilities:

> Women with children can't go out to work like female factory operatives. Because they have to raise their children, they take on piecework. They have no time to spare – which has a great impact on family life. They cannot complete their housework; they cannot take good care of their children. This brings about a lack of joy (*tanoshimi*) in the home and unsanitary conditions.
>
> (Tōkyō Shōkō Kaigisho 1928: 11)[23]

A more charitable estimate of pieceworkers' domestic lives would have noted, not only their participation in income-earning activities, but the effects of the lower-class metropolitan environment as well. Living in cheap hotels or tenements with few amenities amid the humidity, dirt and overcrowding of back alley urban districts also posed many obstacles to smooth management of household tasks.

Household formation and division of labour

From the 1890s until the 1920s, two-fifths of urban lower-class households in Tokyo were formed by consensual, common-law marriages rather than arranged, legally registered unions, but by the 1930s less than 10 per cent of such marriages were unregistered (Nakagawa 1985: 340; cf. Suzuki 1888: 139). The vast majority of these families were formed by migrants from rural areas. Seventy per cent of parents in lower-class households came from outside Tokyo, while 80 per cent of their children were born in Tokyo during these years (Nakagawa 1985: 337). Despite the saying 'And the poor get children' (*Bimbōnin no ko takusan*), surveys revealed that household size among the urban lower classes of Tokyo ranged from 3.0 to 3.5 in the 1890s and 3.2 to 4.2 in the 1920s, averaging 3.5 in the latter years, figures which were generally below the average of the national population[24] (Nakagawa 1985: 339; Taeuber 1958: 108). Furthermore, nuclear composition characterized 80 per cent of poor households during these four decades (Nakagawa 1985: 340). These demographic characteristics suggest that employed wives as a rule could rarely rely on mothers-in-law or senior household members for assistance with housekeeping, child care, or income-earning activities.

Yet should we assume, as did the above middle-class observers, that women alone had responsibility for domestic work? Although urban poor families generally were small in size, children participated in household tasks – and productive work as well – in the early modern and modern eras (see, for example, Thomas C. Smith 1977: 79, 109, 117; Uno 1979; Uno 1991a: 393–4; 1991b: 34–5). Especially before the First World War, homeworkers did not hesitate to ask children, even pre-schoolers, to help at home. In 1900, one woman kept her pre-school daughter out of day care to mind the baby while the mother did piecework 'piled up like a mountain' at the end of the month (Futaba Yōchien 1901: 6). Yet in this case, the child's domestic work was intimately related to her mother's wage work. By assisting her mother with child care, the young daughter freed her mother to earn more at outwork, which raised the family income. Moreover, recent studies suggest that the involvement of early modern peasant, merchant and samurai men in household chores, including child care, was greater than previously imagined (Uno 1987: 15–52; 1991b: 30–34). The attitudes of modern urban lower-class men, especially the self-employed, toward housework and childrearing and their participation in such work, bear further investigation. Finally, many urban lower-class women were recent migrants from the countryside, but throughout the modern era ordinary and poor rural women slighted cleaning, laundry and childrearing in order to engage in income-earning activities, much as they had before the modern era (Hane 1982: 79–101; Smith and Wiswell 1982: xxix–xxxv, 177–84, 202–41).

Furthermore, the earnings of children as well as wives increased household income. Some self-employed women, such as scavengers, took their children along to work because their labour could increase the day's earnings (Suzuki 1888: 145; Matsubara 1896: 84–6). Female operatives, especially single mothers, sometimes brought their youngsters to the factory in order to keep an eye on them, but pre-schoolers engaged in light tasks such as cutting, picking up scrap threads or cleaning, and older children did regular work such as tending bobbins for cut-rate wages (Tsurumi 1990: 154–6). Nevertheless, as school attendance rates of lower-class children rose in response to state pressure (Nakagawa 1985: 337), children's participation in domestic tasks and wage work lessened as the twentieth century progressed (Nakagawa 1985: 351; Uno 1979; 1987: 42–8; 1991a: 392–5). By 1920, one survey reported that no poor (*saimin*) children under age 11 were employed, although by age 14 half the youngsters had entered occupations (Nakagawa 1985: 115).

Urban environment and housing

In the late nineteenth century, the metropolitan lower classes, especially the poor, tended to concentrate in ghettoes (*hinminkutsu*), but as the twentieth century progressed, these dense settlements of the poor gradually dispersed (Nakagawa 1985: 264–76; Chubachi and Taira 1976: 399–407; 412–13). The 'grottoes of the poor' tended to occupy low-lying areas characterized by poor drainage, scarce breezes, and high humidity. And despite the high population density, the low wooden tenements housing the poor lined dark, narrow alleys rather than ordinary streets. Overcrowded, dimly lit, damp and stinking, the urban slums fostered crime and disease. They were hardly a promising environment for busy working women seeking to establish households and raise children.

In the 1890s, amid a general metropolitan housing shortage, urban lower-class women and their families lived in cheap hotels (*kichinyado*) or five-to-ten unit single-storey longhouses (*nagaya*) tucked away in alleys behind the main thoroughfares. Poor households as a rule resided in two-by-three to three-by-four square metre rooms, while working-class families might occupy two small rooms. Not infrequently two households or a household and unrelated persons shared living quarters. Not only did the dwellings of the urban underclass lack private toilets, baths and water supplies; many did not even have windows or cooking facilities (Nakagawa 1985: 343; Nishikawa 1990: 15–28). Needless to say, under these living conditions it was not easy for employed women to manage cooking, laundry, cleaning, and childrearing. None the less, communal facilities such as wells and public baths, which charged admission, had some advantages. They provided opportunities for women to socialize as they did laundry, washed dishes and bathed their children, while no single woman bore responsibility for the daily maintenance or cleaning of the facilities.

By the early 1930s, poor and working-class women and their families tended to occupy larger living spaces, often with amenities such as tiny kitchens, electricity and private toilets, and they owned more household goods – bedding, dining tables, cooking utensils and Shinto or Buddhist family altars (Nakagawa 1985:

345). In sum, the material aspects of urban lower-class women's home lives seem to have changed during the early twentieth century in ways that would ease working women's performance of household chores in a private residence. Yet one may also ask whether opportunities to cook at home instead of purchasing prepared foods and to wash clothes and utensils alone at home instead of in the company of other women truly served the interests of urban lower-class working women. On the contrary, it can be argued that the privatization of household tasks due to diffusion of housing amenities after the 1920s impoverished the social life and increased the workload of poor women who were already hard pressed to maintain their households and care for their children. And greater awareness of middle-class ideals of domesticity for married women may have begun to transform conceptions of womanhood and daily practices of urban lower-class women, particularly those of the working class, whose households were less likely to require wives' economic contributions.

Finances and consumption

By again scrutinizing the household budgets in Tables 3.1 to 3.3 (above) we gain further insights into the domestic world of urban lower-class women. Analysis of expenditures reveals patterns of consumption which shifted over time. The domestic environment of lower-class women, even those who were poor, became richer in material goods as the twentieth century progressed. Knowing who made decisions about purchases and who actually bought the goods that appeared in the home is critical to an understanding of household dynamics and authority. Although the budgets themselves do not reveal much regarding the extent of wives' control over household finances, other sources provide a few clues. Factory operatives earned wages on their own, yet had little free time in which to spend their pay. Yokoyama hints that late nineteenth-century lower-class wives freely disposed of their own earnings from piecework, and that they sometimes spent all of their pay on themselves and their children to the detriment of their husbands (1898: 58). A government report suggests that turn-of-the-century working-class women felt entitled to manage some portion of their husband's earnings, but that male workers contested their wives' authority over their paychecks:

the wives of the workers, anxious as to whether their husbands will really bring home the money on pay-day, gather in a group around the factory gate, demanding that their husbands turn over the wages [before they drink them away].

(Nōshōmushō Shōkō kyoku, *Shokkō Jijō*, 2, 1902: 19–20, cited in Gordon 1985: 28)

In the absence of documentary evidence, one can speculate that wives with independent incomes who spent more time at home than their husbands, that is, those who worked at home as piece-workers or petty entrepreneurs, had greater opportunities to exercise autonomy in making purchases, while wives who worked as unpaid family workers might have exercised less control over household income and expenditures.[25]

During the late Meiji era, urban lower-class women and their families spent a high proportion of their income on bare essentials – between 68 to 72 per cent on food and 10 to 19 per cent on shelter (see Table 3.1).[26] As household economic life revolved around obtaining basic necessities, women could not afford to buy durable goods. Expenses for the rental of bedding under the housing category during the 1890s indicate that many poor families did not even own sleeping mats and quilts (Nakagawa 1985: 345). Many families purchased leftover food, including rice, the staple grain, from vending carts, for several reasons. Used food was cheap, convenient, and, as mentioned previously, their rented rooms in cheap hotels and tenements often lacked cooking facilities (Nakagawa 1985: 343). While working-class budgets of these years shared with budgets of the poor a tendency to allocate a higher proportion of their income to food and to run a net monthly deficit, workers were able to devote somewhat more of their income to shelter and to discretionary expenses such as reading material and educational fees.

Yet by the 1920s, urban poor women spent less of their household budgets on food, 45 to 50 rather than over 60 per cent, while the expenditures of their working-class sisters had fallen to under 40 per cent (see Tables 3.2 and 3.3).[27] Housing expenses, too, came to consume a smaller proportion of urban lower-class budgets, while miscellaneous expenditures for newspapers, baths, educational fees, gifts and entertainment increased. As the domestic life of lower-class women became somewhat less focused on daily struggles for survival, they were able to spend more on clothing, education, and entertainment.[28]

Cleaning

As we have seen, urban lower-class women occupied cramped quarters which were not necessarily tidy or clean. The family members and their few possessions cluttered their small rented rooms, for space per person averaged at most a single one-by-two-metre straw mat per person until the 1930s (Chubachi and Taira 1976: 412; Nakagawa 1985: 28–9, 49–51, 117, 271–5, 286). House-hold members constantly tracked dirt and mud into residences from the unpaved alleys and streets of lower-class districts. Com-ments by teachers and social workers regarding the dirty clothes and bodies of the urban poor suggest that mothers lacked the time, money, or both, to keep themselves and their children clean. It seems unlikely that these hardworking women who worked long hours had the stamina to regularly beat the dust out of bedding and to sweep and scrub floors.[29] Moreover, before the First World War, it is conceivable that poor women who rented bedding, pawned their cooking pots on days when cash was short, and omitted regular clothing expenditures from their budgets could not afford to buy brooms.

Cooking

Lack of time, equipment and proper facilities limited lower-class women's opportunities to develop their culinary skills. Before the Russo-Japanese War (1904–5), the absence of kitchens in the long-houses or cheap hotels rented by the families of many lower-class women prevented them from preparing meals. Thus at the turn of the century poor women and men bought leftover rice (con-sidered the main course) and side dishes from vendors who had purchased their wares from dining halls and restaurants (Matsub-ara 1896: 41–5, 49, esp. illustration, 43; Yokoyama 1898: 53–4). However, improvements in the low tenements rented by poor and working-class households allowed many lower-class women to become more involved in meal preparation over time. By the 1910s, tiny kitchens of wooden tenement apartments, measuring about one square metre to one by two metres, could contain a clay cooking stove, small amounts of kindling and firewood, and a few pots and supplies.

Cooking was a fairly demanding task for women who also worked at paid employment at home or outside the home for ten to twelve or more hours per day. Cooking involved starting a fire in the stove; hauling of water from the well or communal tap outside to wash ingredients, make soup, and boil rice; and returning to the outdoor water supply to clean utensils. Yet a Tokyo survey found that by the early 1920s the poor no longer purchased leftover food and that Japanese white rice (thought to have better flavour than cheaper imported rice) constituted the primary grain in the diet of 88.4 per cent of 286 *saimin* surveyed, while only 10.5 per cent regularly ate rice mixed with barley (Tōkyō-shi Shakaikyoku 1921: 139–40).

Even with tiny private kitchens, cooking was inconvenient for lower-class working women; however, children did not necessarily suffer from hunger or malnutrition. Small shops, markets, and street vendors in lower-class neighbourhoods sold basic foodstuffs – rice, bean paste, salt, soy sauce, bean curd, vegetables, pickles, clams, dried and fresh fish, boiled and fermented beans, baked sweet potatoes and stews. Except rice, most of these foods required little or no cooking. Furthermore, food carts sold meals as well as dishes that could be incorporated into meals eaten at home. These ranged from noodle soups to boiled beans, baked sweet potatoes, stews, grilled chicken and sweets (Matsubara 1896: 60, 64–5; Yokoyama 1898: 27). Husbands and children could buy a wide variety of prepared foods, freeing wives from the need to prepare meals on a daily basis.

Childrearing

Some descriptions of lower-class mothers' child-care practices emphasized mothers' lax supervision of their children. In 1900, a young schoolteacher observed that hard-working poor parents in one of Tokyo's infamous slums allowed even pre-schoolers to roam the streets without supervision, which inspired her to found Japan's first day care centre. The mothers worked such long hours to gain subsistence that they had little choice but to neglect their beloved children (Uno 1987: 65–6). Two decades later, a social observer again reported that urban slum children were unkempt and unsupervised and that child babysitters still shared infant care with mothers. He noted that in the Minami Senjū district on the outskirts of Tokyo, 'babies cried beside housewives (*okamisan*) with untidy hair who were working frantically at piecework', once more depicting the difficulties which lower-class urban women faced in doing paid work and chores at home (Inoue 1922 cited in Uno 1987: 168).

Whether pieceworkers, self-employed, unpaid family workers, or factory hands, lower-class working mothers had little time to spend on the physical care of their children – feeding, clothing and bathing, nor could they devote long hours to the shaping of their children's intellect or character.[30] Mothers in Aisenbashi, an Osaka slum district, did not pour their energies into meal planning and preparation. When they were too busy to cook, children bought dishes from street vendors or went without food. None the less, their teacher noted the Aisenbashi youngsters did not seem mal-nourished and that they were hardy enough to eat spoiled food without getting sick and to avoid illness during the last cholera outbreak (Tomita 1921a). Even in the mid-1920s, descriptions of lower-class children depicted smudged faces, runny noses, rheumy eyes, matted hair with head lice, grimy bodies and dirty clothes (Uno 1987: 168–9). It was not uncommon for children to keep the same schedule as their mothers. Infants were not necessarily put down for naps, and pre-schoolers sometimes stayed up all night while their outworker mothers rolled cigarettes, pasted boxes or sewed sandal thongs.

Employed mothers worked hard for their children – not at caring for them on a daily basis, but at earning income for their food, clothing and shelter. The scant hours spent on child care did not necessarily mean that lower-class women were indifferent to their children's welfare. On the contrary, it is likely that the long hours spent at low-paying occupations suggest lower-class working women's strong concern for the welfare of their children and house-hold.

Observers often commented that lower-class mothers felt much affection for their children, despite having little time to care for, watch over and educate them. Mothers usually took their offspring with them when they left a common-law marriage, in sharp con-trast to prevailing practices in the legally-registered unions of prop-ertied families (Suzuki 1888: 139;[31] Tomita 1921b). Among the prosperous, children remained with the corporate household (*ie*) of their father, unless he was an adopted son, when a marriage dissolved. Lower-class mothers and fathers sent children as young as 7 or 8 to work as servants and apprentices in other households and as wage workers at factories, but such parents were not necessarily engaged in cold-hearted exploitation of their offspring. If the children remained nearby, parents might translate protective feelings into concrete actions. For example, in the early years of industrialization, to managers' dismay, parents of poor children in the Nago-chō slum district of Osaka would rush to the factories to side with their children in workplace quarrels (Yokoyama 1898: 159). Parents would intervene on their children's behalf in street scuffles as well (Uno 1985: 4). Poor and working-class mothers and fathers gave young children allowances (kozukai) that amounted to 3 to 6 per cent of household expenditures (Yokoyama 1898: 51, 262–8; Uno 1987: 86).[32] Finally, it seems that mothers manifested concern for their children in new ways as the twentieth century progressed. Employment of lower-class children under 14 declined and their school enrolment rates steadily climbed after the 1890s, suggesting that lower-class mothers began to accept the modern state's definition of children as dependants in contrast to the older view of children as contributors of labour and income to the household.

CONCLUSION

This chapter has sketched the interrelated work and domestic activities of pieceworkers from the 1890s to the late 1920s, suggesting that their patterns of paid and domestic work and their attitudes toward their work had much in common with those of other urban lower-class women – petty entrepreneurs, unpaid family workers and factory operatives during the same period. As recent migrants from the countryside, pieceworkers and other urban lower-class women very likely regarded participation in income-earning activities as a normal part of a married woman's duties. Moreover, although they might have felt a tension between paid and domestic work, they may not have valued housekeeping over income-earning activities, for both were essential to the survival of their households. In fact, the evidence considered here suggests that paid work had priority over domestic chores. Without money to pay for housing, food, fuel and other necessities, the household and its members would cease to exist, although some domestic work, especially providing food and caring for children, was also necessary to maintain a household.

Rather than performing an extensive range of domestic tasks themselves, lower-class married women relied on substitutes when they could. Children, in-laws (if present), and possibly spouses, could mind babies, clean, wash and cook, while other tasks, particularly meal preparation, could be replaced by purchased goods and services. And housekeeping standards were not very rigorous. It seems likely that urban lower-class women demonstrated their devotion to husband, children and/or home by participation in paid employment rather than painstaking involvement in domestic work. And while poor women were likely to have held such attitudes throughout the period under study, working-class women probably began to shed this view of married womanhood after the First World War.

Significantly, this study suggests that class and urban-rural distinctions in ideals of womanhood as well as differences between manhood and womanhood sharpened in Japan during the modern era, as do previous works treating the early modern and modern periods (Cf. Sakai 1939; Varner 1978; R. Smith 1983; Uno 1987, 1991b). Early modern married women worked on behalf of their households, although in contrast to commoner women, samurai women were barred from active participation in their husband's work – the governing of the lord's territory. As home and workplace separated in the modern era, women whose spouses worked in modern educational, industrial or political institutions found themselves unable to assist the family livelihood by helping their husbands at work. They could, however, raise household income by taking up employment on their own – at home as pieceworkers or petty entrepreneurs or outside the home as wage workers.

In the modern period, conceptions of womanhood became more diverse. One segment of the modern state, some Interior Ministry (*Naimushō*) bureaucrats, encouraged women to be diligent and productive at the beginning of the twentieth century. This view sanctioned behaviour in harmony with early modern ideals of womanly industry and frugality for the sake of the household (Nolte and Hastings 1991). Calling on women to contribute to the imperial state in addition to the private household was novel, but emphasis on the public implications of women's private domestic efforts for women overlapped with exhortations to men to serve the country through energetic participation in the economy and army. Articles in popular magazines concerning piecework in this era echoed these sentiments, encouraging middle-class as well as lower-class women to take up homework, not only to increase household income but also to avoid character degeneration stemming from idleness (Maruoka 1980: 85–92, 94–101; Ogi *et al* 1990: 384–99).

However, a competing conception of womanhood, 'good wife, wise mother' (*ryosai kenbō*), promoted by the Education Ministry (*Monbushō*) in the same period, stressed woman's duties as child-rearer and domestic manager (Fukaya 1977), in contrast to the Interior Ministry's emphasis on female productivity.[33] In defining women's destiny as the home, the 'good wife, wise mother' accented women's differences from men, although it did not pro-scribe the earning of income within households. In addition, the standards of the new domesticity were differentiated by class (Uno 1988). Thus in the pre-war higher girls' schools, middle-class women learned to apply the latest scientific methods of cleaning, clothing construction, nutrition, and childrearing to modernize their homes, because their children, the nation's future leaders, deserved the best possible home environment. While the government desired some improvement in sanitation, nutrition and personal hygiene in lower-class homes, optimum surroundings were not necessary for lower-class children who faced mundane destinies as army conscripts, ordinary workers and mothers. Laxer standards allowed lower-class married women in both city and countryside to live as 'good wives' in the old sense – toiling long hours at income-earning activities at the expense of domestic tasks to ensure the survival of their households and children – preferably at home rather than outside the home.[34] And even if their views of womanhood did not coincide precisely with those of the state, their productivity at home continued to contribute to economic development, which remained an important state goal.

Although urban lower-class women's self-conceptions had changed relatively little, attitudes toward piecework in municipal surveys and magazine articles had shifted by the mid–1920s, probably reflecting slowly-changing views of motherhood. From the 1870s, independent of the Education Ministry's *fin-de-siècle* prescrip-tions for womanhood, the modern western insistence on the import-ance of the mother as primary caregiver for children had begun to infuse the fields of education, child study and welfare as well as popular women's periodicals in Japan (Uno 1992b). Perhaps the confluence of new private and official conceptions of the feminine explains the triumph of the vision of woman as domestic, of woman with a social destiny distinct from that of men, and of the ideas of the Education rather than the Interior Ministry, in written, or elite, culture by the 1920s. Criticism of homework because it interfered with child care and domestic chores became commonplace in surveys and descriptions of outwork, yet it was tolerated as a sort of necessary evil for poor, lower-class and lower-middle-class women whose households needed their earnings. Domestic neglect was better than falling into dependence on relief. However, the enthusiastic recommendations of the 1890s – that women of all classes, including those in the upper reaches of the middle class, take up outwork vanished (Tōkyō-shi Shakaikyoku 1926; Saitama-ken Gakumubu Shakaika 1926; Tōkyō Shōkō Kaigisho 1928). Changes in conceptions of womanhood during Japanese industrialization, then, tended increasingly to stress differences in the attitudes and conduct of middle-class and urban underclass women[35] as well as women's differences from men in the initial decades of the twentieth century.

NOTES

Acknowledgements: I would like to express my gratitude to Tsunoda Katsuhiko, Masako Ohtomo, Michiko Mabashi, Kazuyo Yamamoto, Suwon Kim, Narita Ryūichi and Nakagawa Kiyoshi for assistance with sources, translations, and citations, and to Barbara Molony and Laura Hein for encouragement and comments on earlier drafts of this chapter.

1 The modern era is generally defined as the years between the Meiji Restoration (1868) and the Second World War (1941–5), including the reigns of three emperors, Meiji (1868–1912), Taisho (1912–26) and Showa (1926–89). It is generally said that the preceding early modern era began in 1600 and ended in 1867.
2 That is, from the 1880s to the mid–1920s. In English, see Ishimoto (1935); Sugimoto (1928); K. Molony (1980); Sievers (1983). Among the far more numerous Japanese sources see, for example, the important anthologies Joseishi Sōgō Kenkyūkai (1982), Wakita (1985) and Joseishi Sōgō Kenkyūkai (1990), which lack discussions of the domestic life of modern urban working women. Fuse (1984: 130–62) is exceptional in discussing married women's work. In addition, materials in the pioneering 10-volume *Nihon Fujin Mondai Shiryō Shūsei*, especially vol. 7 (Maruoka 1980), can serve as a useful starting point for such research.
3 Sievers (1983: 64–86); Hane (1982: 172–225); Hunter (1984); Tsurumi (1984); Bernstein (1988); Tsurumi (1990); B. Molony (1991);

Silverberg (1991). Glimpses of the home life of anarchist and socialist married women workers appear in Hane (1988).

4 Regarding the need to overcome dichotomies (also referred to as binary oppositions or dualisms) in studies of Japanese history and society, see Kondo (1990); Uno (1991b, 1992b).

5 Even middle-class status was precarious in an age without adequate social insurance. Because of the differential between men's and women's full-time earnings, the unemployment, illness or death of the primary male earner could easily plunge a comfortable household into poverty.

6 However, female versatility did not preclude male participation in domestic work in the early modern and modern eras (Uno 1987, 1991b, 1992b).

7 For the post-war comparison, see Bernstein 1983.

8 This type of employment is also called homework or outwork. Regarding homework in early modern Japan, see Leupp (1991) and Yokota (1991); regarding homework in post-war Japan, see, for example, Nakayama (1957: 30–33). For discussions of contemporary female pieceworkers outside Japan, including women engaged in white-collar work such as data processing see Boris and Daniels (1989); Benería and Roldan (1987); Joekes (1987); Ward (1990); Roh (1990).

9 Piecework such as machine sewing and embroidery required skills or substantial investment in equipment, but handbooks recommended these to middle-class rather than poor women (Tōkyō-shi Shakaikyoku 1926: 44–7). See also Ogi et al. (1990: 386–99). Regarding rural women's outwork see Yokoyama (1898: 304–8); Saitama-ken Gakumubu Shakaika (1926).

10 Advantages to employers included low labour costs and hiring flexibility (Tōkyō-shi Shakaikyoku 1926; Saitama-ken Gakumubu Shakaika 1926).

11 I know of no earlier estimate of outworker numbers than this 1925 survey which was published in 1926.

12 Middle-class women engaged in Japanese and machine sewing.

13 In descending order the distribution of outwork types, which closely resembled that of the larger sample, was Japanese sewing (482), sandal-thong stitching (423), toy assembling and finishing (284), machine sewing (241), attaching footwear soles (233), paper-bag pasting (187), and knitwear finishing (170) (Tōkyō-shi Shakaikyoku 1926: 84–6).

14 The age categories overlap in the original.

15 Regarding the relationship of pieceworkers to middlemen, see Tōkyō-shi Shakaikyoku (1926: 12–13, 39).

16 One hundred sen equalled one yen.

17 Estimate based on Budget no. 10 in Table 3.2 below. The average monthly income of 1926 pieceworkers surveyed was 70.8 yen per month, while the average real monthly income for the Budget no. 10 sample was 72.4 yen per month.

18 Tables in Fuse (1984: 138) compiled from Nōshōmushō Shōkōkyoku Shokko Jijō (1903) reveal that at the beginning of the twentieth century the percentage of married female factory hands ranged from 3.2 to

39.1 per cent among 2,400 workers in seven textile factories and from 11 to 60.6 per cent among 2,350 women in eight other industries – including brush (60.6), cotton-processing (48.6), match (43.6), knitted goods (31.6) and string (11.2) factories. Fuse (p. 147) also found a 1924 survey indicating that, on the average, 17 per cent of female workers in over 13 industries had spouses, ranging from highs of 71 per cent and 62.4 per cent in the construction and metal industries to a low of 12 per cent in the textile trades.

19 Regarding hours, wages, and working conditions of female factory operatives, see the works cited in note 3 above. For insights into women's work as urban petty entrepreneurs and unpaid family workers in the modern era, see Yokoyama 1898: 122; Maxson 1976; Pelzel 1979; Kikumura 1981: 14–15; Lebra 1991, although as yet, no historical studies exist.

20 The Tokyo Chamber of Commerce reported that the highly-skilled pieceworkers working over ten hours per day could earn a monthly wage of 24–25 yen, far lower than the top monthly earnings of 70 yen for full-time female factory operatives in 1922 (Tōkyō Shōkō Kaigisho 1928: 11).

21 Lower-class male occupations included artisans; manual labourers, including rickshaw pullers; miscellaneous workers (paper scavengers, clam sellers, footwear repairers, pipe menders, metal casters and ash buyers); factory operatives; construction workers; and day labourers, with the latter four occupations predominating by the 1920s. During the Showa Recession (1927–33), those doing miscellaneous work increased. The incomes of the outdoor occupations varied according to the weather (Matsubara 1896: 61; Nakagawa 1985: 53–8, 119–24, 304–11. In English, see Hazama 1976; Taira 1988).

22 Lower-class men typically worked about 25 days per month. Full-time factory operatives might average 25 to 29 workdays per month, while day labourers averaged 22 to 23 days per month (Nakagawa 1985: 57, 119–20). Regular days off numbered only two per month, but bad weather, festivals, and failure to report to work increased the number of workless days.

23 See also Tōkyō-shi Shakaikyoku 1926: 15; Saitama-ken Gakumubu Shakaika 1926: 2.

24 The average number of persons per household was 4.98 in 1920, 4.98 in 1940, and 4.97 in 1950 and 1955 (Taeuber 1958: 108).

25 Thus women who worked outside the home and those who helped their husbands in family businesses may have had less autonomy in making decisions regarding consumption.

26 However, one study estimates that the national population spent 63.5 per cent of their income on food and 8.2 per cent on housing in the decade 1896–1906 (Hazama 1976: 37).

27 Among the upper reaches of the poor, whose incomes were roughly equal to those of the bottom of the working class, the proportion of expenditures on food dropped to 40 per cent.

28 Investigation of the proportions of discretionary expenditures spent on

wives, husbands and children should reveal additional dimensions of domestic life.

29 Standards of cleanliness and personal hygiene were low in villages at this time as well. Rural children too often had dirty clothes, head lice and runny noses, for their mothers toiled long hours at agricultural work and by-employments (Smith and Wiswell 1982: xxxv, 202–4, 211–3, 238–40). For a post-war comparison, see Bernstein 1983.

30 Similarly, the need to gain a livelihood reduced the time available to modern lower-class rural women for child care (see note 29).

31 In stating that 'there is nowhere in the world where more women have children of different fathers', rather than of different mothers, Suzuki implies that children stayed with their mothers when parents separated.

32 This is the equivalent of parents with a yearly income of US $35,000 giving US $1,050–2,152 per year, or about $3–6 per day, to a pre-school child for pocket money.

33 Both ministries, however, emphasized women's contributions to state as well as private households.

34 Discussions of the stigma attached to work outside the home appear in Bernstein 1988 and Tsurumi 1990.

35 However, middle-class ideals of womanhood may have begun to influence working-class women by the 1920s.

REFERENCES

Benería, Lourdes and Martha Roldan (1987) *The Crossroads of Class and Gender*, Chicago, University of Chicago Press.

Bernstein, Gail Lee (1983) *Haruko's World: a Japanese Farm Woman and Her Community*, Stanford, Stanford University Press.

Bernstein, Gail Lee (1988) 'Women in the silk-reeling industry in nineteenth-century Japan', in Gail Lee Bernstein and Haruhiro Fukui (eds) *Japan and the World: Essays in Honour of Ishida Takeshi*, New York, St Martin's Press, 54–77.

Bernstein, Gail Lee (ed.) (1991) *Recreating Japanese Women, 1600–1945*, Berkeley, CA, University of California Press.

Boris, Eileen and Daniels, Cynthia R. (eds) (1989) *Homework*, Urbana, University of Illinois Press.

Chubachi, Masayoshi and Taira, Koji (1976) 'Poverty in modern Japan: perceptions and realities', in Hugh Patrick (ed.) *Japanese Industrialization and Its Social Consequences*, Berkeley, CA, University of California Press, 391–437.

Fukaya, Masatoshi (1977) *Ryōsai Kenboshugi no Kyōiku*, Nagoya, Reimei Shobō.

Fuse, Akiko (1984) *Atarashii Kazoku no Sōzō*, Tokyo, Aoki Shoten.

Futaba Yōchien (1900) *Shiritsu Futaba Yōchien Daiikkai Nenpō* 1 (January–June 1900), Tokyo, Futaba Yōchien.

Futaba Yōchien (1901) *Shiritsu Futaba Yōchien Dainikai Nenpō* 1 (July 1900–June 1901), Tokyo, Futaba Yōchien.

Futaba Yōchien (1908) *Shiritsu Futaba Yōchien Daikyūkai Nenpō* 1 (July 1907–June 1908), Tokyo, Futaba Yōchien.

Gordon, Andrew (1985) *The Evolution of Labor Relations in Japan: Heavy Industry, 1853–1955*, Cambridge, Massachusetts, Harvard University Press.

Hane, Mikiso (1982) *Rebels, Peasants, and Outcastes: The Underside of Modern Japan*, New York, Pantheon Books.

Hane, Mikiso (1988) (ed.) (trans.) *Reflections on the Way to the Gallows: Voices of Japanese Rebel Women*, Berkeley, CA, University of California Press and New York, Pantheon Books.

Hazama, Hiroshi (1976) 'Historical changes in the life style of Japanese workers', in Hugh Patrick (ed.) *Japanese Industrialization and Its Social Consequences*, Berkeley, CA, University of California Press, 21–52.

Hunter, Janet (1984) 'Labour in the Japanese silk industry in the 1870s: the *Tomioka Nikki* of Wada Ei', in Gordon Daniels (ed.) *Europe Interprets Japan*, Exeter, England, European Association of Japanese Studies, 20–25.

Inoue, Teizō (1922) *Roku Daitoshi no Hinminkutsu*, n.p., n.pub.

Ishimoto, Shidzue (1935) *Facing Two Ways: The Story of My Life*, New York, Farrar & Rinehart.

Joekes, Susan (1987) *Women in the World Economy: An INSTRAW Study*, New York, Oxford University Press.

Joseishi Sōgō Kenkyūkai (1982) *Nihon Joseishi*, 5 vols, Tokyo, University of Tokyo Press.

Joseishi Sōgō Kenkyūkai (1990) *Nihon Josei Seikatsushi*, 5 vols, Tokyo, University of Tokyo Press.

Kikumura, Akemi (1981) *Through Harsh Winters: The Life of a Japanese Immigrant Woman*, Novato, California, Chandler & Sharp.

Kondo, Dorinne (1990) *Crafting Selves: Power, Gender, and Discourses of Identity in a Japanese Workplace*, Chicago, University of Chicago Press.

Lebra, Joyce (1991) 'Women in an all-Male industry: the case of sake brewer Tatsu'uma Kiyo', in Gail Lee Bernstein (ed.) *Recreating Japanese Women, 1600–1945*, Berkeley, CA, University of California Press, 131–48.

Leupp, Gary (1991) 'The women of Hanaguruma-cho: gender and wage-labor in Nishijin during the late Tokugawa period', paper given at the conference 'Female and Male Role Sharing in Japan: Historical and Contemporary Constructions of Gender', University of Michigan, December.

Maruoka, Hideko (ed.) (1980) *Nihon Fujin Mondai Shiryō Shūsei* 7 (*Seikatsu*), Tokyo, Domesu Shuppan.

Matsubara, Iwatarō (1896) *Saiankoku no Tōkyō*, repr. 1988, Tokyo, Iwanami Shoten.

Maxson, Mary Lou (1976) 'Women in family businesses', in Joyce Lebra, Joy Paulson and Elizabeth Powers (eds) *Women in Changing Japan*, Stanford, Stanford University Press, 89–105.

Molony, Barbara (1991) 'Activism among women in the Taishō cotton textile industry', in Gail Lee Bernstein (ed.) *Recreating Japanese Women, 1600–1945*, Berkeley, CA, University of California Press, 217–38.

Molony, Kathleen (1980) 'One woman who dared: Ichikawa Fusae and the Japanese woman's suffrage movement', PhD dissertation, University of Michigan.

Naimushō Chihō-kyoku (1912) *Saimin Chōsa Tōkeihyō*, Tokyo, Naimushō.

Nakagawa, Kiyoshi (1982) 'Kakei shiryō ni miru kindai Nihon no toshi seikatsu', *Niigata Daigaku Shōgaku Ronshū* 15 (August 1982), 141–213.

Nakagawa, Kiyoshi (1985) *Nihon no Toshi Kasō*, Tokyo, Keisō Shobō.

Nakagawa, Kiyoshi (1987) 'Urban life in early 20th-century Tokyo', *Nihon Joshi Daigaku Kiyō* 36 (March), 29–51.

Nakayama, Yasu (1957) *Shufu no Seikatsu Jittai*, Tokyo, Yamamoto Shoten.

Nishikawa, Yūko (1990) 'Sumai no hensen to "katei" no seiritsu', in Joseishi Sōgō Kenkyūkai (ed.) *Nihon Josei Seikatsushi* 4 (*Kindai*), Tokyo, University of Tokyo Press, 1–49.

Nolte, Sharon and Hastings, Sally (1991) 'The Meiji state's policy toward women, 1890–1910', in Gail Lee Bernstein (ed.) *Recreating Japanese Women, 1600–1945*, Berkeley, CA, University of California Press, 151–74.

Nōshōmushō Shōkōkyoku (1903) *Shokkō Jiyō*, repr. 3 vols 1976, with an introduction by Tsuchiya Takao, Tokyo, Shinkigensha.

Ogi, Shinzō, Kumakura, Isao and Ueno, Chizuko (eds) (1990) *Fūzoku: Sei, Nihon Kindai Shisō Taikei* 23, Tokyo, Iwanami Shoten.

Pelzel, John (1979) 'Factory life in Japan and China today', in Albert Craig (ed.) *Japan: A Comparative View*, Princeton, NJ, Princeton University Press, 392–405.

Rendall, Jane (1990) *Women in Industrializing England 1750–1880*, Cambridge, Massachusetts, Basil Blackwell.

Roh, Mi-hye (1990) 'A study on home-based work in Korea', *Women's Studies Forum 1990*, Seoul, Korean Women's Development Institute, 25–38.

Saitama-ken Gakumubu Shakaika (1926) *Naishoku ni Kansuru Chōsa*, n.p., Saitama Kyōsaikai.

Sakai, Atsuhiko (1939) 'Kaibara-Ekiken and "Onna Daigaku" ', *Cultural Nippon* 7 (4), 43–56.

Sievers, Sharon (1983) *Flowers in Salt: The Beginnings of Feminist Consciousness in Modern Japan*, Stanford, CA, Stanford University Press.

Silverberg, Miriam (1991) 'The modern girl as militant', in Gail Lee Bernstein (ed.) *Recreating Japanese Women, 1600–1945*, Berkeley, CA, University of California Press, 239–66.

Smith, Robert J. (1983). 'Making village women into "good wives and wise mothers" in prewar Japan', *Journal of Family History* 8(3), 70–84.

Smith, Robert J. and Wiswell, Ella (1982) *The Women of Suye Mura*, Chicago, University of Chicago Press.

Smith, Thomas C. (1977) *Nakahara: Family Farming and Population in a Japanese Village, 1717–1830*, Stanford, Stanford University Press.

Sugimoto, Etsu Inagaki (1928) *Daughter of a Samurai*, Garden City, New York, Doubleday, Doran & Co.

Suzuki, Umeshiro (1888) *Osaka Nago-chō Hinminkutsu Shisatsu Ki*, in Taketoshi Nishida (ed.) *Meiji Shoki no Toshi Kasō Shakai, Seikatsu Koten Sōsho* 2, repr. 1970, Tokyo, Kōseikan, 123–52.

Taeuber, Irene (1958) *The Population of Japan*, Princeton, NJ, Princeton University Press.

Taiga, Koji (1893) *Hin-tenchi Kikankutsu Tanken Ki* in Taketoshi Nishida (ed.) *Meiji Shoki no Toshi Kasō Shakai, Seikatsu Koten Sōsho* 2, repr. 1970, Tokyo, Kōseikan, 65–122.

Taira, Koji (1988) 'Economic development, labor markets, and industrial relations in Japan', in John W. Hall, Marius B. Jansen, Madoka Kanai and Denis Twitchett (eds) *The Cambridge History of Japan* 6, Cambridge, Cambridge University Press, 606–53.

Tōkyō-shi Shakaikyoku (1921) *Tōkyō-shinai no Saimin ni kansuru Chōsa*, Tokyo, Tōkyō-shi Shakaikyoku.

Tōkyō-shi Shakaikyoku (1926) *Naishoku ni kansuru Chōsa*, Tokyo, Tōkyō-shi Shakaikyoku.

Tōkyō Shōkō Kaigisho (1928) *Tōkyō-shi oyobi sono Fukin ni okeru Kanai Kōgyō Jōtai*, Tokyo, Tōkyō Shōkō Kaigisho.

Tomita, Ei (1921a) 'Saiminkutsu no sannen – sono san', *Katei Shūhō* 603, 4 March.

Tomita, Ei (1921b) 'Saiminkutsu no sannen – sono yon', *Katei Shūhō* 604, 11 March.

Tsurumi, E. Patricia (1984) 'Female textile workers and the failure of early trade unionism in Japan', *History Workshop Journal* 18 (autumn), 3–27.

Tsurumi, E. Patricia (1990) *Factory Girls: Women in the Thread Mills of Meiji Japan*, Princeton, NJ, Princeton University Press.

Uno, Kathleen (1979) 'Family strategy in late Tokugawa and early Meiji Japan', unpublished paper.

Uno, Kathleen (1985) 'The family in the city: late Meiji-Taisho urban parent-child relationships', paper given at the Association for Asian Studies annual meeting, Chicago, March.

Uno, Kathleen (1987) 'Day care and family life in industrializing Japan, 1868–1926', PhD dissertation, Berkeley, CA, University of California.

Uno, Kathleen (1988) ' "Good wives, wise mothers" in early twentieth-century Japan', paper given at the joint annual meeting of the Conference of Western Women Historians and the Pacific Coast Branch of the American Historical Association, San Francisco, CA, August.

Uno, Kathleen (1991a) 'Women and changes in the household division of labor', in Gail Lee Bernstein (ed.) *Recreating Japanese Women, 1600–1945*, Berkeley, CA, University of California Press, 17–41.

Uno, Kathleen (1991b) 'Japan', in Joseph Hawes and N. Ray Hiner (eds) *Children in Historical and Comparative Perspective: An International Handbook and Research Guide*, Westport, Connecticut, Greenwood Press, 389–419.

Uno, Kathleen (1992a) 'The death of "good wife, wise mother?" ' in Andrew Gordon (ed.) *Postwar Japan as History*, Berkeley, CA, University of California Press.

Uno, Kathleen (1992b) *Childhood, Motherhood, and State in Early Twentieth-Century Japan*, unpublished manuscript.

Varner, Richard (1978) 'The organized peasant: the wakamonogumi in the Edo period', *Monumenta Nipponica* 32(4), 459–83.

Ward, Kathryn (ed.) (1990) *Women Workers and Global Restructuring*, Ithaca, NY, ILR Press, Cornell University.

Wakita, Haruko (ed.) (1985) *Bosei o Tou*, 2 vols, Kyoto, Jinbun Shoin.

Yokota, Fuyuhiko (1991) 'Kinsei no shakaiteki bungyō to josei,' paper given at the conference 'Female and Male Role Sharing in Japan: Historical and Contemporary Constructions of Gender', University of Michigan, December.

Yokoyama, Gennosuke (1898) *Nihon no Kasō Shakai*, repr. 1990, Tokyo, Iwanami Shoten.

Chapter 4

Textile factories, tuberculosis and the quality of life in industrializing Japan

Janet Hunter

A striking feature of the modern outlook on tuberculosis is the public recognition of its social and economic setting. Tuberculosis is no longer solely a disease of medical significance and relegated to the physician and the surgeon. Its social and economic implications are far-reaching . . . [Researchers] have repeatedly shown tuberculosis to be a source of financial loss to the community in wage-earning power and efficiency, which too frequently brings its victim to poverty and destitution.

(Sir Arthur S.MacNalty, Chief Medical Officer, Ministry of Health, 1939, in Hart and Wright 1939:v)

The incidence of tuberculosis in most of the industrializing countries of the west showed a progressive decline during the late nineteenth and early twentieth centuries, but mortality particularly among young adults remained worryingly high. Nevertheless, recognition of the existence of an etiological relationship between social and economic conditions and tuberculosis, of the kind contained in the above statement, was slow in coming. Doctors in Western Europe and the United States for long failed to agree on the causes of the spread of tuberculosis, let alone on how to cure it. Only from the 1880s did the majority of doctors begin to abandon the belief that tuberculosis was caused purely by hereditary or 'moral' factors in favour of regarding it as a communicable disease spread by bacilli (Smith 1988:47). Even after it was recognized that the disease was communicated by more than one variety of bacillus, introduced into the body by the inhalation of infectious droplets or ingestion of foodstuffs, disagreements continued over how best to prevent the spread of infection and cure the afflicted. Debates raged over the relative importance of heredity and environment in individuals' predisposition to the disease. Correlations between poor working and living conditions, general poverty and high tuberculosis contraction and mortality rates began to be substantiated after the turn of the century, but the results of research were often obscured by vested medical and other interests, while their practical implications were costly and difficult to implement. For both these reasons they failed to have a rapid impact on prevention and treatment strategies (Smith 1988:46ff.; Teller 1988).

In Japan the environmental contribution to the contraction of tuberculosis appears to have been recognized, and exhaustively documented, at a relatively early stage. Doctors in Japan and the west were simultaneously exploring this area of research in the first decade of the twentieth century. While Japanese doctors could not necessarily explain the causality any better than some of their western counterparts, they kept a close eye on advances in European and American research, while also pursuing their own investigations. Researchers enjoyed substantial support from national and local government bodies, and with facilities for treatment virtually non-existent, did not have to contend with powerful vested interest groups. Practical strategies for prevention and cure did not necessarily follow from the publication of research results. Public health policies were in their infancy, and Japan's developing economy could not provide the resources for a national education programme and improved facilities. Nevertheless, the question of health, and of tuberculosis in particular, became the object of considerable debate over the years after 1900.

Over the period 1900–40 Japanese researchers targeted one group in particular – female textile workers. These workers were mostly young (12–20 years of age) and unmarried. Most were *dekasegi* (migrant) workers, who worked at silk or cotton mills for short periods of a year or two, residing in mill dormitories during their period of employment. They would then move on to alternative employment, or return to their native villages, often to marry.[1] The rural link remained strong and contemporaries, at least until the 1930s, viewed these women as temporarily seconded members of the rural proletariat, rather than fully-fledged members of an industrial one.

The focus on workers in an industry which played such a key role in Japan's early industrialization process led researchers and others to consider more widely the links between health and industrialization. Detailed and well-publicized knowledge of the working life of these women, and in particular of their health, at an early stage put mortality and disease on the agenda as one index of the quality of life in Japan. Writers from as early as the 1890s were in effect using health data as a proxy for the quality of life of various population groups during the course of industrialization. It was quickly recognized that the anticipated rising per capital gross national product (GNP) over the long run did not mean that there were not 'losers' in the short and medium term; indeed, it was understood that throughout the early decades of industrialization the human cost of much of the process was bound to be considerable. The health and tuberculosis evidence played a crucial part in promoting the view that female textile workers were some of the most definitive losers of all, and this characterization has persisted ever since.

This paper seeks to explain how the high incidence of illness, especially tuberculosis, among female factory workers became an object of concern, to identify factors in their living and working conditions which may have been conducive to the spread of the disease, and to comment briefly on why the issue assumed both historical and historiographical significance.

MORTALITY AND TUBERCULOSIS IN INDUSTRIALIZING JAPAN

There are conflicting views over trends in Japanese mortality in the Meiji period (Umemura 1988; Okazaki 1986; Saitō 1989; Nishikawa and Abe 1990:45–59),[2] but at least after 1920 the process of industrialization was accompanied by declining death-rates. However, the aggregate national figures conceal variations in the death-rates of different age and occupational groups, and in different regions. During the early decades of the twentieth century, contemporaries observed that while female life expectancy in almost all areas of the country was greater than male life expectancy, in certain age groups female mortality rates were much higher than for males. This was particularly true of cities. In 1925–6 death-rates of girls aged 10–14 in big cities were 148 per cent of the rates for boys in the same age group. Ten years later the figure was still 143 per cent. Outside the cities it was only marginally less – 139 per cent and 134 per cent. This disparity existed for all age groups up to 40 (Taeuber 1956:306). During the years up to the late 1930s, female mortality in the puberty to 30 age group exceeded male mortality in the same age group by about 20 per cent. Available data suggest that only a very small part of this excess can be explained by problems arising out of pregnancy and childbirth.[3]

Pre-Second World War Japan also experienced a marked shift in the major causes of mortality. Following the breach of what has been called the 'cordon sanitaire' by increasing western contacts from the 1850s, there was a wave of epidemics of illnesses such as cholera and measles (Jannetta 1986:206). There was then a relative decline in deaths from complaints which could be curbed by environmental control or by direct medical action, such as diarrhoea and gastro-enteritis, dysentery, pneumonia, bronchitis, cholera, smallpox, typhus and typhoid. Significantly, over the same period registered deaths from tuberculosis increased, and from 1934 to 1950 the disease was the leading single cause of death, accounting for 12–14 per cent of all deaths (GHQ SCAP n.d.:18–38).

Tuberculosis had long been prevalent in Japan, and the absence of reliable data pertaining to any years prior to the twentieth century make an accurate assessment of the situation very difficult. What is absolutely clear, though, is that the mortality rate from all forms of tuberculosis in Japan, which stood at 160/100,000 around 1900, a level comparable with that in Western Europe, increased dramatically thereafter, reaching a peak in 1918 of 253/100,000. A comprehensive anti-tuberculosis law in 1919 provided for measures such as disinfection and subsidies for sanatoria, but the fresh air, rest and improved nutrition deemed by doctors to be the best treatment were largely unavailable to the poor, and medication was only patchily effective (Powell and Anesaki 1990:44). The death rate did decline to 179.5/100,000 in 1932, only to rise to 280/100,000 in the appalling circumstances of 1945–6. After 1950, largely due to more effective drug treatment, the rate fell dramatically, though it remained somewhat higher than in many other industrialized countries.

Moreover, mortality statistics cannot necessarily be regarded as a true indicator of the spread of infection. Many Japanese doctors were insufficiently trained to make accurate assessments of patients, and, in Teller's words, 'the diagnosis of incipient tuberculosis was a challenge even to the best clinician' (Teller 1988:86). Tuberculosis was not a legally notifiable disease and, in an

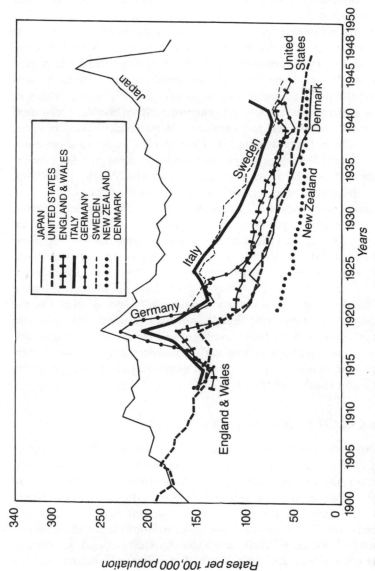

Figure 4.1 Comparative tuberculosis death rates: 1900–48
Source: GHQ SCAP n.d.: 39

environment where the pattern of infection was ill understood, contraction often led to social ostracism. It was often concealed if at all possible. To save face doctors were often thought to attribute death from pulmonary tuberculosis (phthisis) in particular, to illnesses such as pneumonia and bronchitis. The official figures available may therefore be taken as a substantial underestimate of the real situation.

Over the same period, in most of the industrialized countries of the west, rates of tuberculosis mortality were declining. In Britain, the US and many countries of Western Europe there was a progressive decline from the mid-nineteenth century onwards, well before the introduction of any preventive BCG or other immunization programme or effective chemotherapy. Having recognized a correlation between the incidence of tuberculosis and poverty, authorities in the west noted that this decline in tuberculosis mortality parallelled rising living standards, as measured by conventional indices such as real earnings (Hart and Wright 1939:20ff.). They disagreed, however, on the cause of the decline.

A significant feature of tuberculosis is that the highest incidence was found among younger age groups (Teller 1988:35; Hart and Wright 1939:1ff.). Tuberculosis mortality patterns by age show that in early twentieth-century Japan this was true for both males and females. It became apparent, however, that more girls contracted tuberculosis at a younger age than did boys.[4] Medical researchers began to suspect a particularly high incidence of the disease among the young female industrial workers who laboured in the nation's numerous textile mills. In the years after 1900 research on morbidity and mortality among this group was undertaken, and detailed surveys carried out of days lost through illness in a large number of textile mills.

RESEARCH INTO FACTORY HEALTH

The debate over the significance of tuberculosis in Japan must be seen in the context of concern over working conditions and pressure for factory legislation (Kobayashi 1965; Dore 1969; Taira 1970). This pressure developed in Japan from the late 1890s, and was fuelled by the publication of reports such as Yokoyama Gennosuke's *Nihon no Kasō Shakai* (The Lower Social Strata of Japan) (Yokoyama 1898), and the Agriculture and Commerce Ministry's *Shokkō Jijō* (Conditions of Workers) (Nōshōmushō Shōkōkyoku 1903). As factory owners showed continuing resistance to state intervention in working conditions, investigators became increasingly concerned about the state of health of workers in the nation's factories. Doctors drew strong and unfavourable contrasts with the western working environment, castigating Japanese employers for their failure to improve the situation (Yamane 1911:3–5). One writer commented that workers would normally leave bad conditions for better, but because women workers were young and unable to resist the use of force, normal labour market conditions could not operate, so employers had a 'paternalistic' duty towards their employees (Kubota 1902:4). For the most part improvement in worker welfare was argued not for its own sake, but for the sake of national efficiency. Reports frequently mentioned the dire effect on factory productivity of the huge numbers of days lost through worker illness (for example, Koinuma 1925:22), and the profits which could accrue from prevention of illness (Kose 1926:214).

Reports on worker health proliferated after 1900, a large number concentrating on the situation relating to female textile workers. A very comprehensive study was carried out 1909–11 by Ishihara Osamu, who was to become particularly famous for his work on tuberculosis (Ishihara 1913a). By the inter-war period the government's own statistics clearly showed that the sickness rate for women in all large factories in Japan was much greater than that for men, and was particularly high in textiles (ILO 1933:243)[5]. Four surveys selected here, two in the cotton industry and two in silk, well represent researchers' findings. One investigator in 1911 conducted a general medical inspection of 1,300 workers in a cotton-spinning mill. It appears that health inspection standards on entry were rigorous, and conditions relatively good. While the rate of acute illness was not particularly high, the extent of less acute ailments was immense. No fewer than 42 per cent (546) were suffering from trachoma (of whom 200 had contracted the disease since entering the factory), and some 13 per cent had tonsil or throat infections. Large numbers were hospitalized for some period for a range of ailments, including bronchitis and pneumonia. Figures on average height, weight and chest measurements of workers indicated a relatively good state of affairs, but were far below those found in surveys of the admittedly more advantaged students in Ministry of Education schools (Ōhashi 1911:22–35). The writer said that the definition of occupational diseases should be extended to include flat-footedness, kerosene-induced nausea and noisy breathing, often a sign of incipient pulmonary tuberculosis.

A later survey carried out in ten Kansai spinning mills in the year to August 1924, reported that nearly half the total number of c.12,000 workers in the survey became sick at some point during the period, resulting in an estimated loss of over 50,000 working days. The most common ailments were colds and flu, followed by stomach ailments and beriberi. Tuberculosis figured low on the scale, but still accounted for 43 per cent of all worker deaths at the mills, and 30 per cent of all workers discharged owing to sickness. There was a strong seasonal pattern in mill sickness, with illness peaking in January-March, when colds and flu were most common, and again in July-September, when intestinal problems were widespread (Koinuma 1925:21–3).

Patterns in silk mills were similar. An extensive health inspection of over 80,000 Nagano silk workers, the results of which were published in 1924, again showed very high rates of trachoma, respiratory disease and digestive problems. Tuberculosis accounted for a very small number of those inspected, but the survey remarked that it was common knowledge that most workers with suspected tuberculosis were rapidly discharged.[6] Significantly, this survey shows clearly a higher sickness rate for female than male workers (see Table 4.1).

The disparity was attributed by the Nagano Factory Inspectorate to the fact that men's work in silk mills was relatively light by comparison with women's, and that most girls' living conditions at the mills were very poor (*Rōdō Jihō* 1924:11ff.).

Table 4.1 Nagano factory inspections, 1920–3

	1920	1921	1922	1923
No. of mills inspected	413	463	395	354
No. of workers	80,789	74,937	85,409	81,103
No. of sick	3,605	3,615	2,774	2,240
Sickness rate per 1,000	44	48	32	28
No. of women sick	3,356	3,474	2,619	2,108
No. of men sick	249	141	155	132
Sick men per 1,000	26	22	15	16
Sick women per 1,000	49	53	36	29

Source: *Rōdō Jihō* 1924: 12

A further survey published in 1926 on the basis of sickness notifications issued by silk mills in Nagano drew the same picture of twice-yearly peaks, prevalence of colds, flu, respiratory ailments and gastro-intestinal disorders, and, in all, a substantial number of working days lost through illness (Kose 1926:179–95).

The picture suggested by this data was of a mortality rate higher than average, against a background of recurrent disorders and infections, of both major and minor order. Tuberculosis accounted for a substantial minority of deaths at the mill, but the absolute numbers of such deaths were very small. However, when morbidity and the health of discharged workers were analysed, tuberculosis was found to assume a far greater importance, as will be shown in the next section. Conditions in the textile mills, argued these researchers, were a major contributory factor to the higher-than-average mortality and morbidity rates among this female age group, and hence the nation-wide excess of female over male deaths in these particular age groups.

TUBERCULOSIS

The spread of tuberculosis was a matter of concern in Japan by the turn of the century. One doctor, writing in 1902, spoke of the spread of pulmonary tuberculosis as a primary area where research was needed, as the available data were totally inadequate. He referred to the fact that it was 'well known that all forms of tuberculosis, but particularly pulmonary tuberculosis, were spreading in factories using large numbers of women'. This, he said, was likely to be critical for the health and welfare of the nation (Kubota 1902:8). Ten years later Ishihara Osamu, who conducted the most important research work in this area, was able to comment that all factories, but especially big ones, were at their wit's end over what to do with the tuberculosis problem (Ishihara 1913b:134). Unfortunately, however, as Taeuber poignantly comments, 'families did not analyse the statistics on tuberculosis before they sent a daughter to a textile dormitory' (Taeuber 1958:293).

Ishihara Osamu's writings on the tuberculosis question, known collectively as *Jokō to Kekkaku* (Mill girls and tuberculosis), resulted from extensive research carried out at the request of the Ministry of Agriculture and Commerce over the years 1909–11.[7] Ishihara estimated that one out of every six to seven mill girls returning to the countryside did so with serious illness (13,000 out of 80,000 surveyed in 1910). Of those workers discharged because of serious illness, around one-quarter (3,000) had tuberculosis (see Table 4.2).

Table 4.2 Factory workers discharged due to illness, by disease, 1910 (%)

	Cotton-spinning	Silk-reeling	Weaving
Pulmonary tuberculosis	26.6	3.4	20.0
Suspected pulmonary tuberculosis	21.7	4.7	38.0
Other tuberculosis	5.2	2.5	0.0
Beriberi	1.8	4.3	11.3
Gastro-enteric illness	6.7	28.4	2.0
Other	38.0	56.7	28.7
Total	100.0	100.0	100.0

Source: Ishihara 1913b: 135

Note: Ishihara also give figures for hemp workers, but the distribution does not total 100 per cent, and these have been omitted

Most came from the cotton-spinning industry. Comparing estimated death-rates for these factory workers with national mortality rates, Ishihara concluded that the death-rates for 16- to 20-year-old returnees were 14.86 per 1,000 dekasegi (migrant) workers, more than double the national average for the age group. For 20- to 25-year-olds it was 11.67 per 1,000, around a quarter above the national average (Ishihara 1913b:141). Average mortality rates would imply a figure of 4,000 deaths among this group (female dekasegi workers), whereas the actual rate was 9,000, giving 5,000 'extra' deaths (ibid.:142). Of these 9,000 deaths, 70 per cent (6,300) were caused by tuberculosis, of which over a third (2,700) were due to pulmonary tuberculosis (Ishihara 1913b:142) (see Tables 4.3 and 4.4).

Some prefectures were particularly badly hit. In Yamanashi, for example, 80 per cent of the returnees who died had tuberculosis, while many other areas reported problems as the disease spread to rural families (Ishihara 1913b:138, 143). Unlike his superior in the Agriculture and Commerce Ministry, Oka Minoru, Ishihara was very explicit on the connection between factory health and the countryside. It was not just in textile dormitories that tuberculosis was becoming one of the most feared diseases, but in the countryside as well.

Table 4.3 Factory worker mortality by cause of death, 1906–8 average (%)

	Cotton-spinning	Silk-reeling	Weaving	Hemp-working
Pulmonary tuberculosis	34.5	16.5	16.3	18.8
Suspected pulmonary tuberculosis	12.6	14.2	3.8	12.5
Other tuberculosis	7.1	3.8	12.5	1.9
Beriberi	8.2	3.8	8.8	12.5
Gastro-enteric illness	4.1	10.3	8.8	6.3
Other	33.5	51.4	49.8	48.0
Total	100.0	100.0	100.0	100.0

Source: Home Ministry figures given in Ishihara 1913b: 144

Table 4.4 Returnee deaths by occupation and illness, 1910 (%)

	Cotton-spinning	Silk-reeling	Weaving	Other	Total
Pulmonary tuberculosis	41.3	37.4	35.4	33.8	39.0
Suspected tuberculosis	31.2	33.4	29.2	32.4	31.3
Beriberi	9.9	2.4	5.0	8.8	6.4
Gastro-enteric illness	6.6	11.4	11.8	4.4	8.6
Other	12.1	16.6	18.5	22.6	14.6
Total	100.0*	100.0*	100.0*	100.0*	100.0*

Source: Ishihara 1913b: 142–3

Note: * Ishihara's own figures, given here, do not total 100. The reason for this is not explained.

These mortality figures without doubt understated the true extent of tuberculosis and other illnesses. Ishihara himself noted that the way in which respiratory diseases were categorized in the Statistics Office figures he used meant that the tuberculosis rate was probably greater than actually appeared (ibid.:144). Moreover, rapid turnover and resignations due to ill health restricted mortality in the factory itself (ibid.:138).

The results of Ishihara's research seemed to confirm what many had suspected. Published in stages in subsequent years, the findings were not always popular, and most mills were slow to act upon them. However, many contemporaries considered them to provide incontrovertible proof of the existence of higher tuberculosis morbidity and mortality rates in textile factories than prevailed in the nation as a whole. By implication the results also suggested that the conditions experienced by young female textile workers, especially in cotton-spinning, were a contributory cause of those higher morbidity and mortality rates. This conviction seemed to be borne out by later researchers' discovery of similar patterns in other parts of the textile industry. One 1938 report on workers in the Hyōgo silk industry indicated a tuberculosis contraction rate far higher than the prefectural average (Ōtsuka 1938:79). Weavers' families seemed particularly prone to the disease (Sanpei 1961:541).

It was in the cotton industry, though, that concern was concentrated, as it was here that Ishihara had assigned the greatest blame. The better mills sought to improve health inspection and working conditions, but tuberculosis remained a serious problem for management throughout the inter-war years. The depth of concern is revealed in a confidential report drawn up by medical staff at the cotton giant Tōyōbō in 1929, as part of a larger survey mandated by the Home Ministry. The research identified a disproportionately high tuberculosis rate among 1,743 former Tōyōbō workers previously discharged sick. Explaining differential tuberculosis rates between Tōyōbō factories by disparities in skill of diagnosis, the research showed that there was also an immense variation according to the area of recruitment. Looking at the three major areas of Tōyōbō recruitment, it was found that tuberculosis rates in Toyama and Okinawa were much higher than in Niigata, suggesting that it was not just in the factories that the cause and cure had to be sought. Nevertheless, the existence of a tuberculosis death rate among company workers of 2.5 times the national average, and the fact that the death-rate increased with the length of service, could not be ignored. Castigations of the failures of Japanese public health policy could not conceal the distress of the doctor who compiled this report (Tōyō Bōseki 1929:1–28).

The concern with tuberculosis among industrial workers demonstrated by official sponsorship of Ishihara's own research continued for most of the inter-war years. The government's Social Affairs Bureau took steps to find out the state of research in the west, and pressed for better working conditions. While some bureaucrats were no doubt motivated by humanitarian considerations, an overwhelming concern continued to be national economic efficiency. By the 1920s it was a matter of concern that Japan's tuberculosis death-rate was so much higher than those in countries such as France and Germany. Officials sought to publicize their own investigations, which continued to show that young female factory workers were particularly vulnerable to the disease. Graphic illustrations of the kind shown in Figure 4.2 could hardly fail to have an impact. Although these are actual recorded numbers, and tell us nothing about mortality rates (there were still many more women than men in large factories at this time), the intent of the graph was unambiguously to shock.

The authorities pressed for preventive measures, the rejection of vulnerable workers through stringent health inspections, and methods of early detection, which, German research suggested, vastly improved the overall recovery rate. It was openly admitted that tuberculosis was encouraged by poor nutrition and overwork (Naimushō Shakaikyoku 1926:31–6).

Despite efforts of this kind, a later survey on the post-mill experience of female cotton-spinning workers, carried out in 1936 by members of the factory inspectorate, continued to show the same kind of story. This survey included both those who left, and those who were discharged, a small sample of 204 in all. Of these, thirty-one had been ill on departure. Fourteen recovered, nine continued sick and eight had died. Of the eight deaths, seven were from tuberculosis. Several of those sick also had tuberculosis. The inspectorate noted that selection standards in the mills covered in the survey were fairly strict; the quality of workers was good, and the mills possessed good medical facilities and managements with a constant eye to tuberculosis. The report expressed concern that tuberculosis patients were being discharged from mills with good

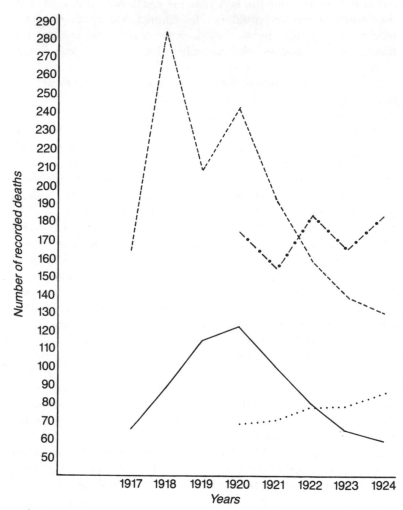

Figure 4.2 Recorded deaths from tuberculosis in textile and other
         factories, 1917–24

Source: Naimushō Shakaikyoku 1926: 40 (modified)

Key: ――――― Men (all large factories)
       ---------- Women (all large factories)
       ············ Men (textiles)
       ―•―•― Women (textiles)

Note: Data for all large factories applies to factories with 50 or more workers
        up to 1921, and factories with 500 or more workers from 1922 onwards.
        Since many textile workers (especially weavers) were in small
        workshops they are thus excluded from the post-1921 industry figures.

medical facilities to families lacking the means to pay for medical care (Tanino 1937:28–30). The writer commented seriously that the prevalence of illness, especially tuberculosis, among these girls indicated the existence of social problems 'which must be taken seriously by intellectuals seeking a better future in which productive work is a joy' (Tanino 1937:32). By 1948 the head of Tōyōbō's welfare section, a medical doctor, was able to make the doubtful claim that the number contracting tuberculosis in cotton mills was *lower* than the national average (Itō 1948:11), but the national circumstances were distinctly unusual, and national rates also beginning to decline.

THE ETIOLOGY OF TUBERCULOSIS AND JAPANESE TEXTILE WORKERS' WORKING AND LIVING CONDITIONS

The relationship between tuberculosis and the standard of life is still inadequately understood, but there is no doubt that living and working conditions can be more or less conducive to the spread of infection. For example, sputum or water droplets containing the bacillus may be allowed to lie around; hence the ordinances relating to spitting in much of Europe and the US. The temperature may be kept at a level which causes the bacilli to be preserved and to multiply (38–41°C). Conditions which reduced the resistance of the individual to infection could include poor diet and exhaustion. As mentioned earlier, however, in the west many doctors and officials were slow to recognize any connection between tuberculosis infection and living and working conditions. Little attention was paid to psychological and emotional factors in tuberculosis contraction, and even after 1900 substantive research in Europe and the US was on a piecemeal basis, though there was a growing interest in the relationship between occupational conditions and the disease. In this context, the wide-ranging and systematic investigations carried out by Ishihara in the first decade of the twentieth century were of a path-breaking nature. In Ishihara's view, and in the view of his successors, the correlation between inferior living and working environment and tuberculosis, especially in the cotton-spinning industry, was quite unambiguous. While the implications and costs of accepting these findings were considerable, mill doctors, managers and the state were forced to take note. While some of the causality could be disputed, it proved virtually impossible to explain away or ignore the actual research results.

It is well known that, from the 1890s onwards, contemporaries were describing working conditions which they regarded as unacceptably poor, even by contemporary standards (for example, Yokoyama 1898; Nōshōmushō Shōkōkyoku 1903; Hosoi 1925). Conditions of life among female textile workers appeared to compare unfavourably both with those of male industrial workers, and with the conditions most of these women would have experienced had they remained in the rural sector. Conditions improved over the years up to the 1930s, but in many places remained poor. Even allowing for some exaggeration of the horrors of new and unfamiliar conditions, or for anti-urban bias, there is plenty of evidence that, on a variety of counts identified by medical opinion as conducive to the spread of tuberculosis, conditions in the mills provided ideal breeding ground for the illness.

There are several environmental factors which historically show a strong correlation with the spread of tuberculosis (particularly pulmonary tuberculosis), and which are now recognized by doctors to be of significance. The next section will seek to identify how far these factors may have been relevant in the case of Japanese textile workers. It is not my intention here to assign an exact causality for high rates of tuberculosis among mill workers, since it is not possible to determine which factor was most significant. It is important to note that both in Japan and elsewhere these factors have invariably gone hand in hand, and together act as an important determinant of higher rates of tuberculosis among the less well off. It is apparent from any such analysis of environmental tuberculosis causality that textile workers do pretty badly. The total package of living and working conditions experienced by these workers would make them 'score', to whichever of the various factors was attributed the most importance.

WORKING ENVIRONMENT

Both in Japan and in the west some occupations had much higher tuberculosis rates than others. In Britain metal-workers, tailors, shoemakers, bakers, seamstresses, masons and printers appeared particularly vulnerable (Smith 1988:212). In Japan, apart from textiles, rubber workers experienced high rates of tuberculosis; rates increased with length of service in the industry, giving a different profile from national tuberculosis contraction rates (Ōtsuka 1938:77–8). The disease seemed most prevalent in small workshops, and in dirty and ill-ventilated workrooms. Significantly, it was suggested in the 1890s that female cotton operatives in the UK were comparatively healthy, because they were not in huddled workrooms (Smith 1988:213). In the US, by contrast, it was found that, with the exception of English and Irish males, the tuberculosis death rate of cotton-mill operatives was higher than among non-operatives, especially for women. This was attributed to the stress of the double burden which married women workers had to bear (Teller 1988:105).

If we look at the working environment of Japanese factories in the pre-Pacific War years, we find that they were generally overcrowded and ill-ventilated, especially up to the First World War. Silk-reeling mills were constantly full of steam from cocoon boilers, while humidity levels in cotton-spinning factories were intentionally kept at a high level. Temperatures tended to rise to very high levels, reaching 35°C or even higher in summer. In winter cotton workers moved quickly between temperatures little above freezing and the 22°C of the mill (Koinuma 1925:22). Poor ventilation kept the level of carbon dioxide in the air very high, and the stench of oil combined with the build-up of carbon dioxide both caused lung damage and led to shallow breathing. In young people in particular this caused ill-developed and vulnerable lungs (*Rōdō Jihō* 1925:5). High levels of dust in the air in parts of the cotton-spinning process promoted a variety of lung infections. By injuring lungs, dust and fumes assisted the invasion of the tuberculosis bacillus. The June 1929 Safety Regulations for Factories included stipulations for the control of dust (ILO 1933:257). The relationship between dust and tuberculosis was the subject of debate, which focused on the size of cotton dust grains, but by the 1920s research seemed to confirm that most days were lost to illness in the most dusty preparation and pre-spinning departments (mixing, ginning, carding, and so on), results which researchers claimed were borne out by investigations in Germany as well (Koinuma 1925:23; *Rōdō Jihō* 1925:2). Even where doctors denied any connection between dust and tuberculosis, they were forced to acknowledge some connection between dust and respiratory problems (Itō 1948:11–12). Given that tuberculosis infection was passed on in water droplets, that dust in the air often forced workers to spit, and the bacillus was favoured by high (human body) temperatures, these conditions are significant. Fumes, poor ventilation and heat reduced vitality. With girls forced to wear damp working clothes outside the mill as work clothing was rarely provided, and subject to sudden temperature changes, resistance was clearly further lowered.

LENGTH OF WORKING HOURS AND EXHAUSTION

Western research again shows an occupational pattern here, with the disease disproportionately prevalent among workers with irregular hours and long shifts. Fatigue and overwork, often consequent on piecework rates, were deemed to make individuals lose strength, thereby making them more vulnerable to tuberculosis, but this was difficult to prove. Contemporary research in Japan confirmed this view. For example, a survey of bus conductresses carried out in the late 1930s indicated that their exhaustion over lengthy periods was of significance in the contraction of tuberculosis (Ōtsuka 1938:77). In all branches of textiles, working hours were very long and exhaustion common. One 1902 survey spoke of an eighteen-hour day in Suwa during the peak silk season (Kubota 1902:6), and another in 1901 found 12- to 13-year-olds sleeping perhaps three-four hours out of twenty-four, ending up so tired that they could not eat (Yamane 1901:15). In the early cotton mills days off might be as little as three per year at this time (New Year, Obon and a local festival). By 1938 the number had risen to about two per month (Ōtsuka 1938: 79), but this still left frequent seven-day working weeks. Seasonal operation in silk meant a long winter break, but over time the industry moved towards year-round operation. The extensive use of night shifts in cotton-spinning up to 1929 resulted in shortage of sleep and progressive weight loss (Ishihara 1913b:126), which was especially critical when most workers were immature young girls.

OVERCROWDED LIVING AREAS

Poor housing was well established as an agent of tubercular infection from the turn of the century (Teller 1988:100; Hart and Wright 1939:34). In overcrowded housing, infection was more easily communicated from one individual to another. It was proved that prolonged contact was the most common origin of clinical tuberculosis. Work on Glasgow (McFarlane 1989) has indicated the importance of tenement-living in contributing to a continuing high rate of tuberculosis in the city when rates were falling elsewhere. In the Japanese textile industry, the majority of workers resided in company dormitories. Many were of a substantial size. The Nagano Factory Department in 1928 reported that there were 257 dormitories in the prefecture with over 100 residents each (Kō 1928: 2). Some of the larger mills sought to improve dormitory conditions, and firms such as Kanebō were well known for their efforts to monitor workers' health (Tōyō Bōseki 1929: 24), but these were in the minority, and the reputation of most mill residential facilities remained poor. Most dormitories were very crowded. One 1926 survey of 534 silk textile mills reported a single dormitory room for 708 occupants (Sasamura 1926:617). Many workers enjoyed space of less than 1 jō (about 6' by 3'), especially in Nagano, and for warmth in winter shared bedding with one other girl (Ishihara 1913b:129–30). Rapid turnover of workers meant that the same bedding could be used by six to seven girls a year. One report in 1926 stated that in half the mills surveyed bedding was shared between two or even three girls, and similar complaints were still being made as late as 1938 (Sasamura 1926:623; Ōtsuka 1938:79). The use of continuous double shifts in spinning meant not just that bedding could be in constant use by four girls every twenty-four hours, but that even during the day doors, windows and curtains were never opened, so bedding was never exposed to light or fresh air. Since bacilli contained in sputum and particles exhaled by infected individuals were more likely to be killed by light and exposure, or dispersed by good ventilation, such conditions encouraged the persistence of infectious dust and particles. In Nagano in the late 1920s it was still felt necessary to issue injunctions that bedding should be regularly changed and aired outside at least once every three months (Kō 1928:6). Even where management wished, this was not always easy without considerable capital expenditure. Buildings tended to be very dark. Four factories surveyed in 1926 had dormitories without any windows whatsoever (Sasamura 1926:10). Washing and cleaning conditions were often inadequate, and disinfectant frequently unavailable. Some reporters regarded the washing of utensils by each girl after communal meals as inviting the spread of infection (Kose 1926:210ff; Ōhashi 1911:24).[9] There seems no doubt, therefore, that lack of ventilation, light and heating exacerbated conditions of dirt and overcrowding already identified by Ishihara as fostering infection (Ishihara 1913b:130–1).

NUTRITION

> Of all the factors involved – housing, fatigue, anxiety, uncleanliness – poor nutrition with the impaired resistance that accompanied it, seems to have been the crucial divider between exposure and active manifestation of the disease.
>
> (Smith 1988:19)

This view was borne out by the fact that at times of inadequate food supply the incidence of tuberculosis increased. In Europe during the First World War, for example, tuberculosis mortality rates rose, particularly in Germany, where nutrition standards were especially bad. However, the nutrition factor was very difficult to measure. It did gradually become apparent, however, that a low protein intake could weaken an individual's resistance and immunity. In the west there was also a clear link with bovine tuberculosis, through the widespread consumption of beef and milk (Smith 1988:172–80). This latter feature was of far less relevance to Japan, despite the growth in meat consumption from the Meiji period, but a low quality of nutrition was a significant issue.

Diet varied tremendously from mill to mill. An early survey in 1901 spoke of a scant weekly diet consisting of basic foodgrains, pickles, *hijiki* (a kind of seaweed), bean curd (*tōfu*) with leeks (*negi*), dried sardines, *daikon* (white radish) and beans. It was a diet with very little protein, especially animal protein, as there was no meat (Yamane 1901:15). However, another a year later spoke of fish or meat two to four times weekly (Kubota 1902:7). Ishihara in his survey reported that the food was quite good, and much improved over the previous ten years, as factories were improving diets to help overcome problems of recruitment (Ishihara 1913b:129). Some workers compared the diet they found favourably with what they might otherwise have consumed at home (Yamamoto 1972:337). Many workers did not, however, receive this kind of diet, getting little more than pickled *daikon*, watery *misoshiru* and basic foodgrains. Diets in general were short of protein and fresh food, which was particularly important in the context of teenagers who were still growing. Even in relatively good mills nutrition was frequently inadequate for the harsh labour demands made on workers. The high rates of beriberi shown in the more comprehensive health surveys mentioned earlier point clearly to nutritional deficiency.

Whether in the case of Japan nutrition was as critical as western writers have suggested is debatable. The high incidence of diseases such as beriberi was clearly related to diet (increasing through the shift to polished or half polished rice), but Japanese researchers concluded that it was difficult to extend the connection directly to tuberculosis (Koinuma 1925:21). It may well be, though, that as one scholar has suggested, we should be looking not at the quantity, but at the quality of nutrition, and analysing the effects of the high dependence on rice grain, and the low intake of both animal and other proteins (Saitō 1989:350). Whatever the case, it is likely that poor nutritional standards among many textile workers helped to undermine resistance.

LOW WAGES AND POVERTY

In the west tuberculosis was clearly not restricted to the poor, but its incidence among the poor was higher than among the better off. Most of the occupational groups among which tuberculosis was particularly prevalent consisted of low-waged workers. Such workers were in addition more likely to experience one or more of the above environmental factors, identified as conducive to the spread of infection. They were also less likely to be able to pay for medical care which might help to combat the disease in its early stages. Textile workers were in general poorly paid, not least because they were women. With competitive piece rates normally operating, some workers were bound to be especially badly off. A system of forced savings was implemented by many companies, and constant pressure to remit substantial parts of their earnings to their homes, and to repay advances made, meant that most workers had relatively little left over to supplement their meagre diet by purchases from the factory shop or to pursue other courses of action which might have enhanced their resistance. Substantial improvements did occur in the 1920s to 1930s, but it was not easy to break out of the vicious cycle of long hours, low wages and poor conditions. It is very hard to draw a direct connection between the low wages earned by textile workers and the high rates of tuberculosis and other illnesses. Where financial poverty is particularly relevant is in the spread of infection, and the ability to pay for medical care. Sanpei Kōko, writing as late as 1941, noted that the particular poverty of weavers' families led to low nutritional standards and susceptibility to tuberculosis. She recounted how weavers from Ashikaga contracting tuberculosis were returned to their families in neighbouring hamlets, where they were compelled to sleep on straw, unable to afford a *futon* (bedding). They were ineligible for free medical care since they lacked the necessary *futon* and clothing to be admitted (Sanpei 1961:542–3). In Nagano it was reported that some doctors gave a 20 per cent discount on prices to sick workers, but this could still mean payments of 30–40 sen per day, the equivalent of half to two-thirds the average daily wage in the area (Kose 1926:213). For the unwaged, such payments were clearly quite out of the question. Low wages and poverty may not have been the cause of tuberculosis, but it was closely correlated with the factors significant in its contraction, and the failure to treat it adequately.

CONCLUSION

The conditions found in late nineteenth- and early twentieth-century Japanese textile mills were highly detrimental to the physical well-being of those who worked in them. Sickness rates, death-rates, body weights and heights and other assessments of physical health all indicate that this was the case. Tuberculosis was only the most lethal and most conspicuous of their ailments, and as such caused unusual concern in a society long accustomed to relatively high mortality and morbidity rates. At a time when many of the formerly 'fatal' illnesses were on the wane, this particular one, closely identified with the industrialization process, seemed to be out of control. Yet high rates of illness and tuberculosis were far from being the monopoly of female textile workers. We have seen that other occupational groups, such as rubber workers, bus conductresses and weavers also experienced a high incidence of tuberculosis. Many other population groups experienced the environmental factors identified above. One 1940 survey found cotton-mill workers complaining that work at home in the countryside was far harder, because they were no longer used to it (*Sangyō Fukuri* 1940: 66). Reports on village homes in the 1940s spoke of them as overwhelmingly dark, dirty and ill-ventilated.[12] General nutrition was poor, with beriberi a nation-wide affliction for most of the pre-war and early post-war periods. Many other workers enjoyed minimal incomes. The same conditions which researchers highlighted could be found in varying degrees in the life and work of many Japanese. If the conditions female textile workers lived and worked in were conducive to the spread of tubercular infection, then so were the same conditions in both city and countryside, where exhaustion, overcrowding, dirt and poverty were also prevalent. Ninety per cent of the silk workers interviewed by Yamamoto Shigemi said that they were glad to have gone to the mills, and that it was on balance preferable to staying at home (Yamamoto 1972:337).

Why, then, did the issue of tuberculosis among female mill workers assume such a particular prominence in a society not normally noted for its altruistic and humanitarian concern with its female labour force? Several reasons may be suggested. The first relates to the whole industrialization process itself. Japan was a late industrializer, and policy-makers felt themselves under immense pressure to industrialize the country with great rapidity. This resulted in economic and business strategies which were recognized to have considerable costs in human terms. They nevertheless came to realize that for a variety of reasons – for example, foregone profits, labour discontent, low labour productivity, an unhealthy female population leading to unhealthy children – high sickness and mortality rates among industrial workers were not conducive to enhanced national efficiency. The key role of the textile industries in the pre-war industrialization process highlighted this concern. Ishihara and his colleagues were effectively saying that the ill-health and mortality of these workers was the price of national progress, but that this cost could not over the long term be justified in either economic or humanitarian terms. The campaign for factory legislation, spearheaded by members of the bureaucracy, argued along the same lines.

Factory managements, however, also claiming to operate within limits imposed by Japan's position as a late industrializer, were unable or unwilling to eradicate the conditions which appeared to encourage the spread of tuberculosis and other diseases. They blamed capital shortages and the pressure to 'catch-up' for the non-availability of funds to improve working and living conditions. They could persuade themselves, and others, that young country girls on temporary contracts could endure the undoubted hardships of mill life (Tsurumi 1990:172). In cotton, where tuberculosis was most rampant, turnover was already high, workers relatively quickly trained, and managers assumed (sometimes erroneously) that there was an ample supply of labour. With one or two exceptions, it was only after the First World War that some companies even started to recognize the value of investment in improved labour conditions to reduce recruitment costs and raise productivity. Better approaches to tuberculosis in large mills were just one aspect of this strategy. The worker health issue was thus for managers a sensitive issue whose implications they were compelled to acknowledge, but which, they claimed, was thoughtlessly brandished by strident critics ignorant of the economic realities under which companies had to operate.

Perhaps the most powerful reason for the prominence of the tuberculosis issue in contemporary thinking, however, is its importance for the rural community. As stated at the beginning, most female textile workers were migrants, whose patterns of life and work can only be understood in the context of their agrarian background. Contemporary Japanese researchers and policymakers, faced by a population still largely agrarian, identified in this rural link consequences for the economy and society which they saw as far more tragic than the deaths and illness of the workers themselves. This was the rapid spread of tuberculosis through the rural area, which, it was argued, would threaten population growth, increase poverty, harm agricultural production and undermine the very foundations of Japanese society. Figures do give support to a relative increase in contraction in the countryside. While tuberculosis remained more of an urban phenomenon, partly due to the concentration of young people (the worst affected age groups) in the cities, there was evidence that the disparity between urban and rural tuberculosis mortality rates was less than previously thought, and of increasing rates in the countryside (Yoshioka 1941:259). Female textile workers were viewed as a major agent for the damaging spread of tuberculosis in rural areas.

The evidence for this claim was largely anecdotal. It proved easy to find stories of families and villages which had lost half or more of their members to tuberculosis after a girl had returned from a mill suffering from the disease (for example, Tōyō Bōseki 1929:19ff.). It proved more difficult to provide statistical evidence of such a link. The area where the disease was acquired was not necessarily that where death occurred. Mills invariably discharged workers in the early stages of tuberculosis. Often they did go back to their home village to recover, or, in many cases, to die, but sometimes they stayed in the cities, trying to keep on earning a living. As a result, tuberculosis was not necessarily focused on areas with a high incidence of textile mills. Moreover, sick workers were rarely listed according to area of origin.[13] Very few surveys looked at the post-work health of textile workers, and while peasant household surveys proliferated in the inter-war years, they provided relatively little documentary evidence on this particular relationship.

Nevertheless, regional concentrations of tuberculosis infection existed, and national statistics showed that concentrations of deaths from tuberculosis came in areas of previous high outmigration (Taeuber 1958:308). Research correlated high tuberculosis death-rates not just with industrialization, the degree of population concentration and the level of income, but also with the rate of *dekasegi* occurring in a region (Yoshioka 1941:267). While *dekasegi* might be a high risk occupation, belonging to a *dekasegi* family appeared to be equally dangerous to one's health. Moreover for much of this time migrant labour played a crucial part not only in the growing industrial sector, but in sustaining the rural sector itself.

The continuing high rates of tuberculosis despite rising national income distinguishes Japan from other countries industrializing in the pre-Second World War years. The industrialization process in Japan, as elsewhere, clearly produced substantial changes in the living and disease environment. This affected not just female textile workers, but the population as a whole. Although living and working environments may have improved in certain respects, in other facets of life there was a deterioration, or at least a change, which proved to be of particular relevance to the spread of tubercular infection. That the issue of tuberculosis gained such prominence was due not just to the high rates, but to their implications for national efficiency, economic management and rural life.

The health and tuberculosis debate thus had a significance which went far beyond medical and humanitarian considerations. As such it has provided powerful evidence for a whole school of historiography. Medical research helped to reinforce the enduring perception of female textile workers as the archetypal exploited work-force found in so many texts on labour history (for example, Nakamura 1976; Ōkōchi and Matsuo 1965; Tsurumi 1990). The tuberculosis issue helped to reinforce the view of many Japanese historians that textile workers were the victims of inhuman exploitation, whose experience was powerful evidence of the iniquities of the emergent capitalist system.

NOTES

An early version of this paper was presented at the Institute of Economic Research, Hitotsubashi University. I would like to express my gratitude to Professors Saitō Osamu, Odaka Kōnosuke, Satō Masahiro and others for their helpful comments, also to Dudley Baines and Leslie Hannah at LSE.

1 Contemporaries assumed that almost all returned to their villages after mill employment, there to marry, but research suggests that this was not the case (Tanino 1937; Tsurumi 1990: 172–3; Molony 1991:224).
2 The relationship between mortality rates and economic growth has been a significant element in debates over the standard of living in western industrialization (see, for example, Wrigley and Schofield 1981; Fogel 1986).
3 Data prior to the first full census in 1920 are very patchy, but this gender disparity in mortality rates for specific age groups existed at least from 1900 (Taeuber 1958: 305–6). The levels here were also subject to regional variation, and definitive conclusions were rendered more difficult by the constant process of in- and out-migration.
4 A similar disparity was found in the early twentieth-century in England for girls under 24, but for the older age groups there was a considerable excess of male over female deaths from tuberculosis (Hart and Wright 1939:12). The peak age for women dying of tuberculosis was 25–35, for men it was older (Smith 1988:17). One suggestion was that this was partly because more women were entering industrial occupations (Hart and Wright 1939:93).
5 This report cites the government-produced Kōjō Kantoku Nenpō (Factory Inspection Yearbook).
6 Even in the 1930s relatively few mills had special facilities for tuberculosis sufferers.
7 Ishihara's work is discussed at some length in Kagoyama Takashi's introduction to the 1970 edition of Ishihara's writings (Kagoyama 1970:1–46). Useful comment in English of its findings' importance can be found in Tsurumi 1990:169–72).
8 There is no evidence that Ishihara's findings were ever translated into English, and one can only speculate on the impact had this happened.
9 The view was that because of the hurry in which they ate, washing was totally inadequate, and would be better handed over to specialized staff. At the very least, the use of disinfectant was required.
10 This fact was not taken seriously in Europe until after 1900 (Smith 1988:168), but was widely acknowledged by the inter-war years.
11 Long-term trends in wage rates can be found in Umemura et al. 1966 and Ohkawa et al 1967. Wage rates varied according to the branch of the industry, length of service, and so on, and were not necessarily

poor in relation to what the same worker might have earned had she stayed in the agricultural sector. In general, women textile workers earned around 50 per cent of their male counterparts, and earned far below the average male wage.

12 I am grateful to Professor M. Sato of the Institute for the Documentation of Japanese Economic Statistics, Hitotsubashi University, for drawing my attention to this information.

13 Sick workers rarely seem to be categorized by both nature of illness and place of origin. One exception is Ōtsuka 1938, which lists factory workers suffering from syphilis according to regional origin.

REFERENCES

Dore, R. P. (1969) 'The modernizer as special case: Japanese factory legislation, 1882–1922', *Comparative Studies in Society and History* 11 (4).

Fogel, R. W. (1986) 'Nutrition and the decline in mortality since 1700: some preliminary findings', in S. L. Engerman and R. E. Gallman (eds.) *Long Term Factors in American Economic Growth*, Chicago, Chicago University Press.

General Headquarters Supreme Commander for the Allied Powers, Public Health and Welfare Section (GHQ SCAP) (n.d.) *Public Health and Welfare in Japan*, 1, Tokyo, SCAP.

Hart, P. D'Arcy and Wright, G. Payling (1939) *Tuberculosis and Social Conditions in England, with Special Reference to Young Adults*, London, National Association for the Prevention of Tuberculosis.

Hosoi, Wakizō (1925) *Jokō Aishi*, repr. 1976, Tokyo, Iwanami Shoten.

International Labour Office (ILO) (1933), *Industrial Labour in Japan*, Studies and Reports Series A (Industrial Relations) No. 37, Geneva, International Labour Office.

Ishihara, Osamu (1913a) 'Jokō no eiseigakuteki kansatsu', *Kokka gakkai Zasshi* 322 (November).

Ishihara, Osamu (1913b) 'Jokō to kekkaku', *Kokka Igakkai Zasshi* 322 (November).

Itō, Minoru (1948) 'Bōseki to kekkaku', *Nihon Bōseki Geppō* 12 (February).

Jannetta, Ann B. (1986) *Epidemics and Mortality in Early Modern Japan*, Princeton, Princeton University Press.

Kagoyama, Takashi (1970) 'Introduction' to Ishihara Osamu, *Jokō to kekkaku*, no. 5 of *Seikatsu Koten Sōsho*, Tokyo, Kōseikan.

Kō, Isaburō (1928) 'Jokō kishukusha no shakan ni tsuite', *Sangyō Fukuri* 3 (11).

Kobayashi, Tango (1965) *Kōjōhō to Rōdō Undō*, Tokyo, Aoki Shoten.

Koinuma, Engo (1925) 'Bōseki jokō no shippei', *Rōdō Jihō* 2 (12).

Kose, Yasutoshi (1926) 'Jokō no kanbō oyobi ichōbyō ni kansuru kōsatsu', *Shakai Seisaku Jihō* 67 (April).

Kubota, Seitarō (1902) 'Kōjō eisei ni tsuite', *Kokka Igakkai Zasshi* 188 (December).

McFarlane, Neil (1989) 'Hospitals, housing and tuberculosis in Glasgow', paper presented at the Economic History Society Conference, Exeter.

Molony, Barbara (1991) 'Activism among women in the Taishō cotton textile industry' in G. Bernstein (ed.) *Recreating Japanese Women, 1600–1945*, Berkeley, CA, University of California Press.

Naimushō Shakaikyoku (1926) *Kōgyō to Kekkaku*, Tokyo, Sangyō Fukuri Kyōkai.

Nakamura, Masanori (1976) *Rōdōsha to Nōmin*, vol. 29 of *Nihon no Rekishi*, Tokyo, Shōgakkan.

Nishikawa, Shunsaku and Abe, Takeshi (1990) 'Gaisetu – 1885–1914', in S. Nishikawa and T. Abe (eds) *Sangyōka no Jidai – Jō*, vol. 4 of *Nihon Keizaishi*, Tokyo, Iwanami Shoten.

Nōshōmushō Shōkōkyoku (1903) *Shokkō Jijō*, repr. 3 vols 1976, with an introduction by Tsuchiya Takao, Tokyo, Shinkigensha.

Ōhashi, Mamoru (1911) 'N, S. bōseki kabushiki gaisha eisei jōkyō', *Kokka Igakkai Zasshi* 289 (May).

Ohkawa, Kazushi et al. (eds) (1967) *Bukka*, vol. 8 of *Long Term Economic Statistics of Japan*, Tokyo, Tōyō Keizai Shinpōsha.

Okazaki, Yōichi (1986) 'Meiji Taishō ki ni okeru Nihon jinkō no dōtai', *Jinkō Mondai Kenkyū* 178.

Ōkōchi, Kazuo and Matsuo, Hiroshi (1965) *Nihon Rōdō Kumiai Monogatari*, 3 vols, Tokyo, Chikuma Shobō.

Ōtsuka, Kanō (1938) 'Fujin rōdō mondai hōkoku', *Rōdō Kagaku Kenkyū* 15 (1).

Powell, Margaret and Anesaki, Masahira (1990) *Health Care in Japan*, London, Routledge.

Rōdō Jihō (1924) 'Seishi shokkō no kenkō shindan seiseki', *Rōdō Jihō* 1(10).

Rōdō Jihō (1925) 'Menshi Bōseki Kōjō no Eisei', *Rōdō Jihō* 2(6).

Saitō Osamu (1989) 'Keizai hattatsu wa mortality teika o motarashita ka? – Ōbei to Nihon ni okeru eiyō – taii – heikin yomei', *Keizai Kenkyū* 40(4) (October).

Sangyō Fukuri (1940) 'Kurihara bōshoku gōmei kaisha ni okeru joshi kōin seikatsu zadankai', *Sangyō Fukuri* 15 (10).

Sanpei, Kōko (1961) *Nihon Kigyō Shi*, Tokyo, Yūzankaku.

Sasamura, Etsuo (1926) 'Sen'i kōjō fuzoku kishukusha no eiseiteki kansatsu', *Shakai Igaku Zasshi* 477 (October).

Smith, F.B. (1988) *The Retreat of Tuberculosis*, London, Croom Helm.

Taeuber, Irene B. (1958) *The Population of Japan*, Princeton, NJ, Princeton University Press.

Taira, K. (1970) 'Factory legislation and management modernization during Japan's industrialization 1886–1916', *Business History Review* 44 (1).

Tanino, Setsu (1937) 'Bōseki jokō taishokugo no kisū ni kansuru chōsa', *Sangyō Fukuri* 12 (11).

Teller, Michael E. (1988) *The Tuberculosis Movement: a Public Health Campaign in the Progressive Era*, New York, Westport and London, Greenwood Press.

Tōyō Bōseki Kabushiki Gaisha Eiseika (1929) *Tōyō Bōseki Jokō Igakuteki Kenkyū*, Tōyō Bōseki, September.

Tsurumi, E. Patricia (1990) *Factory Girls: Women in the Thread Mills of Meiji Japan*, Princeton, NJ, Princeton University Press.

Umemura, Mataji *et al.* (ed.) (1966) *Nōringyō*, vol. 9 of *Long Term Economic Statistics of Japan*, Tokyo, Tōyō Keizai Shinpōsha.

Umemura, Mataji (ed.) (1988) *Rōdōryoku*, vol. 2 of *Long Term Economic Statistics of Japan*, Tokyo, Tōyō Keizai Shinpōsha.

Wrigley, E. A. and Schofield, R. S. (1981) *The Population History of England 1541–1971*, London, E. A. Arnold.

Yamamoto, Shigemi (1972) *Aa Nomugi Tōge*, Tokyo, Asahi Shinbunsha.

Yamane, Seiji (1901) 'Kōgyō eisei shisatsu dan', *Kokka Igaku Zasshi* 175 (November).

Yokoyama, Gennosuke (1898) *Nihon no Kasō Shakai*, repr. 1976, Tokyo, Iwanami Shoten.

Yoshioka, Hirohito (1941) 'Honpō haikekkaku no ekigakuteki tokuchō', *Nihon Rinshō Kekkaku* 2(2).

Chapter 5

Female labour in the Japanese coal-mining industry

Regine Mathias

INTRODUCTION

Studies on female labour in pre-war Japan mostly focus on the female workers in the textile mills. There can be no doubt that these women, who around 1910 accounted for more than one-third of the whole industrial labour force (male and female) were especially important for Japanese industrialization. However, there were many other occupations in which women played an important role as well. One example which has been somewhat neglected so far is the female labour force in the coal-mines.

Women miners worked in Japanese coal-mines from the middle of the nineteenth century. They were employed not only on the surface but also below ground. It was only after the end of the Second World War that women were finally banned from mines. Even though the history of female labour in the coal-mines thus spans more than a hundred years, very few Japanese nowadays can conceive that there was a time in Japan when women worked in the pits. The important contribution of women miners in the collieries to Japanese industrialization seems to be completely forgotten.

THE HISTORY OF COAL-MINING IN NORTHERN KYŪSHŪ

Coal is one of the few natural resources found in Japan. The biggest coal-fields are located in northern Kyūshū and Hokkaidō, while the mining districts of Ube-Ōmine and Jōban are of less importance (see Figure 5.1). The history of coal-mining in Japan begins in northern Kyūshū and dates back to the seventeenth

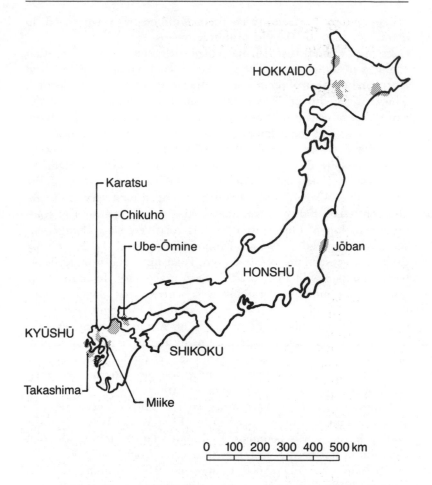

Figure 5.1 Location of coal-fields in Japan

century.¹ In this early time it was mostly undertaken by peasants from nearby villages, who tunnelled holes into hills and dug for the 'burning stones' (*moe ishi*) which they used as house coal. In the eighteenth century coal was increasingly used as fuel for salt production in the coastal areas of the inland sea, and therefore became an important commodity. Coal-mining came under the control of the respective feudal lords and was carried out in a more regulated way. Even so, however, it remained a spare-time occupation for peasants and their families, who continued to extract the coal by the old primitive means.

In the second half of the nineteenth century the situation changed to some extent. The number of coal-mines increased, and a growing number of them were managed by early 'entrepreneurs', who, vested with privileges from their feudal lords, pursued the extraction of coal in a more systematic way. For more and more people, many of them migrant workers, who toured the coal districts alone or with their families, mining became a full-time occupation. Despite this, on the whole coal-mining was still regarded as a seasonal occupation for the unskilled labour force of the surrounding villages,[2] and this image changed only very gradually later on, when industrialization led to a great expansion of coal-mining in Japan. One reason for this relatively slow change was the limited spread of technical innovations. Until the 1890s only the two biggest mines of Miike and Takashima (both in Kyūshū) were equipped with shafts and modern machinery. In most of the other mines mining operations were carried out through slope openings. The digging of the coal as well as its transport relied solely on human labour. From the 1890s a number of mines were taken over by zaibatsu-enterprises. Owing to the consequent capital infusion, shafts were sunk to exploit new coalfields, but except in a very few parts of the haulage and drainage systems, mechanization of mining operations progressed rather slowly.

Around the turn of the century coal production grew rapidly; growth culminated in the years of the First World War, when the mining business was booming. In Japan's largest mining district, Chikuhō in northern Kyūshū, output grew from 1,000,000 tonnes in 1894 to over 11,000,000 tonnes in 1919 (Mathias 1978:95, Sumiya 1968:295). This enormous increase in production was reached mainly through rapid expansion of the labour force, which increased tenfold from 23,000 to 225,000 miners over the same period. It was not until the post-war recession in the early 1920s, when mine operators were forced to carry out extensive rationalization, that mechanization was extended in many of the bigger mines. In particular, the replacement of the stall-and-pillar system by the more efficient method of longwall mining changed the working conditions underground, leading to a restructuring of the work-force there.

In this period many of the bigger mines also started to adopt a modern system of personnel management. Until the First World

War the so-called *naya seido*,[3] a subcontracting system, prevailed among the mines in northern Kyūshū. Under the *naya* system workers were not directly employed by the mining company, but by subcontractors (*nayagashira*), each of whom was in charge of a certain number of miners. The subcontractors had to recruit these workers, provide them with board and lodging, supervise their work and distribute their wages to them. By such means as recruitment bounties and advance payments the miners were tied to their subcontractor, often to the extent of effectively losing their personal freedom. Their dependence on the subcontractor was strengthened further by the feudalistic ideology, based on Confucianism, which underlay the paternalistic relationship between subcontractor and miners. This system was only gradually given up in favour of a modern personnel-management system based on direct employment. Even then a certain kind of paternalism was retained.

FEMALE LABOUR IN THE JAPANESE MINING INDUSTRY: A HISTORICAL OUTLINE

The importance of womens' contribution to Japan's industrial development before the First World War can hardly be overstated. In 1909 women made up more than half of the labour force in industry and mining. The female workers in the textile industry were, without doubt, the largest single group, but in many other branches of production women accounted for 20–30 per cent of the labour force. Around 10 per cent of all women employed in 1909 worked in mines and collieries (see Table 5.1), and their number greatly increased when the First World War boom further boosted the number of miners. However, the importance of collieries as working places for women was even greater than these figures suggest, because of the geographic concentration in the mining districts. In these areas mining was *the* most important and sometimes the only possible gainful employment for women.

The typical female job in a colliery was haulage work, and the Japanese word for these women, *atoyama* (literally, 'backstage in the pit'), became a synonym for women miners in general. While the predominantly male hewers (*sakiyama*, literally, 'at the working face') extracted the coal with pickaxes, the *atoyama* drew the coal in tubs or baskets from the working face to a loading point, where the coal was reloaded into wheeled tubs, and then pushed by hand to central haulage machines or directly to the surface. Until the

Table 5.1 Number of male and female workers, by industry, 1909[1]

Industry	Male workers	%	Female workers	%	Total	%
Silk-reeling	9,611	5.2	174,786	94.8	184,397	100
Cotton-spinning	21,347	20.5	81,639	79.3	102,986	100
Weaving	17,648	13.8	109,793	86.2	127,441	100
Textile industry total	60,896	13.8	381,273	86.2	442,169	100
Food production	43,534	60.2	19,333	30.8	62,867	100
Machine industry	51,863	94.6	2,947	5.4	54,810	100
Chemical industry	42,668	64.7	23,298	35.3	65,966	100
Others	40,509	64.4	22,349	35.6	62,858	100
State-owned factories	92,875	79.2	24,384	20.8	117,241	100
Total	271,449	74.6	92,311	25.4	363,760	100
Ore mining	61,657	83.2	12,448	16.8	74,105	100
Coal-mining	113,957	74.7	38,558	25.3	62,515	100
Mining total	184,766	78.4	51,043	21.6	235,809	100
All industries Total[2]	517,766	49.6	524,627	50.4	1,041,738	100

Source: Sakamoto (1977: 32)

Notes:
1 Factories, mines with 10 or more workers
2 The total sum includes the total of 'other industries', which is not listed in the table

1920s hewing and haulage work was mostly done by small teams, consisting of one or two hewers and the same number of drawers. Such teams were usually made up of married couples, parents and children, or brothers and sisters. Female mining labour was not restricted to the collieries of northern Kyūshū. Women miners worked in other mines as well, and in other parts of the country. Owing to the long history of coal-mining in northern Kyūshū, however, there developed special labour conditions, which proved to be more adapted to the use of female and child labour than those in other branches and areas.

There is no exact date for the beginning of women's work in the pits of northern Kyūshū. In the 1850s, however, sources reporting on female workers in the collieries become more frequent. In 1852, for example, a chronicle from the village of Kajiyama near the Karatsu mining district mentions male and female miners working in two nearby pits. A more detailed account of the labour force of three pits is given in another source from 1862 (cited in Morisaki 1974:117):

Pit A: 36 miners: one family of five, two families of four persons, five couples and 13 singles.

Pit B: 33 miners: one family of five, five families of four, one family of three persons and one single.[4]

Pit C: 14 miners: two families of four and two families of three persons.

This account clearly shows that coal-mining at that time was carried out as a kind of family work, and must therefore be regarded as the extension to a new kind of side-line of the usual kind of family work in rural communities. Over the course of time, for many men and women this side-line turned into their main occupation. Nevertheless, it is important to bear in mind the fact that female labour in mining evolved within the framework of family work, and was therefore quite different from, for example, women's work in the textile mills.

As far as the nature of women's work at that time is concerned, we have only a few sparse hints. One document from the village of Kanada (Fukuoka prefecture) mentions that in the nearby Hayashigatani pit female day labourers worked as drawers (Chikuhō Sekitan 1973:41). There seems, therefore, to be a long tradition of the employment of women miners in haulage work.

When coal-mining started to expand in the second half of the 1880s, and then grew rapidly after the turn of the century, this tradition enabled the mine operators, through the subcontractors, to meet the ever-growing demand for labour by tapping the large labour reservoir of women and children. Family work, including women's work, was actively promoted by many mining companies. Two leaflets used by the Miike colliery for the recruitment of miners in the years 1907 and 1910 give clear evidence of this trend; single miners are not explicitly excluded from the labour force, but the colliery stresses its preference for 'couples or families with as many members as possible joining the labour force'.[5] The reasons for the promotion of this personnel policy lay in its obvious advantages for the employer:

1 By employing women and children the size of the potential labour force was doubled. This was quite important in mining, which was still carried out as a labour-intensive operation.
2 At the same time, the policy helped to save costs, since wages for women and children were much lower than wages for men.
3 The recruitment of couples and families was thought to have a stabilizing effect on the highly mobile labour force in the coal-mines, since the turnover rates of single workers were twice or three times as high as those of married colliers.[6]
4 The employment of families was seen as a means of securing the future labour force, as the children of miners tended to join their parents in the mines early on and mostly became miners themselves.

The time of the First World War is often called the 'golden age' of coal-mining in northern Kyūshū. An ever-growing amount of coal was needed to fuel the rapid expansion of the economy. In the decade between 1909 and 1919 the number of female colliers in Japan increased from 38,000 to more than 95,000, the highest point ever in the history of coal-mining women in Japan. A comparison of the growth rates of the number of male (104 per cent) and female (147 per cent) colliers in this decade shows that women's contribution to this expansion of the labour force, and thus to the large increase in coal production, was much greater than that of men. The proportion of women in the labour force in coal-mines rose to 27 per cent on average. Out of 271,828 colliers in Fukuoka prefecture, where the mining district of Chikuhō is located, 81,861, or 30%, were women in 1920. In other words, in Chikuhō at that time every third miner was a women (Shindō 1974:275).

The recession after the First World War caused mass dismissals in the coal-mines. These affected female colliers more than male. Rationalization measures like, for example, the above-mentioned transition from the stall-and-pillar system to the longwall system led to a reorganization of the mining process, making the work of many women redundant. It also meant, in the long run, the end of family work in the mines. At the same time pressure from national and international labour organizations meant that the need to protect women and children from the hardships of under-ground work became a topic of heated discussion, culminating in the drafting of protective labour laws, by which women and minors were forbidden from working underground. The law was passed in 1928 and was to come into force after a transition period of five years in 1933. Owing to this situation many women found employment in jobs above ground, or went into small collieries in which coal was still hewed and hauled in the traditional way, and where labour laws could be more easily circumvented. This, however, usually meant a cut in wages, and working conditions worse than in the bigger collieries.

After 1937, when the Japanese economy increasingly shifted on to a war footing, the demand for coal grew rapidly, and a severe labour shortage was soon felt. To cope with this situation, women were again 'allowed' to work in coal-mines. The labour protection law, already undermined by a growing number of 'special per-missions', was finally put aside in 1939. Five years later, in 1944, more than 50,000 women were again employed in the mines, though 'only' one-fifth of them worked below ground. They were mostly used as unskilled workers for drilling and timbering, whereas haulage work was now carried out by Korean forced labour. The return of women to the coal-mines was not just a means of increasing production; women were also used to replace men who had been drafted into the army.

After the Second World War women were again banned from underground work. By March 1947 the last women were reported to have been removed from the mines (Natural Resources Section 1948:103–21). Above ground they continued to work at the picking belts and in the offices. The closing down of many coal-mines in the late 1960s, and the complete mechanization of the sifting pro-cess, brought to an end the history of coal-mining women in Japan.

WORKING CONDITIONS OF WOMEN IN THE MINES: FROM FAMILY LABOUR TO INDUSTRIAL LABOUR

Working conditions were in general quite bad in the coal-mines. The narrow width of the coal seams and poor facilities in the pits made the work there hard and dangerous. On top of this wages were low and living conditions inadequate. Therefore in the early phase of industrialization, work in the collieries was attractive only for those unable to make a living otherwise. Despite this, however, the surplus population of the rural areas provided a nearly inexhaustible supply of mine labour. In the second half of the nineteenth century miners' families working in the pits of northern Kyūshū came mostly from the surrounding villages and the neighbouring prefectures. When the demand for workers increased, recruitment was extended to other parts of western Japan. The majority of miners came from the lower stratum of the rural population. Those who went to work in the coal-mines had usually lost the means of making a secure living in the village. A significant minority belonged to the discriminated minority of the *burakumin*. Many were lured into mining by the promise of a secure job and good wages made in the brochures issued by the big mining companies, only to discover afterwards the grim reality of colliery work.

Many male and female members who worked full-time in the collieries had started work there as children. A typical example may be found in the life of Sakamoto Tatsu, a coal-mining woman in Kyūshū. Sakamoto was born in 1898 in a poor tenant family in Kumamoto prefecture. When she was 4½ years old her parents died. Her brothers went to work in the Miike colliery, and took her along. Only a few years later, she started to work underground, working under the guidance of an experienced woman as a drawer in a team with her brothers. At the age of 14 or 15 Sakamoto herself was a fully-fledged collier. When she was 21 she married a collier, and worked with her husband in the pit until the birth of her second child (Shindō 1974:256–8).

Among female workers in the collieries the high proportion of women working underground is very conspicuous. Even in 1924, when the peak number of female workers in the mines had already passed, more than 60 per cent of female miners worked as hewers, drawers (putters), haulage women, and timberwomen. Above ground women mostly worked at the picking belts. Others were employed as unskilled labour. Only very few were engaged in technical or craft jobs (see Table 5.2).

The work of the drawers was very hard. Creeping along low passages they pulled baskets (*battera*) or tubs (*sura*) of coal from the working face to the loading point for coal cars, harnessed by a rope which was put over both shoulders. One basket held 60–100 kg, one tub 150–250 kg, and two or three tubs were needed to fill a coal car (*tansha, hako*). An experienced hewer was able to fill two or two and a half coal cars per shift, so the drawers had to creep back and forth four to six times per shift, hauling up to one ton of coal. When owing to sickness or an accident the hewer could not work, the drawers would themselves sometimes take the pick, hewing the coal and hauling it to the loading point. Among old coal-mining women there are many who claim with pride that they were as good hewers as the men (Shindō 1974:17–18).

Around the turn of the century coal production was expanded and mining advanced to deeper seams. This process was accompanied by several changes in the organization of labour, which especially affected women miners. The usual working day in the Meiji and Taishō periods was twelve hours starting at 3a.m. or 4a.m.. Nevertheless, during most of the Meiji period, female colliers could, within the given time-frame, determine their own working hours fairly freely. They often went underground later than their husbands or brothers and came out earlier, in order to prepare meals and care for the children (Yamamoto 1973:23). The introduction of shift systems and a more strictly regulated form of labour organization in many mines, as well as the growing distance between the surface and the working face as mining advanced to greater depths, made this relatively flexible time disposal possible.

At the same time there was an extension of daily working times. Many collieries introduced a shift system, with two twelve-hour shifts, but the actual time spent underground could be much longer. If, for example, the empty coal cars did not come back to the loading point in time, drawers had to have a break and wait for them. However, as wages were on piece-rates, with payment according to the number of filled coal cars, and since teams had to fulfil a certain quota in order to get any wages at all, women often stayed below the surface for sixteen hours or more. Restrictions in working hours for women and minors were set out in the Factory Act of 1911, which became law in 1916, but owing to the

Table 5.2 Share of women in various occupations in coal-mining, Japan, 1924

Occupations	All colliers	Female colliers	%	Portion of this occupation among female colliers (%)
(a) Below ground:				
Hewer	79,045	7,208	9.1	11.1
Drawer, putter	43,894	30,228	68.9	46.4
Timber (wo)men	22,475	5,357	23.7	8.2
Haulage (wo)men	27,475	1,188	4.3	1.8
(b) Below and/or above ground:				
Coal-sorting	15,159	12,382	81.7	19.0
Machine operator	9,488	154	1.6	0.2
Crafts (wo)men	11,916	340	2.9	0.5
Electrician	1,688	18	1.1	0.02
Unskilled worker	25,523	6,490	25.4	10.0
Others	8,350	1,782	21.3	2.7
Total	245,013	65,147	26.6	100.0

Source: Tōyō Keizai Shinpōsha (1927: 591)

granting of many exemptions actual working time in the mines changed little until the 1930s.

This development signifies one radical change; namely, mining was no longer typical family work. Its organization of labour became industrialized, in the sense that the organization of work became more strictly regulated along the lines of a modern factory system. Even though families continued to work in the mines, the work was no longer compatible with a 'normal' family life. For women the double burden of work and domestic responsibilities became increasingly heavy during the period of industrial development from the 1890s. Owing to this burden, as well as to factors such as childbirth, women colliers worked fewer days per annum than men. There was also a taboo against women entering a mine during menstruation. However, women often ignored this taboo, because they feared the loss in income caused by such a forced break every four weeks (Morisaki 1974:24).

The women at the picking belts above ground also worked in two twelve-hour shifts. In contrast to the conditions of female drawers and timberwomen, who worked together with and sometimes even competed with men, work at the picking belts was a solely female occupation. For this work mostly young and unmarried women were employed. Wearing colourful short kimonos, and often some make-up, they had the reputation of being attractive. They therefore constituted quite a different type of colliery woman from those working underground.

Wages for female labourers in the collieries varied greatly depending on the region, the size of the company and the kind of work. For underground work miners were paid on piece-rates, consisting of a basic wage plus a performance-related wage measured by the amount of coal produced. As stated earlier, those who did not produce a certain minimum amount did not get even the basic wage. Young and inexperienced miners therefore often had difficulties earning enough to support their families. For work on the surface, women were paid by the hour. On the whole, wages for underground work were much higher than those for work on the surface, and the differential between male and female wages was smaller than, for example, it was in the factories.

For male colliers wages were lower than the equivalent average wage in a factory, but for female colliers working underground wages were higher than in factories. Women working underground obtained on average between 58 per cent (1930) and 78 per cent

(1933) of the male wage, whereas those on the surface earned not more than half. In the factories the difference was much more striking: female wages there were for the most part not more than 29–35 per cent of the average male wage. A woman working underground could earn nearly twice as much as a female factory worker, and sometimes her wage came close to male wages for work on the surface (see Table 5.3). The fact that underground work was heavy labour and was carried out by men and women working in teams, was probably one reason for the relatively high female wage and the relatively small gender-related wage differ-ence. On the other hand, women working on the surface often earned less than their colleagues in the factories.

When comparing wages one has, however, to keep in mind that the stated wage figures do not always represent the real income. There were wage deductions for forced savings, advanced pay-ments had to be repaid, while tools, implements and food, which the miners obtained from the company, had to be paid for by instalments. *De facto* wages were therefore often much lower. More-over, until the end of the First World War, wages were often not paid in cash, but in *kippu* (a kind of money substitute), which could be exchanged for goods in the company-owned store and in nearby shops, but were not valid beyond the area.

The income of female miners, especially that of drawers, was an important part of a family's income. As male wages in mining tended to be lower than, for example, in other factories, and were often reduced by various additional factors, the income of the household head alone was not enough to support the family. A survey carried out in the Mitsui Tagawa colliery in 1922 clearly shows that in twenty-nine out of a sample of thirty families the income of the household head was not sufficient to cover living expenditures, amounting only to between 23 per cent and 77 per cent, depending on the kind of work and the size of the family (see Table 5.4; Kawada 1923:149). The work of women and children was therefore a financial necessity for miners' families, which could not have survived without this contribution to the family income.

As has been mentioned, most female colliers were married[7] and had to care for their families besides working at the mine. Preg-nancy and childbirth usually meant that women would cease work-ing, and that the family income would therefore drop, in some cases below the minimum for subsistence. Due to this women

Table 5.3 Average daily wages in selected industries, 1930–8, in yen

Year	manufacturing industry		coal-mining below ground		coal-mining above ground		traffic, communication		gas, water supply electricity	
	m.w.	f.w.	m.w.	f.w.	m.w.	f.w.	m.w.	f.w.	m.w.	f.w.
1930	2.55	0.91	1.91	1.49	1.45	0.73	2.03	1.04	2.49	1.28
1931	2.43	0.82	1.64	1.12	1.36	0.67	2.05	1.05	2.36	1.28
1932	2.51	0.77	1.54	0.95	1.31	0.64	2.05	1.07	2.36	1.27
1933	2.45	0.74	1.65	0.96	1.38	0.66	2.05	1.05	2.47	1.26
1934	2.49	0.73	1.80	1.07	1.46	0.69	2.03	1.04	2.49	1.26
1935	2.43	0.73	1.88	1.11	1.52	0.72	2.01	1.04	2.18	1.29
1936	2.41	0.74	1.99	1.31	1.56	0.74	2.01	1.03	2.45	1.19
1937	2.48	0.78	2.26	1.59	1.68	0.80	2.07	1.11	2.50	1.25
1938	2.49	0.85	2.68	2.04	1.90	0.96	2.04	1.15	2.46	1.13

Source: Kawauchi (1972: 110)

Note:
m.w. = male worker
f.w. = female worker

Table 5.4 Average income and living costs in selected mining families, September 1922, in yen

Household size	Number of households	Average income		$\frac{(a)}{(b)} \times 100$	Average expenditure
		Head of household (a)	Total (b)		
3 pers.	5	41,183	53,418	77.1	57,402
4 pers.	8	44,766	97,566	45.9	87,378
5 pers.	6	32,082	80,035	40.1	74,846
6 pers.	4	73,768	135,245	54.5	107,935
7 pers.	5	39,682	122,796	32.3	117,460
8 pers.	2	24,025	102,185	23.5	140,920

Source: Kawada 1923: 149

would often try to work for as long as possible during pregnancy. 'It was quite usual to pull the basket or the tub until shortly before delivery. The better one could control one's body, the easier the delivery was', explained one old coal-mining woman regarding the situation at that time (cited in Shindō 1974:24). In some cases time was even too short to ascend from the mine and children were born underground. After the delivery women normally had a break of fifty to seventy days, a period for which they had often provided by extra shifts during pregnancy.

Even it we take into consideration the fact that working until shortly before childbirth was quite usual for many women at that time, drawing coal was physically extremely hard and demanding work. Its harmful effect on maternity can be guessed from the fact that in 1927 twenty out of every hundred female colliers 'suffered from diseases of the urogenital organs, the majority being diseases of the womb' (International Labour Office 1933:248). Laws and regulations for the protection of motherhood, such as those of the ILO conventions of 1919, were not introduced to Japan before 1926, and even then only in a limited version. The laws included provisions for maternity leave for four weeks before and up to six weeks after childbirth, and the employers had to grant women breaks of thirty minutes twice a day to breastfeed their children. In collieries where the faces being worked were too far away to come up twice a day, day nurseries had to be set up (Ayusawa 1966:194–5). Big collieries like Miike provided day nurseries and kindergartens as early as 1906, but in many of the smaller mines women had to rely on grandparents or neighbours as babysitters, or in some cases, even take their babies with them, when they went down the pit (Ishimoto 1935:169).

Life in the collieries was hard and full of privations. Accidents or sickness would frequently plunge families into deep misery. A survey taken in 1927 of diseases among miners shows that collieries had the highest sickness rate of all mines. The most frequent diseases were those of the digestive organs (men 21 per cent, women 37 per cent), followed by those of the respiratory organs (men 21 per cent, women 31 per cent), and the urogenital organs (men 4 per cent, women 21 per cent) (International Labour Office 1933:249). It can be seen that women were more affected by these sicknesses than men.

In her book *Looking Two Ways*, Baroness Ishimoto Shizue, whose husband was working in the coal-mining districts of northern

Kyūshū in 1915–1917, describes the life of miners under the heading: 'Are miners human beings?' She obviously has difficulty in giving an affirmative answer to this question:

> It would be hard to tell the difference between the life of pigs and the life of these miners. Certainly the human beings were living like animals in barns . . . Women who were already fully tired from their long day's labour in the mines returned home to carry pails of water from a distant well to their kitchens. They cooked, washed and nursed like other women whose energies are only spent on such domestic tasks. Naturally they were abnormally nervous and exhausted. They often beat their . . . children . . . Nothing could be compared to the sight of these crowded nests of ignorance, poverty and misery.
>
> (Ishimoto 1935:167–9)

Probably not all female colliers would have agreed with this dark picture of their daily life. Old coal-mining women who were interviewed by the Japanese writer Morisaki Kazue in the 1970s tended to stress the good human relations in the mines, the solidarity among the miners, and the helpfulness of their neighbours (Morisaki 1974:318–19, 321). Their view of the past culminated in the exclamation: 'Ah, we had a lot of fun, but it was also very hard sometimes!' (Shindō 1974:18). Even if we concede that memory may be kind to these women, the truth probably lies somewhere between Ishimoto's description of the evils, influenced doubtless by her urban upper-class upbringing, and the romantic views of the former colliery women.

One striking thing about the interviews with the old coal-mining women is the pride they had in their work, and their feeling that they were quite capable of competing with the men. 'Whatever one says about it, it is a fact that the work of the drawers, who pulled the tubs, was much more demanding than the work of the hewers' (Shindō 1974:17). Many of the women considered themselves independent wage earners contributing substantially to the family income. As a result they possessed a strong self-confidence seldom found in women working on the surface or in other typical women's occupations.

To what degree this self-confidence manifested itself in political actions is hard to tell. After 1918 women who worked underground participated in the labour movement, but they did not obtain leading positions. Their participation in strikes was limited to providing food for the men and encouraging them by singing labour songs. The labour movement in the coal-mining district of Chikuhō demanded in its programme equal pay for equal work, but as female labour was hired because it was cheap there was little chance of realizing such claims.

PROTECTION OR PREVENTION: LABOUR LEGISLATION AND ITS EFFECT ON THE SITUATION OF FEMALE COLLIERS

The basic legislation governing the general question of woman and child labour consisted of the Factory Act of 1911 and the Factory Act (Amendment Act) of 1923. The Factory Act, which came into force in 1916, contained special rules for so-called protected workers, namely women and young persons, as far as working hours, shifts, night work, rest periods and minimum age were concerned. Owing to many exemptions, however, the law was not very effective. This led to the Amendment Act in 1923, which came into force in 1928.[8]

As regards work in mines, the first law to be effectively applied, at least to some degree, for the protection of labour was the ordinance 'Regulations for the Aid of Mining Workers' (*Sekitan kōgyō rōeki fujo kisoku*) promulgated in 1916, the provisions of which resembled those of the Factory Act. The working hours of women and young miners were restricted to twelve per day, night work between 10p.m. and 4a.m. was in principle forbidden, and rest periods were fixed. However, this ordinance, too, contained so many exemption clauses that its protective value is doubtful.

After the First World War, not least owing to the growing pressure from the International Labour Organization, discussion about the need for protective labour legislation flared up again. This time it included not only demands for a total prohibition of night work for women and young persons, but also demands for a complete ban on underground work by women and young persons. At first, mine operators were opposed to this demand and claimed exemption for women, arguing that mining was carried out as part of a harmonious family labour system. However, during the depression starting in March 1920, the mining industry underwent a serious decline, and the number of miners steadily decreased. The number of women miners decreased from 111,849 in 1919 to 76,199 in 1922 (Ayusawa 1926:12, 60; figures relate to all mines, not just coal-mines). Old women still remember that the end of female colliers' work in coal-mines did not come all of a sudden. Instead, the idea slowly spread that working in coal-mines was not suitable for women. Many women therefore ceased to work in the mines, but when men's wages were not sufficient to support the family, they had to go back again.

In 1926 the Mining Workers' Regulations were revised, but as important problems like night work and underground work were not touched upon at all, a second revision soon became necessary. In 1928 the Home Ministry promulgated revised regulations, under which night work for women and young persons between 10p.m. and 5a.m. was forbidden. Underground work by women and young persons was also to be totally banned after a period of grace of five years. The promulgation of these revised regulations resulted in a dramatic decrease in the number of female miners. Some were transferred to jobs on the surface, but many others were dismissed. Especially in the larger coal-mines, women colliers had to leave underground work. A survey of various mines in Fukuoka prefecture shows that their number shrank from 12,194 in 1929 to less than 400 in 1934, whereas in small and medium collieries the number of women working underground actually grew between 1932 and 1934 (Koeda 1936:13ff; Mathias 1978:278). Thus, as an immediate result of the revised regulations, female colliers were either driven into small and medium mines where working conditions were bad, and social and welfare provisions poor, or they became part of the mass of unemployed workers. Moreover, since the loss of the women's income was not compensated for by any rise in the wages of male colliers, many families became destitute. Therefore, when the content of the revisions became known, many miners staged strikes and other forms of protest[9] (Shindō 1974:137–9).

As dismissals coincided with the Great Depression and a wave of mechanization and rationalization in the collieries, many women felt that the ban on underground work was intended less for their protection than for the smooth implementation of rationalization measures. Their doubts were confirmed when, as late as 1933, shortly before the revised regulations came into force, the Home Ministry stated that exceptions would be made for collieries where coal seams were too thin to be mined by modern methods, and for mines where remnant coal was extracted. Because of such

exceptions quite a large number of women continued to work underground, and under even worse conditions than before.

After the beginning of the Sino-Japanese conflict in 1937,
Japan's coal-mines suffered from a severe labour shortage. In
Fukuoka prefecture a shortfall of more than 16,000 mining workers
was reported in 1938 (*Manejimento* 1939:25). One way of overcom-
ing this shortage was the (forced) employment of Korean workers
in growing numbers. At the same time other solutions were sought;
in this context the re-employment of women, including for underground work, was discussed. Finally, in 1939 the revised regulations of 1928 were partially suspended, and women were once
more called upon to work underground. In 1942 the special permission given in 1939 for the employment of women in underground work was extended until 31 March 1947 ('Kōseishōrei dai
18 gō,' *Kanpō* 4565, 31 March 1942). At the same time several
government orders concerning the improvement of health care for
female miners were promulgated by the newly-founded Ministry
of Welfare (for example, *Kanpō* 4565). In view of the worsening
general situation, however, it seems doubtful whether these orders
were actually carried out.

Owing to the development of the political situation the inten-
tions behind the labour legislation relating to women colliers were
actually reversed. Between 1928 and 1933 the laws provided mine-
owners with an efficient tool for rationalization and the reduction
of workers. Later on, when the economic situation changed because
of the growth of the war economy, the laws were suspended. The
women who were to be protected by these laws, were at first
dismissed, or transferred to positions with much lower wages, and
then, in response to economic need, were again 'allowed' to return
to underground work. Such repeated volte-faces in social and
labour policy made many women miners suspect that the labour
laws were a means not for their protection, but for the protection
of Japanese industry.

CONCLUSION

If, in more recent years, a woman wanted to visit a Japanese
coal-mine and go underground, she was usually told that women
underground would bring disaster for the colliery. The reason
given was the jealousy of the mountain goddess, who was said to
be female. It is evident that most Japanese have completely

forgotten the important role women played in the labour force of the collieries before the war, and their major contribution to the development of the coal-mining industry in Japan.

It is not just to overcome this ignorance and do justice to the tens of thousands of women who pursued this hard and dangerous work underground that female labour in the Japanese coal-mines should be studied more extensively. It is also important in that the situation of these workers differs in many respects from the usual image of female workers in pre-war Japan, which is closely associated with the existence of young unmarried textile workers.

In contrast to female labour in the textile mills, female labour in the mining industry did not develop in response to modern industrial development, but rather evolved in the broader context of family work in the rural areas, long before industrial development started in the coal-mines. Work in the collieries was therefore at first an accepted part of the domestic activities of women, and quite compatible with the traditional family role which female colliers were expected to discharge.

The translation of mining from side work for peasant families to full-time occupation, accompanied by a tightening of the organization of labour and the introduction of a shift system, caused a complete change in the working and living rhythm of miners. For women a relatively flexible division of their time between work and domestic responsibilities was no longer practicable. They were more and more drawn into an industrial production process which left them little time to care for their families. The growing conflict between the traditional domestic role of women and their role in the labour force was for a long time ignored, since mining companies greatly profited in various ways from female labour. It helped them to keep male wages low. At the same time, by maintaining the cheap labour of women (and children), they kept costs low and also expanded their reservoir of labour during a period of fast growth.

On the other hand it has to be conceded that without the exploitation of cheap female labour many of the smaller mines in Kyūshū could not have survived in the first place, and many employment opportunities in this area would have been lost. Moreover, in the eyes of many female colliers, working underground was not always to be regarded as severe exploitation. Sometimes it was also a step towards emancipation as an independent wage-earner, as their pride and their self-confidence show. Thus, as long as coal-mining was carried out as a labour-intensive production process, with a low degree of mechanization in most of the small and medium-sized collieries, and relying largely on an unskilled and semi-skilled labour force, family labour, and especially the employment of women in the collieries, was maintained. With the spread of mechanization and rationalization measures cheap female labour lost its function of reducing production costs. That is why, after some initial protest, employers – at least in the big firms – gave up the concept of 'harmonious family work in mining' in favour of protective labour legislation, which forced women out of the mines.

On the whole, female labour in the coal-mines has to be regarded as a remnant of the pre-industrial era. Therefore, in contrast to the 'modern type' of female workers in textile industries, female colliers represent a more traditional type of working women. This traditional kind of female labour was – to some degree – successfully integrated into the early stages of industrial production in the coal-mines. It did not, however, fit smoothly into the modernized production process of the 1920s and 1930s. It was only then that, supported by the public debate on protective labour legislation, the use of female labour in the coal-mines was questioned on the grounds of health and morals.

NOTES

1 Material on coal-mining in northern Kyūshū is mainly collected in the Sekitan Shiryō Kenkyū Sentaa of Kyūshū University. Among the numerous studies on this subject and on coal-mining in general only a few can be mentioned here (Sumiya 1968; Ueno 1971; Chikuhō Sekitan 1973; Murakushi 1976; Mathias 1978; Tanaka 1984).

2 This is clearly shown by examples of petitions by villages to get permission for the mining of nearby collieries, which are cited, for example, in Sumiya (1968:82,85).

3 The *naya seido* took its name from the *naya* or barracks-like quarters, in which the colliers' families lived. While the term *naya seido* prevailed in Kyūshū and was associated with the type of family labour described, in Honshū and Hokkaidō the term *hanba seido* was more frequently used for a subcontracting system, centred around single male workers. Both systems functioned quite similarly and can be characterized as premodern paternalistic forms of labour management.

4 This is as stated in Morisaki's original text. Notwithstanding an obvious omission, the importance of family labour groups is clear.

5 Unpublished material 'Kōfubōshū kankei shiryō' Miike sōmu 387,

Mitsui bunko, Tokyo (German translation of both pamphlets in Mathias 1978:210, 216ff.).

6 These first three points are explicitly stressed by the employer side in the unpublished manuscript 'Yamano kōgyō enkaku shi', XI:64, Kōzan gojūnen shi kōhon 123, Mitsui bunko, Tokyo.

7 Whereas the bulk of the female labour force in the textile factories consisted of young, unmarried women, the majority of female colliers were married. In 1910, for example, approximately 70 per cent of female colliers were married (Nōshōmushō 1913:76–7).

8 A very comprehensive study on the debate centring around the question of women's night work, especially in the textile mills, is given in Fuchs (1970).

9 Shindō (1974:139) mentions the example of a strike in May 1931, during which miners demanded the re-employment of dismissed female colliers.

BIBLIOGRAPHY

Ayusawa, I. (1966) *A History of Labour in Modern Japan*, Honolulu, East-West Center Press.

Chikuhō Sekitan Kōgyō-shi Nenpyō Hensan Iinkai (ed.) (1973) *Chikuhō Sekitankōgyō Shi Nenpyō*, Fukuoka, Nishi Nihon Bunka Kyōkai.

Fuchs, Karl-Peter (1970) 'Das Problem der Frauennachterbeit in Japan und die Argumentation der japanischen Unternehmer', in *Nachrichten der Gesellschaft für Natur- und Völkerkunde Ostasiens/Hamburg*, 107/108, 71–136.

International Labour Office (ed.) (1933) *Industrial Labour in Japan*, Studies and Reports Series A (Industrial Relations) no. 37, Geneva, International Labour Office.

Ishimoto, S. (1935) *Facing Two Ways: The Story of My Life*, London, Cassel.

Kawada, T. (1923) 'Tankō rōdōsha no seikei', *Keizai Ronsō* 16(5)146–52.

Kawauchi, N. (1972) *Taku Sekitan no Hanashi*, Taku, Taku-shi Kyōiku linkai.

Koeda, H. (1936) *Fukuoka-ken ni okeru Tankō Kasegidōsha no Shujusō*, Fukuoka (author's publication).

Manejimento (1939) 'Kyū o tsuguru – Kōzan no rōdō mondai – fusoku taisaku' 16(6):25–8.

Mathias, R. (1978), *Industrialisierung und Lohnarbeit. Der Kohlebergbau in Nord-Kyūshū und sein Einfluß auf die Herausbildung einer Lohnarbeiterschaft*, Beiträge zur Japanologie, 15, Wien, Institut für Japanologie.

Morisaki, K. (1974) *Naraku no Kamigami*, Tokyo, Yamato shoten.

Murakushi, N. (1976) *Nihon Tankō Chinrōdō Shi Ron*, Tokyo, Jichōsha.

Natural Resources Section (ed.) (1948) *The Coal Fields of Kyūshū* Natural Resources Section Report 103, Tokyo, General Headquarters, Supreme Command for the Allied Powers.

Nōshōmushō (Kōzan-kyoku) (ed.) (1913) *Kōfu Chōsa Gaiyō*, Tokyo, Nōshōmushō.

Sakamoto, F. (1977) *Nihon Koyō-shi, 2 Nenkōsei e no Nagai Michinori*, Tokyo, Chūō Keizaisha.

Shindō, T. (1974) *Chikuhō no Jokōfutachi*, Kyoto, Buraku Mondai Kenkyūsho.
Sumiya, M. (1968) *Nihon Sekitan Sangyō Bunseki*, Tokyo, Iwanami shoten.
Tanaka, N. (1984) *Kindai Nihon Tankō Rōdō Shi Kenkyū*, Tokyo, Sōfu kan.
Tōyō Keizai Shinpōsha (ed.) (1927) *Meiji Taishō Kokusei Sōran*, Tokyo, Tōyō Keizai Shinpōsha.
Ueno, H. (1971) *Kindai Minshū no Kiroku*, 2 *Kōfu*, Tokyo, Shinjinbutsu Ōraisha.
Yamamoto, S. (1973) *Chikuhō Tankō Shi Emaki*, Fukuoka, Ashi Shobō.

Chapter 6

Equality versus difference: the Japanese debate over 'motherhood protection', 1915–50

Barbara Molony

'Motherhood protection' (*bosei hogo*) has an eighty-year history in Japan. The phrase has been used by politicians, bureaucrats, feminists, labour union officials, women workers, social reformers and business managers. It has been used both to deny women workplace equality and to facilitate mothers' continued employment. It has played a powerful and evocative role in political discourse since the early twentieth century. Somewhat dormant during the 1950s and 1960s, it re-emerged in the late 1970s as the dominant issue in the national debate over the Equal Employment Opportunity Law implemented in April 1986.

The phrase 'motherhood protection' (and its related but subtle variants, 'protection of the mother's body', 'mother-child protection', and 'motherhood security') has had multiple meanings. Both 'motherhood' and 'protection' have been understood in differing ways, and the combination of these two words in various contexts and by variously interested individuals has produced a dynamic discursive environment for 'motherhood protection'. 'Motherhood' could mean ability to bear children, pregnancy and childbirth, rearing children, or any combination of these and other conditions. The definition of 'protection' depended on the particular understanding of motherhood under discussion and had political implications, as it suggested the implementation of policy. 'Protection' was variously reified through such policies as limiting work hours for women, removing women from 'dangerous' (to whom? to bodily or moral health?) work, prenatal and childbirth leaves, economic assistance to indigent mothers, and menstruation leave. Thus, the discourse on 'motherhood protection' was complex and was addressed in many different ways by feminists and others. With each reinterpretation of the term, its discussants explicitly raised the issue of equality and difference, most finding no incompatibility in both recognizing 'motherhood' as a distinct category and facilitating meaningful work for women, but others arguing that equality and difference were mutually exclusive.

In the pre-Second World War era, feminists and labour-union women debated the desirability of stressing gendered differences or equality, calling their discussion the 'motherhood protection debate' and arguing primarily in economic terms. In general, they sought ways to help women who were already mothers to support their children, either by facilitating mothers' employment or by demanding state grants to mothers in recognition of their reproductive contributions to the state. Feminists' discussion acknowledged the socially- and politically-defined responsibility of mothers to rear (or educate) their children and thus focused on mothers' economic ability to do so. On the other hand, male politicians and social reformers more often called for a 'motherhood protection' that focused on women's bodies, on their fecundity, on protecting women's physical (and moral!) potential to bear children. Thus, while many feminists sought a motherhood protection that *facilitated* women's access to work by removing impediments to mothers' employment (which would help them carry out their socially-defined role as supporters of their children), male social reformers and politicians sought to *deny* access to some types of work to protect the bodies of potential mothers. These protections were gradually reified in law as limitations on women's work hours and work sites. Because the limitations advanced politically were of work conditions believed dangerous not only to women's fertility but also to women and girl workers themselves, however, many feminists bought into the body-centred discourse on motherhood protection moulded by politically- and bureaucratically-powerful men.

Nevertheless, feminists and women labour activists did not abandon their interest in the economic aspects of motherhood protection – that is, seeking ways to permit women to work or otherwise support their children or future children – resurrecting them in the economically desperate times of the late 1930s and late 1940s. After a discussion of pre-war motherhood protection debates which created the discourse within which post-war debates were framed, I shall focus on one significant post-war work 'benefit' for women, menstruation leave. Regular menstruation leave of, initially, three and, later, two days monthly had economic origins; that is, it permitted women to work in a particular historical context and under specific conditions. It eventually came to be viewed as part of a body-centred form of motherhood protection, a discourse increasingly central to post-war Japanese feminist concerns until the late 1970s. Unions and feminist groups tenaciously held on to menstruation leave as a fundamental right of women workers until the mid-1970s (Herold 1974:184–95). Although by the late 1970s most commentators, noting menstruation leave was a benefit that had little if any bearing on either job performance or fertility, dropped it as an essential part of motherhood protection, feminists have continued to stress the need to enforce other types of motherhood protection, some related to health, but most – such as paid maternity leave, better hours of operation at day-care centres, and most important, women's ability to remain on their companies' promotion tracks despite time off for childrearing – related to mothers' ability to support and raise their children. Thus, while reformers and politicians have conducted their discussion of motherhood protection in terms of women's bodies – that is, a discourse that did not necessarily require consideration of employment equality – feminists and women labour activitists have, at various times, used both body-centred and economic arguments in either recognizing or downplaying difference in order to achieve equality.

PRE-WAR ANTECEDENTS TO POST-WAR MOTHERHOOD PROTECTION

Fearful of rising social discontent and labour unrest, bureaucrats and social reformers began advocating protective legislation in the 1890s (Gordon 1988:64–5; Garon 1987:Ch.1; Hunter 1989:248–52). The Factory Law (passed the Diet in 1911, enforced in 1916, revised in 1923, revision enforced in 1926) was intended to promote labour-management harmony. The sections of the Factory Law that focused on such workplace protections for women and children as prohibition of night work and limitation of length of the workday were far more controversial among industrialists than the non-gender specific clauses providing sick leave or workplace medical facilities. The strong opposition of major employers of women and children won a postponement of implementation of the clause prohibiting night work until 1929.

Despite the opposition of major employers of women, the advocates of the Factory Law usually argued in terms of motherhood protection in campaigning for the bill. The law contained explicitly gendered provisions; women and minors alone were barred from night work and from a workday longer than twelve hours (complete texts of Factory Law, enforcement edicts and revision in Akamatsu 1977:291–304). No comparable restrictions were placed on male labour; to be sure, night work routinely scheduled for economic reasons was, at that time, predominantly a female phenomenon, being concentrated in the cotton textile mills where most workers were young women. The majority of workers whose maternity was being protected by the Factory Law were, therefore, young girls without children of their own. Male labour activists had ambivalent attitudes about protecting women's maternity. Though they agreed with reformers that employers ill served the state by exploiting future mothers, they were reluctant to threaten their own position by endorsing limits on women's work hours, as men's hours were already usually shorter than the stipulated limits for women (Hunter 1989:254–5).

Concern about the moral and physical compromise of the future maternity of young women workers lay behind many bureaucrats' and reformers' arguments for the Factory Law. One intellectual wrote in 1911: 'If we subject our fragile womenfolk to the extremes of harsh employment we cannot have healthy mothers' (Toda Umiichi, *Nihon no Shakai*, quoted in Hunter 1989:250). Journalist Ushiyama Saijirō warned of moral threats to young women workers on the night shift caused by their being sexually harrassed by male supervisors and co-workers (Hunter 1989:251–2).

The provisions of the Factory Law dealing with future mothers' physical and moral health, as Japan's first legislation regarding maternality, played a significant role in creating the discourse on motherhood protection. There was no question of women's equality, only their difference, a difference that both required 'protection' and demanded women's fulfilment of their duty to the state to bear *healthy* children. Feminists during the 1910s, on the other hand, began explicitly to use the term 'motherhood protection' with entirely different meanings and raising different issues. Most focused on mothers' economic ability to support children. Moreover, the debate centred on women who were already mothers rather than on potential mothers.

As middle-class intellectuals, the main feminist protagonists in the 'motherhood protection debate' argued within the dominant discourse on womanhood in the pre-war period – that of the 'good wife and wise mother' (*ryōsai kenbo*). Much has been written in English about *ryōsai kenbo* (see, for example); Uno 1988, 1992; Nolte and Hastings 1991; Ueno 1987; Tocco 1990; Sievers 1983:109–13), but for our purposes just a few strands of that intricately-wound skein need to be unravelled. While elite women were historically valued for their reproductive contributions to their husbands' lines of succession, non-elite women, in contrast, were expected to be 'good wives' who furthered the economic well-being of their families (Uno 1991). Explicit policy changes in the late nineteenth century demanded that women also be 'wise mothers', although anything more than rudimentary education was possible only for women of the middle and upper classes. Because of universal and compulsory elementary education, the state did not expect wise mothers to give primary instruction to their children, but rather to guide them, socialize them, and care for them properly. While ruing – and, in fact, mounting political struggles against – the limitations of the *ryōsai kenbo* role, feminists also accepted its premise that mothers were responsible for the moulding and well-being of their children. The 'motherhood protection debate' of 1918–19 was framed by feminists' acknowledgement of that responsibility.

The main protagonists in the debate were acclaimed poet Yosano Akiko (1878–1942), feminist theoretician and notorious 'new woman' Hiratsuka Raichō (1886–1971), socialist-feminist theoretician and activist Yamakawa Kikue (1890–1980), and rescued Seattle prostitute-turned-'feminist' translator Yamada Waka (1879–1957). The debate ranged over a four-year period from 1915–1919, but was most heated during its last two years when approximately 115 articles addressing women's rights, about one-third dealing explicitly with motherhood protection, appeared in general-circulation intellectual periodicals like *Taiyō* (Sun), *Fujin Kōron* (Women's Review), *Fujo Shinbun* (Women's News), and others (Kouchi 1984:326–31). The main protagonists were occasionally joined by other feminist writers or journalists for mass-circulation daily newspapers; the motherhood protection debate was widely known and its arguments influential. Excellent treatments of the debate among these four women exist (Rodd 1991; Maruoka 1976:154–5; Nakatori 1979:192–4; Sakurai 1987:48–51; and Kouchi 1984, this last being an extensive collection of documents and articles from the debate); I shall summarize the debaters' major theses, especially in so far as they helped create the discourse on motherhood protection.

The strongest advocate of the need for equal treatment of men and women in economic life was Yosano Akiko. She repeatedly called, in her numerous articles, for 'economic independence' for women, adding, on at least one occasion, that men should also be independent. Good marriages were based on the ability of both husband and wife to avoid 'dependency' (*iraishugi*) and stand on their own two feet economically. The desirability of autonomy was not just an affectation for elite women, but a necessity for proletarian women as well. The latter had to work because two incomes were necessary to feed the couple's children. In an interesting reversal of the protection advocates' contention that excessive work harmed women's reproductive abilities, Yosano, who had given birth to eleven children herself, argued that without the income earned by working, women would be unable to maintain their health and would therefore produce unhealthy children (Yosano 1918c:166–7). In answer to those who stressed women's and men's biological differences, Yosano acknowledged the differences in sexual organs but added that both were necessary for reproduction, making men and women equal in that task (Yosano 1916:51).

'The liberation of women' (Yosano 1918d:178) would be achieved not by 'protection' – a term Yosano found pejorative and dismissive (ibid.: 189) – but by education to advance women's lagging skills to the level of men's (Yosano 1918a:81–2). The protection advocated by European and American feminists was not progressive, Yosano stated, but conservative; Japanese women had already proved they could succeed in numerous fields like medicine, teaching, journalism, scholarship, science and business (Yosano 1918c:161). Indeed, dependence on the government for grants during pregnancy and childbirth was no better than dependence on a husband, which Yosano equated with 'slave morality' (*dorei dōtoku*) (Yosano 1918b:85). Rodd (1991:192) also translates *dorei dotoku* as 'slave morality'. Should working mothers need funds to cover income lost during pregnancy and childbirth, they should receive insurance payments similar to those for any other health-related work absence (Yosano 1918d:187; Rodd 1991:197).

Hiratsuka Raichō, who had one child, disputed Yosano's contention that protection was a form of dependency (Hiratsuka 1918: 86–91). Under contemporary conditions in Japan, she said, it was impossible to run a household – part of a mother's role – and hold a job at the same time. While economic independence was generally laudable, she was concerned about those women who were unfairly labelled unproductive (presumably by Yosano) because they had not achieved independence (Hiratsuka 1919:207). Most important, she wrote, children were not the possessions of mothers who could do with them as they pleased, but rather belonged to society or the state. The state, therefore, had an interest in the number and quality of children (*kodomo no kazu to shitsu*) produced, and should give mothers funds to produce healthy children. Hiratsuka agreed with Yosano that women's liberation would be advanced by greater opportunities for women, but disagreed with her on the issue of maternity; in the case of motherhood, women were not to be seen as fulfilling individual needs but rather as esteemed contributors to the larger society. Indeed, on the basis of that contribution, Hiratsuka stated at the time of her co-founding of the suffragist New Woman Association (Shin Fujin Kyōkai) in 1919, women deserved civil rights and the vote.

Hiratsuka's arguments, like those of the other participants in the motherhood protection debate, were primarily economic; mothers needed funds to carry out a socio-economically defined role as supporters of their children on behalf of the state. But she advanced her argument by focusing on body-centred issues after the founding of the New Woman Association. In particular, she fought for legislation permitting women to terminate contracts to marry men who were diagnosed with syphilis. Because it threatened the patriarchal family system, the campaign was presented as part of the motherhood protection movement, but the real beneficiaries were healthy women saved from disease (K. Molony 1978:17).

Yamakawa Kikue agreed with Yosano's support of better education for women and their need for good employment (Yamakawa 1918a:141), but said it was 'impossible for women to harmonize (*chōwa*) home life and work life' under current conditions of capitalism (Yamakawa 1918b:192). Unlike Hiratsuka, who resolved the contradiction by advocating that women leave work and be paid for maternity, Yamakawa called for social revolution to solve the problem of inequality. As we shall see below, by 1925 Yamakawa modified her position and came to accept, in the absence of a socialist revolution, the desirability of improving work conditions to facilitate mothers' access to work. Yamada Waka argued that men and women were not meant to be independent, as Yosano contended. Mothers' role was to educate their children for the sake of the state, and fathers' was to earn money to support their families. Yamada, quoting numerous European examples and particularly citing her major inspiration, Ellen Key (1849–1926), wrote that the demand for mothers' entitlement to support either from their husbands or from the state was progressive and feminist (Yamada 1918:153). Yamada's views, though dressed up in chic European finery, were hardly new, but a fairly close approximation of *ryōsai kenbo* ideology.

Though the 'motherhood protection debate' had died down by the end of 1919, it left a significant legacy. Most important, the debaters introduced to political and social discourse many of the terms of motherhood protection, including the phrase itself, that would be frequently remoulded during the next six decades. But issues were raised that went beyond questions of protection and maternality. For one, in the early 1920s, the disputants became involved in another debate played out in the press, that time over the issue of birth-control (Suzuki 1985:13–56). For another, mothers' contributions to the state by giving birth to healthy children and educating them became one basis for the demand for women's suffrage.

Women labour activists, led by Yamakawa Kikue, soon resurrected the debate within the labour movement. As feminists and socialists, they had to find a way of defining women's demands without appearing to stress gender. The communist union Hyōgi-kai, founded in May 1925, was one vehicle for attempting to further both maternity benefits and equal employment for women.

Short-term health leave before and after childbirth had first been granted to women teachers in Nagano prefecture in 1908, and extended to women teachers nation-wide in 1922 (Sakurai 1987:52) Hyōgikai advocates of maternity leave for all women workers thus had a precedent on which to build. But the struggle for body-centred maternity benefits as well as employment conditions that would permit women (and men) workers to be attentive parents while being employed was conducted in a misogynist environment in the labour movement. Not only were male workers concerned lest protections for women erode their own entitlements, but the term 'worker' (*rōdōsha*), used to define membership, in some unions only implied 'male workers' (Yamanouchi 1975:44). Even the leftist Hyōgikai rejected its women members' call for a separate *fujinbu* (women's division) at the national level, preferring to keep the women divided into politically weaker regional women's divisions and claiming that the organizational structure the women desired was divisive of the larger movement (Ōba 1988:182). The rejection of the women's demand for a *fujinbu* by the male leaders of the Hyōgikai led to the dismissal of the whole packet of demands, including provisions for equality and for protection, put forward by Yamakawa Kikue and other feminist socialists in 1925. Women workers' demands until the end of the Second World War were conditioned by the failure of the feminists' struggle for political position within the Hyōgikai.

The 1925 'Women's Division Thesis', as the women's demands came to be known, contained clauses dealing with conditions in dormitories that housed workers, enforcement of the prohibition of night work and restrictions on child labour, leave with pay before and after childbirth, an eight-hour work day, and equal pay for equal work (Ōba 1988:182). All of these provisions were intended to address the real problems of women workers, although only maternity leave and prohibition of night work were unambiguously gendered. The dormitory demand was, in effect though not explicitly, gendered. Dormitories mainly housed young women textile workers, and although the purpose of dormitories was to prevent workers from escaping, employers claimed that they protected workers' future maternality by guarding their morals. The other provisions were intended to help women gain economic equality and help mothers (and fathers) carry out their parental responsibilities. The eight-hour day would permit mothers who could not rear children while working a twelve-hour day to retain their jobs and be good wives and wise mothers. Equal pay for equal work would enable mothers to improve their care for their children. Equal pay had been called for in the Versailles Treaty, and was advanced by egalitarian feminist Ichikawa Fusae (1893–1981) when she was a member of Japan's ILO committee. The failure of the Hyōgikai women to persuade the union men to accept the demand for equal pay led other women to abandon this issue until 1945 and to focus on motherhood protection provisions in lieu of equality. Ironically, working-class feminists who suffered their male colleagues' criticism for seeking 'separate' interests in their quest for both equal pay and political empowerment within the movement were more successful in persuading the men to join their demands based on women's bodily differences (motherhood protection). Textile workers' strike demands in the latter part of the 1920s, for example, often included maternity leave (B. Molony 1991:234).

Feminist groups that had devoted their energies in the 1920s and the early 1930s to the struggle for political rights and civil equality turned to motherhood protection in the mid-1930s. Recognizing that the growing militarism in Japanese political life made it risky for them to advocate women's suffrage for its own sake, the Women's Suffrage League created the Women's Association to pass a Mother-Child Protection Bill (*Boshi hogo seitei sokushin renmei*) in 1934. Suffragist Ichikawa Fusae recognized that feminists had to find a cause that would advance the interests of women but not be threatening to conservatives. She wrote that both the poverty of the depression years and the loss of income of fathers sent overseas with the Japanese military severely harmed mothers and their children, contributing to the shocking rash of mother-child suicides in the early 1930s (Ichikawa 1934:4). Moreover, she connected the demand for women's suffrage to the need to support the economic well-being of mothers and children. The feminists' argument avoided body-centred discourse and focused on economic issues, although it dealt less with employment than with survival.

The Mother-Child Protection Law, which passed the Diet in March 1937, and which granted economic support to single mothers of children under age thirteen, focused state ideology on the mother as the centre of the family (Miyake 1991:272–3). Single fathers were not similarly protected. Despite the state's expressed interest in the welfare of children, as recognized in the title of the law, the law's realization most affected mothers. That is, the law reinforced women's role as supportive mothers, this time as economically supportive, supplementing the earlier stress on educational support implied in the term 'wise mother'. The increasing peripherality of the father in the mother-child Japanese family was influenced by the spread of the ideology about the mother's role as reflected in the law. Subsequent discussions of motherhood protection in Japan, whether during the economically difficult times of the immediate post-war period, or during the affluent years of the 1990s, have focused on protecting mothers' abilities to rear their children while making the money necessary to do so.

Confusing and contradictory rhetoric about motherhood protection abounded during the Second World War (Miyake 1991:277–88). Women were to produce numerous children for the state; birth-control was outlawed and reproduction came under state control. At the same time, women were to produce armaments for the state in the absence of conscripted male workers. To increase female labour in the armaments plants, the government eliminated 'motherhood protection' clauses of the Factory Law which had restricted night work, had mandated minimum ages of workers, and had barred women workers from hazardous work sites (Sakurai 1987:62–4). Women were also discouraged from taking maternity leave; according to survey data, few if any took prenatal leave and more than half took fewer than three weeks *postpartum* leave. Infant mortality reported in another survey was shockingly high: 19.4 per cent (ibid.:63). At the same time the government was empowered to mandate day-care facilities in factories employing more than 200 workers (Miyake 1991:287). Feminists borrowed patriotic rhetoric; a collection of articles written by a group of feminists identified with the egalitarian, suffrage position reconceptualized civil rights for women in terms of their contributions to the state as workers and mothers (Ichikawa 1944). The inconsistency of policies regarding maternity resulted from women's double duty of production and reproduction, and highlighted the variety of policy approaches possible in a particular discursive environment.

MOTHERHOOD PROTECTION IN THE POST-WAR YEARS

Motherhood protection policies were debated and created in an atmosphere of both desperation and cautious optimism in the immediate post-Second World War years. The optimism resulted from women's sense that change was imminent. Japan was occupied by a foreign power that subscribed to the Potsdam Declaration with its call for male-female equality; steps toward equality had been taken with the granting of suffrage to women in 1945 and the promulgation of the new Constitution in 1946 mandating equal political rights. Laws were being rewritten, and women anticipated legal changes for women workers as well. Labour unions, newly freed from wartime oppression, were enjoying rapid growth and found women's issues convenient causes around which to organize.

At the same time Japan was desperately poor. Agricultural production was down 60 per cent, many factories were either destroyed by bombing or closed by Occupation orders, six million

Japanese were being repatriated from military, political, or commercial posts in China or South-east Asia, housing stock was
severely depleted in the fire- or nuclear bombings of 100 cities,
and health and sanitation facilities were virtually non-existent.
Policies concerning women workers were discussed and formed
using both the new vocabulary of gender equality and the pre-war
rhetoric of special sexual protections in a historic context in which
widows, orphans and wives required employment while repatriated
men encountered job shortages. These factors all contributed to
the types of legislation concerning women workers, particularly
such motherhood protections as maternity leave, restriction of work
sites, and menstruation leave, passed in the early post-war years.

Within three months of the beginning of the American military
Occupation of Japan, the Japanese government, the Japan
Communist Party and feminist labour advocates were ready with
policies regarding women. On 6 December 1945, the Welfare Ministry issued an order to women to 'go back into the home' to open
up jobs for returning men (Ōba 1988:24). When women failed to
comply, the government used pressure tactics. For example, in
July 1946 the Transportation Ministry told the National Railroad
(Kokutetsu) to take 'cost-cutting measures' like firing 'weak and
inefficient' workers, especially those hired when protections had
been eliminated during the war and who could no longer be freely
assigned to night work. Women workers knew exactly who was
being fired, and wanted their union to call for a twenty-four-hour
strike. But there was no consensus in the national union to strike;
moreover, the women's section of the railroad union was shut out
of labour-management negotiations, and women's interests failed
to be protected by male labour leaders (Ōba 1979:76; 1988:27–35).
Government opinion generally applauded the removal of women
from factory jobs as a means of controlling inflation and of bribing
male workers into labour peace. Ironically, some women forced
from railroad or factory work due to the enforcement of the prohibition of night work were pushed into prostitution (Ōba 1988:25).
Moreover, although women had begun to make inroads into a
greater diversity of industries during the war, the reinstitution
of protections reconcentrated women in female-dominated, poorly
remunerated, dangerous jobs like those in textiles for which the
protections of the Factory Law had been created in the first place.[1]

The Japan Communist Party (JCP), interested in recruiting
women into the labour movement and the party, called for a

comprehensive protection programme in an article in its party organ, *Akahata*, on 5 December 1945 (Sakurai 1987: 70–2). The JCP advocated prohibition of dangerous work, two months prenatal and *postpartum* leave, medical facilities for pregnant women at factories, one-week paid menstruation leave per month, and free hospitalization and child care.

Feminist labour activist Akamatsu Tsuneko, later head of the Women's Division of the non-communist Sōdōmei union and member of the Diet's House of Councillors, also strongly supported maternity leave and menstruation leave, although she preferred not to let employers avoid making improvements in labour conditions by taking stop-gap measures like menstruation leave (Ōba 1988:103; Sakurai 1987:95). Her official role in the deliberations over the Labour Standards Law of 1947 privileged her particular interpretation of women workers' rights.

Labour unions also began to demand motherhood protection – although not guarantees of job security – for their women members. In December 1945 the Japan Crane Operators' Union (whose female membership was probably small) became the first union to demand three days menstrual leave and one month prenatal and *postpartum* leave for women (Sakurai 1987:75). Menstruation leave was a bargaining issue in about one-tenth (70 out of 739) of the contracts negotiated in 1945–6. The peak month for such demands was April 1946, when 23 of 153 contracts included the benefit (Ōba 1988:101). By 1946, menstruation leave was an acceptable topic for negotiation and would soon be part of the discourse on motherhood protection. The short-lived but influential Communist-led Sanbetsu Kaigi union (Congress of industrial unions), founded in August 1946 and bringing together 43 per cent (1.63 million members) of Japan's unionized workers, demanded both equality and protection in its platform. Along with equal pay for equal work, the union advocated prohibition of hazardous and underground work for women, a workday of six or fewer hours, maternity leave of fifty-six days, menstruation leave of three days, nurseries and schools in factories, and time off for infant nursing (Sakurai 1987:79). Though public discussion of menstruation had been somewhat taboo in the early twentieth century, its frequent mention in late–1940s negotiations made it seem a 'symbol of women's liberation' to some feminists (Ōba 1988:104–5) and at least acceptable in wider discourse. But not too acceptable; the term 'menstruation' was rarely used in most discussions on the subject in the late 1940s. Rather, the discussion revolved around *seiri kyūka* (lit. physiological leave), the euphemism currently used in legal discourse.

Menstruation leave was not entirely new in the post-war years, although conditions at that time made the demand for menstruation leave more salient. The first mention of menstruation leave had been in 1928, when 500 women bus conductors, staging a strike against the Tokyo Municipal Bus Company, demanded menstruation leave. The particular conditions of the conductors' work – long hours on their feet, with little or no opportunity to use a toilet – inspired this demand (Sakurai 1987:58–61). These women were not protecting their motherhood, they were trying to protect their livelihood; short of improving menstrual pads or supplying buses with toilets, the Municipal Bus Company could do no better than to grant time off.

The April and May 1937 issues of *Fujin Kōron* carried articles under the title 'Let's have menstruation leave!'. In April, a (male) physician wrote that menstruation leave was medically necessary, and noted that women in various occupations – bus conductors, teachers, nurses, office workers, telephone operators, candy makers, printers and typists – had clamoured for the benefit. In May, eminent intellectuals and feminists, including Yamakawa Kikue, writer Miyamoto Yuriko, and suffragist and journalist Kaneko Shigeri, joined the chorus of support for menstruation leave (Sakurai 1987:65).

Menstruation leave ceased to be an issue during the Second World War, but re-emerged in the gloomy conditions of the post-war factories. In October 1945 the American Occupation demanded that protections for women be restored, but enforced that order quite selectively. For example, although the Factory Law's ban on underground work for women was restored, mine operators requested a postponement of the implementation of that ban; an eleven-month postponement was granted by the Occupation (Ōba 1988:98). But menstruation leave was a simpler matter. Without menstruation leave, women factory employees, like their counterparts among the Tokyo bus conductors two decades earlier, could not work. Women had no menstrual pads; there was no cotton available for that purpose. Rags were few. Factories had no heat or clean toilets, and many had broken or missing windows (ibid.:98). Menstruation leave was not inspired by women feeling weak or cramped or in need of protection for future maternity, but by women who had no easy way to deal with the physical aspects of their periods.

Menstruation leave came to be seen as an important 'quality of life' issue. Of course, it was gendered as well. Other gendered demands, inappropriate today though explicable in the context of a destitute, bombed-out Japan with inadequate social services and a destroyed economic infrastructure, included time off for shopping – stores, where they existed, rarely had goods, forcing housewives to spend hours each day shopping or gathering food in the surrounding countryside (ibid.:99) – and a 'living wage' for heads of families, usually male, instead of the equal pay for equal work demanded by women in the early post-war period before that demand was suppressed by male union leaders between the late 1940s and late 1950s (ibid.:185). Shopping time was not formally institutionalized as was menstruation leave, although caring for the family, of which shopping was a part, was viewed as one aspect of a mother's responsibilities. Had shopping time been granted, it would have had economic consequences for mothers by facilitating their employment. Men's 'living wage' was instituted in a variety of ways, including differential rates of pay, housing allowances, special medical benefits, vacation privileges and so on, for 'heads' of families. This gendered 'living wage', which was blatantly based on the worker's age and the number of his family members, paralleled motherhood protection in its protection of the privileges of fatherhood. Few women workers in the post-war years were old, and fewer yet were heads of household.

Post-war poverty made 'quality of life' more attractive than 'equality of gender' to union leaders already wary, despite their egalitarian rhetoric, of political women. And many women, though reluctant to abandon the struggle for equal pay, agreed that improvement of the quality of life and of conditions of work (except, apparently, for pay) were of paramount immediate importance. The inherent gendering of 'quality of life' issues was, therefore, overlooked and, if anything, interpreted as beneficial to the needs of women. While most working-class women desired protections for economic reasons – that is, so they could continue to work even in unsanitary and cold conditions or while carrying out the maternal chores they rarely problematized – union spokeswomen explicitly raised the issue of protection versus equality. Typical of their opinion was Sakurai's: 'The right of motherhood protection must be recognized as the premise of male-female equality' (Sakurai 1987:15).

The Labour Standards Law of 1947 codified a variety of protections. Those for women were, like those in the pre-war Factory Law, centred on present and future maternity.[2] A survey of business managers and workers (data not disaggregated by sex of respondents) conducted in the summer of 1947 indicated their agreement with the law's focus on reproduction rather than on caring for children. While a majority of workers agreed that maternity and menstruation leaves were necessary and approved of restrictions on night work for women, only a minority of workers surveyed believed child-care leave and day-care facilities were necessary (*Shiryō Rōdō Undōshi* 1952, reprinted in Akamatsu 1977:749). The survey might have indicated otherwise had the respondents all been women, but that is impossible to determine.

With labour unions demanding some type of protective legislation, the American Occupation forces insisting on reinstitution of protections, and women's groups calling for social, political and economic rights, the government felt constrained to deal with labour beyond telling women workers to return to the home. The Welfare Ministry first proposed drafting a new Labour Standards Law in early March 1946, and put bureaucrat Matsumoto Iwakichi in charge of the project (Ōba 1988:106). Matsumoto was inexperienced in the area of labour legislation, as the Welfare Ministry (the Labour Ministry had not yet come into existence) had not been directly responsible for labour policy before the war. The Interior Ministry (Naimushō), which had been responsible, had been disbanded by the Occupation. Matsumoto was proud that the Occupation played only an indirect role in the framing of the Labour Standards Law (ibid.:106–7), but other sources indicate the significance of the Occupation's Golda Stander, a labour specialist from the United States (Sakurai 1987:85; Nishi 1985:142).

Matsumoto was responsible for co-ordinating work on the law, but much of the framing of the sections dealing with women was done by Tanino Setsu (Ōba 1988:108). Tanino was Japan's first female factory inspector, with a career stretching back to the 1920s. Appointed the first head of the Women and Minors' Section of the Labour Standards Bureau of the Welfare Ministry in 1947, she was Japan's most experienced bureaucrat concerned with women workers. Her support for menstruation leave made it certain that

that benefit would be included in the Labour Standards Bill. The drafting committee worked with dispatch, reporting out a bill on 26 July 1946. The initial wording of the clause dealing with menstruation leave read: 'Women who have unusual (*ichijirushii*) difficulties working on days of menstruation may request leave' (ibid.:109). The wording was ambiguous, engendering heated debate from all sides.

The way laws are made in Japan encouraged this debate. After a law is drafted, usually within the bureaucracy rather than by elected politicians, specially constituted interest groups called deliberative councils (*shingikai*) representing the variety of opinion likely to be expressed about a particular issue debate the draft, fine-tuning it with their comments before and during the Diet's debate on the bill. The deliberative council for the Labour Standards Bill was confused about menstruation leave: Was a physician's consultation necessary to show 'unusual difficulties?' Were certain types of jobs to be designated as 'injurious to menstruation?' A citizens' group (*kōtokukai*) of labour and business leaders was next consulted. This group could not reach a consensus. The labour leaders' views paralleled a 1946 survey in which women workers showed strong support for a menstruation-leave policy to cover *all* women, not just those with 'unusual difficulties'. Businessmen replied that menstruation leave was not needed by all women, and that sick leave could cover those with unusual difficulties. Moreover, the businessmen said, ominously warning women who wanted protection for workers in particular industries, perhaps 'women should be prohibited from workplaces like buses and trains that are injurious to menstruation' (Ōba 1988:111). Statements like this placed equality and gendered protection in sharp contrast.

Another significant citizens' group met in all-day session and reported its conclusions to the government. This was an all-women deliberative group, divided in two sections meeting in separate sessions. The morning session brought together eight veterans of the women's movement, all located in Tokyo and the surrounding prefectures, including Ichikawa Fusae, educator Hani Setsuko, consumer advocate Oku Mumeo, and pioneer physician Yoshioka Yayoi. The afternoon session assembled sixteen working women from a variety of industries, including medicine, transportation, electronics, textile manufacture, retailing and banking. Bus conductors spoke persuasively about needing menstruation leave (ibid.:111).

Regardless of the persuasiveness of the transportation workers' arguments, Japan was a country under foreign military occupation and, therefore, in need of the Americans' support. Bureaucrat Tanino Setsu and labour activist Akamatsu Tsuneko led a group of working women to Golda Stander's office to convince her of the merits of menstruation leave (Sakurai 1987:85). Stander had never heard of such policies, but decided that if Japanese women really desired menstruation leave – and its frequent inclusion in strike demands in 1946 indicated they did – they should have it. The Occupation offered no objection to menstruation leave.

After recasting most of the provisions of the Labour Standards Bill, the Welfare Ministry sent it to the Diet in February 1947. Labour discontent had been building throughout the winter of 1947, and women workers, who suffered unemployment disproportionately, were as anxious as male workers to carry out a nation-wide general strike on 1 February. The government and the Occupation prohibited the strike, but soon thereafter, to quiet potential dissent, sent the Labour Standards Bill to the Diet. The House of Representatives considered the bill in February, and the (now defunct) House of Peers discussed it in March. Both majority and opposition representatives questioned the logic of permitting special menstruation leaves for women while requiring employers to give equal pay for equal work.[3] The Diet members' questions prompted the Welfare Minister to state that because workplace conditions for Japanese women were poor, the only way to guarantee male-female equality in the workplace was to recognize and make allowances for women's differences. This paralleled the argument of union women that protection of women's unique motherhood potential was a prerequisite for gender equality. Despite the pointed questions raised by members of the Diet, the bill's protections were, if anything, strengthened; in addition, it was recognized that women must be appointed to the committee to oversee and enforce the implementation of the Law because 'women workers faced difficult problems that only women could understand' (*Shiryō rōdō undōshi* 1952 in Akamatsu 1977:762). The Labour Standards Law, which has been amended frequently since 1947, passed the Diet on 5 April.

Passage of the law guaranteeing menstruation leave did not imply its immediate implementation, however. The Sōdōmei union gave ambivalent support to the struggle to implement the leave because they feared it would both let companies with bad labour conditions off the hook and jeopardize the principle of equal pay for equal work (Sakurai 1987:95). By contrast, the women's sections of many other labour unions campaigned hard to force companies to grant the leave and to educate women workers about their entitlement to it. But the ability of the women's sections was limited, as they themselves came under attack by the late 1940s. The Occupation, fearing the growing radicalism of the increasingly empowered and autonomous women's sections, permitted no expansion of women workers' rights either to workplace protection or to political strength within the labour movement (ibid.:97–8). At the same time, budgetary problems caused the government to reduce the number of menstruation holidays from three to two days monthly and maternity leave from fifteen weeks to twelve weeks.

How thoroughgoing was the implementation of motherhood protection provisions? According to a Tokyo Municipal Government survey in 1949 (ibid. 101–2), only 27 per cent of labour contracts permitted menstruation leave and 21 per cent permitted prenatal and *postpartum* leave. Just 2 per cent gave time off for nursing. While the rate of compliance was low, most of those who did comply with the law – that is, 96 per cent of the compliers in the case of menstruation leave and 98 per cent in the case of maternity leave – gave full or partial pay during these holidays. In a nation-wide survey in the same year, the Women and Minors' Bureau of the Ministry of Labour found that the average woman worker took menstruation leave 1.4 times per year, and the average length of the leave was 1.7 days (total 2.3 days of menstruation leave per year). By contrast, 41.2 per cent needed child-care leave in 1949 (59.6 per cent needed it in 1948), a far greater socio-economic need not adequately addressed in the body-centred motherhood protections repeatedly reified in law during the preceding half century.

Even the body-centred protections began to be eroded soon after their codification. In 1950 and 1951, major business and employers' associations repeatedly petitioned the government to revise the Labour Standards Law to remove menstruation leave, as Japan was becoming increasingly independent of the Occupation and needed to rebuild its economy. Companies began pressuring women to 'go back to the home' in the belief that protected women were too expensive to retain on the payroll. Some companies decided to force women to leave by making them work on their feet for long hours and firing those unable to stand during their periods (ibid.:113). Support for protection was rapidly waning among employers and certain parts of the government, and women labour leaders were worried. In December 1951 they recruited concerned feminists and women students, 1,000 of whom met in Tokyo to begin a concerted campaign against proposed restrictions of menstruation leave (ibid.:122). Originally established to help women workers keep their jobs, menstruation leave was increasingly a part of the feminist agenda for motherhood protection. Ironically, few women took menstruation leave, and those who did took fewer days than they were entitled to. Many claimed to be embarrassed to request leave (ibid.:115). But after years of struggle to obtain the benefit – fighting sexism, capitalism and conservatism – women labour activists were reluctant to abandon menstruation leave ('a symbol of women's liberation'), even though the availability of menstrual pads removed one reason for its establishment in the first place, and despite the fact that menstruation leave did nothing to combat the real problem of institutionalized discrimination and sexism in Japanese employment practices.

By the mid–1950s, Japanese women shifted the discourse on motherhood protection. Women's sections of unions began to negotiate for child-care breaks and for maternity leave before and after childbirth.[4] They recognized that these demands focused less on women's bodies as producers of babies than on their ability to rear children. The job of childrearing was still gendered – no paternity leave was advocated at that time. Those women whose contracts granted maternity leave usually received compensatory funding, so the problem was less one of money than one of promotion and – except for the six-week period after the childbirth during which mothers were protected from being fired – retention.

Women labour advocates began to make the explicit argument that maternity should be no ground for discrimination in the workplace (Ōba 1988:120). At the same time, many argued that it was premature, in the mid–1950s, to remove protections for mothers and non-mothers. A majority of the members of the Japanese Association of Women Reporters (*Nihon fujin kishakai*) – a group that might get its best stories at night! – replied to a questionnaire in 1954 that women should continue to be protected from night work because blending housework and employment was difficult (ibid.:140). In Diet debate in 1954, veteran egalitarian feminist-turned-member of the Diet Ichikawa Fusae fought against removal of protections. Clearly, feminists and professional women had ambivalent attitudes toward the question of difference and equality. While egalitarian feminists struggled to accommodate protectionism, protectionists began to come to terms with equality, thereby altering the rhetoric of discussion. In 1962, for example, the labour union Sōhyō dropped the phrase *botai hogo* (protection of the mother's body) from its list of demands, replacing it with *bosei hoshō* (motherhood security) (ibid.:118). *Bosei* was more inclusive than *botai*, suggesting more than merely the physical ability to bear a child; and *hoshō* (the term is the one used in the phrase 'social security') does not carry the paternalistic connotations in Japanese that *hogo* does.

That working women's primary identification was with the home and motherhood was not questioned from the mid–1950s until the early 1970s when the post-war ' "women at home" movement was at its peak' (Saso 1990:99). In fact, the number of mothers of small children remaining in the workplace gradually dropped during that period, climbing rapidly only since the mid–1970s. Spurred by the International Women's Year in 1975, the Japanese women's movement grew rapidly and took on the eradication of employment discrimination as a major cause. By 1978 protection had come under attack, and feminists split over whether protections permitted women a level playing field or kept women from being taken seriously. Menstruation leave was finally abandoned by most feminists, and the Labour Standards Law has been amended to permit leave only in extraordinary cases, thereby medicalizing menstruation. But maternity provisions have claimed centre stage in renewed debates over equality and protection, although the terms have shifted from protecting women in the weeks before and after childbirth (Japanese law is already quite generous in that regard) to creating a workplace in which women (and, many feminists add, men) on the promotion track can expect to be home in time to see their children. (Since the passage of the Equal Employment Opportunity Law, evidence has mounted that companies are making particularly stringent demands for out-of-town travel and overtime on women, attempting to persuade women to abandon their quest for promotion-track job opportunities.) In affluent contemporary Japan, 'motherhood protection' has come to mean protecting the right to a full life, including work and the enjoyment of one's family,[5] and although it is still primarily a gendered demand, some feminists have sought to extend it to men.

CONCLUSION

'Motherhood protection' has been an important part of labour and political discourse in the twentieth century in Japan, and continues to have meaning for contemporary women. As we have seen, that meaning must be historicized as it has changed in varying contexts. It has had both economic interpretations – safeguarding the livelihoods of mothers and their children, either by state grants for maternity or by legislation permitting women to return to work after taking health breaks for childbirth or (presumed) related reasons like menstruation – and body-centred interpretations – safeguarding mothers' bodies by limiting their access to work in order to assure a good supply of physically healthy children.

Few feminists and no labour advocates (that I have discerned) degendered the functions of childbirth, infant care, and childrearing during the pre- and early post-war period. Those functions were to be mothers', and mothers should be permitted to carry them out without losing their jobs. In addition, many feminists and labour advocates supported menstruation leave as a necessary part of motherhood protection. Although menstruation leave was but one part of the larger motherhood protection package, I have focused on it in this paper because its international rarity (and eventual elimination in Japan) force a re-examination of all naturalized aspects of motherhood.

Proponents of protections knew that their concern for motherhood, translated into legislation, was hardly unique to Japan. Middle-class Japanese reformers in the early twentieth century voiced arguments that reminded listeners of European discourse. Pre-war Japanese feminists (and some non-feminists masquerading as feminists) consciously referred to American and European rhetoric of motherhood protection in their debates. Although post-war discussions were conducted under conditions of extraordinary material and spiritual impoverishment that altered the framework for discussion, many of the protagonists had been involved in pre-war debates.

The most interesting comments were those of the women (and some men) claiming to be advancing the interests of women. While some feared that emphasizing reproduction would undermine the cause of women's rights and preferred to stress the basic identity of men and women,[6] most focused on reproduction as a basic right of women. Some, like Hiratsuka, saw motherhood as ennobling and a good reason to extend civil rights to women as the producers of healthy babies for the state and the transmitters of nurturant values in art and culture.[7] Others, such as Ichikawa, were made uncomfortable by a focus on motherhood and generally emphasized equal political rights for women, but even Ichikawa worked before the war to establish welfare payments for single mothers and after the war to maintain the protections of the Labour Standards Law in the face of business opposition. Socialist feminists continued to advocate shortened work hours to help mothers rear their children as well as body-centred protections. The relative weight given by particular feminists and other advocates of women workers to different types of maternalist[8] policies and ideologies shifted in varying contexts. And, of course, some feminists eschewed maternalism altogether, whereas bureaucrats, muckrakers and other reformers espoused it while rejecting other types of political rights for women.[9]

The motherhood protection debate is not a relic of the past but continues in contemporary contexts. Most feminists were bitterly opposed to the Equal Employment Opportunity Law (implemented in 1986), both because it was toothless and because it called for equal treatment of men and women by employers; 'equal treatment' essentially meant male work norms would be applied to women whose particular social function as mothers would be devalued (B. Molony 1990). Identical treatment would produce discriminatory results, many argued. As we can see in the motherhood protection debate, Japanese feminism and women's rights advocacy are evolving, and their study offers important insights into these issues in a broader international context.

NOTES

I wish to thank Kathleen Uno for her helpful comments on an early draft of this paper.

1 Despite this reconcentration of women workers in female-dominated jobs, Japan has a low level of job segregation by gender compared to other industrial countries (Saso 1990:55).
2 Many of these protections have been eliminated or modified since the implementation of the Equal Employment Opportunity Law in 1986.
3 To be sure, equal pay, despite its legal requirement, was a moot point in the absence of unions' struggle for it. The 'living wage' gave employers and male workers a way of retaining gendered inequality in

pay without violating the letter of the equal-pay provisions of the Labour Standards Law.

4 Many employers failed to implement labour benefits required by law except when forced to do so by union negotiations or legal decisions.

5 Similar concerns are addressed by many feminists in the United States over the issue of pregnancy leave. Although many argue that pregnancy should be treated as any other temporary disability in order to maximize the similar treatment of men and women, others argue that 'the gender-neutral approach to pregnancy devalues its special biological and social nature' (Vogel 1990:23). Japanese feminists would endorse the view of those American feminists who maintain that 'the phenomenon of childbearing ... marks all women, constituting a strength and source of unity but also creating specific needs' (ibid.:23). Denial of women's right to rear children, Japanese feminists would add, constitutes a denial of women *as they are*.

6 Much has been written on the tensions among feminists in the United States over the issue of 'pure' equality, as represented in the campaign for the Equal Rights Amendment in the 1920s, versus protectionism (see, for example, Cott 1987:Ch. 4; 1990).

7 'Relational feminism' – a term coined by Karen Offen to describe an ideology of women's liberation based on the complementarity of the genders which was successful in overturning many types of male dominance in the late nineteenth and early twentieth centuries (Offen 1988:152–5) – aptly describes Hiratsuka's ideology.

8 'Maternalism' is an effective term used by Seth Koven and Sonya Michel in their insightful comparative article on the origins of welfare states in France, Germany, Great Britain and the United States. Maternalists campaigned for welfare benefits for mothers and children, 'generat[ing] searching critiques of state and society' (Koven and Michel 1990:1077). Koven and Michel

> apply the term to ideologies that exalted women's capacity to mother and extended to society as a whole the values of care, nurturance, and morality. Maternalism ... extolled the private virtues of domesticity while simultaneously legitimating women's public relationships to politics and the state, to community, workplace, and market.
>
> (ibid.:1079)

9 Cott's caveat that 'not ... all activities undertaken by women who claim to have women's interests at heart ... are ... feminist' (Cott 1989:826) would be well to keep in mind here.

REFERENCES

Akamatsu, R. (ed.) (1977) *Nihon fujin mondai shiryō shūsei*, vol. 3, *Rōdō*, Tokyo, Domesu.

Cott, N. F. (1987) *The Grounding of Modern Feminism*, New Haven, CT, Yale University Press.

Cott, N. F. (1989) 'What's in a name? The limits of "social

feminism": or, expanding the vocabulary of women's history', *Journal of American History* 76, 809–29.

Cott, N. F. (1990) 'Equal rights and economic roles: the conflict over the equal rights amendment in the 1920s', in L. K. Kerber and J. S. De Hart (eds) *Women's America: Refocusing the Past*, New York and Oxford, Oxford University Press.

Garon, S. (1987) *The State and Labor in Modern Japan*, Berkeley, CA, University of California Press.

Gordon, A. (1988) *The Evolution of Labor Relations in Japan: Heavy Industry, 1853–1955*, Cambridge, MA, Harvard Council on East Asian Studies.

Herold, R. (1974) 'Seiri kyūka o kangaenaosu', in *Onna Erosu* 3,184–5.

Hiratsuka, Raichō (1918) 'Bosei hogo no shucho wa iraishugi ka?' *Fujin Kōron* May 1918, reprinted in N. Kouchi (ed.) *Shiryō: Bosei hogo ronsō*, Tokyo, Domesu.

Hiratsuka, Raichō (1919) 'Gendai katei fujin no nayami', *Fujin Kōron* January 1919, reprinted in N. Kouchi (ed.) *Shiryō: Bosei hogo ronsō*, Tokyo, Domesu.

Hunter, J. (1989) 'Factory legislation and employer resistance: the abolition of night work in the cotton-spinning industry', in T. Yui and K. Nakagawa, *Japanese Management in Historical Perspective*, Tokyo, University of Tokyo Press.

Ichikawa, F. (1934) 'Fusen to bosei hogo seitei undō', *Fusen* 8.

Ichikawa, F. (1944) *Fujinkai no dōkō*, Tokyo, Bunshōdo.

Kouchi, N. (ed.) (1984) *Shiryō: Bosei hogo ronsō*, Tokyo, Domesu.

Koven, S. and Michel, S. (1990) 'Womanly duties: maternalist politics and the origins of welfare states in France, Germany, Great Britain, and the United States, 1880–1920', *American Historical Review* 95(4),1076–108.

Maruoka, T. (1976) 'Byōdō to hogo to', in N. Suzuki (ed.) *Shiryō: Sengo bosei no kōhō*, Tokyo, Domesu.

Miyake, Y. (1991) 'Doubling expectations: motherhood and women's factory work under state management in Japan in the 1930s and 1940s', in G. L. Bernstein (ed.) *Recreating Japanese Women, 1600–1945*, Berkeley, CA, University of California Press.

Molony, B. (1990) 'The 1986 equal employment opportunity law and the changing discourse on gender', paper presented at the annual meeting of the Association for Asian Studies, Chicago, IL, April 1990.

Molony, B. (1991) 'Activism among women in the Taishō cotton textile industry', in G. L. Bernstein (ed.) *Recreating Japanese Women, 1600–1945*, Berkeley, CA, University of California Press.

Molony, K. (1978) 'Feminist ideology in prewar Japan', in M. White and B. Molony (eds) *Proceedings of the Tokyo Symposium on Women*, Tokyo, International Group for the Study of Women.

Nakatori, Kuni (1979) 'Boseiron no keifu', in N. Suzuki (ed.) *Shiryō: Sengo bosei no kōhō*, Tokyo, Domesu.

Nishi, K. (1985) *Senryōka no Nihon fujin seisaku*, Tokyo, Domesu.

Nolte, S. H. and Hastings, S. A. (1991) 'The Meiji state's policy toward women, 1890–1910', in G. L. Bernstein (ed.) *Recreating Japanese Women, 1600–1945*, Berkeley, CA, University of California Press, 151–74.

Ōba, A. (1979) 'Rōdō kijunhō kenkyūkai no hōkoku', in N. Suzuki (ed.) *Shiryō: Sengo bosei no kōhō*, Tokyo, Domesu.
Ōba, A. (1988) *Danjo kōyō kikai kintōhō zenshi*, Tokyo, Miraisha.
Offen, K. (1988) 'Defining feminism: a comparative historical approach', *Signs* 14(1), 119–57.
Rodd, L. R. (1991) 'Yosano Akiko and the Taishō debate over the "new woman" ', in G. L. Bernstein, (ed.) *Recreating Japanese Women, 1600–1945*, Berkeley, CA, University of California Press.
Sakurai, K. (1987) *Bosei hogo undōshi*, Tokyo, Domesu.
Saso, M. (1990) *Women in the Japanese Workplace*, London, Hilary Shipman.
Shiryō Rōdō Undōshi (1952), reprinted in R. Akamatsu (ed.) *Nihon fujin mondai shiryō shūsei*, vol. 3, Rōdō, Tokyo, Domesu.
Sievers, S. L. (1983) *Flowers in Salt: The Beginnings of Feminist Consciousness in Modern Japan*, Stanford, CA, Stanford University Press.
Suzuki, N. (ed.) (1985) *Shiryō: Sengo bosei no kōhō*, Tokyo, Domesu.
Tocco, M. (1990) 'Before *Ryōsai Kenbo*: women's educational traditions in the early Meiji period, the example of Tōkyō Joshi Shihan Gakkō', paper presented at the Eighth Berkshire Conference on the History of Women, New Brunswick, NJ, June.
Ueno, C. (1987) 'Genesis of the urban housewife', *Japan Quarterly* 34:132–42.
Uno, K. S. (1988) ' "Good wives and wise mothers" in early twentieth century Japan', paper presented at American Historical Association – Pacific Coast Branch Conference, San Francisco, CA, August.
Uno, K. S. (1991) 'Women and changes in the household division of labor', in G. L. Bernstein (ed.) *Recreating Japanese Women, 1600–1945*, Berkeley, CA, University of California Press, 17–41.
Uno, K. S. (1992) 'The death of good wife, wise mother?', in A. Gordon (ed.) *Postwar Japan as History*, Berkeley, CA, University of California Press.
Vogel, L. (1990) 'Debating difference: feminism, pregnancy, and the workplace', *Feminist Studies* 16(1), 9–32.
Yamada, W. (1918) 'Bosei hogo mondai', *Taiyō*, September 1918, reprinted in N. Kouchi (ed.) *Shiryō: Bosei hogo ronsō*, Tokyo, Domesu.
Yamakawa, K. (1918a) 'Bosei hogo to keizaiteki dokuritsu', *Fujin Kōron*, September 1918, reprinted in N. Kouchi (ed.) *Shiryō: Bosei hogo ronsō*, Tokyo, Domesu.
Yamakawa, K. (1918b) 'Yosano Akiko-shi ni kotae', *Fujin Kōron*, December 1918, reprinted in N. Kouchi (ed.) *Shiryō: Bosei hogo ronsō*, Tokyo, Domesu.
Yamanouchi M. (1975) *Yamanouchi Mina Jiden*, Tokyo, Shinjuku Shobō.
Yosano, A. (1916) 'Danjo no honshitsuteki byōdōkan', *Taiyō*, August 1916, reprinted N. Kouchi (ed.) *Shiryō: Bosei hogo ronsō*, Tokyo, Domesu.
Yosano, A. (1918a) 'Joshi no shokugyōteki dokuritsu to gensoku to seyo', *Jogaku sekai*, January 1918, reprinted in N. Kouchi (ed.) *Shiryō: Bosei hogo ronsō*, Tokyo, Domesu.
Yosano, A. (1918b) 'Joshi no tettei shita dokuritsu', *Fujin Kōron*, March 1918, reprinted in N. Kouchi (ed.) *Shiryō: Bosei hogo ronsō*, Tokyo, Domesu.

Yosano, A. (1918c) 'Rōdō to fujin', *Yokohama Bōeki Shinpō*, October 1918, reprinted in N. Kouchi (ed.) *Shiryō: Bosei hogo ronsō*, Tokyo, Domesu.
Yosano, A. (1918d) 'Hiratsuka, Yamakawa, Yamada sanshi ni kotae', *Taiyō*, November 1918, reprinted in N. Kouchi (ed.) *Shiryō: Bosei hogo ronsō*, Tokyo, Domesu.

Chapter 7

Japanese care assistants in hospitals, 1918–88

Eiko Shinotsuka

ANALYTICAL APPROACH

Occupations related to the provision of welfare, such as those of nurse and midwife, have long been regarded as specialist occupations for women workers. However, the need for workers in welfare goes far beyond the tasks performed by this kind of qualified specialist, a need which has led long since to the appearance of women working as domestic workers (home helps) or 'care assistants' (practical nurses, *tsukisoifu*). They are what are called 'workers doing unskilled work', employed through the medium of public or private employment agencies to look after the physical needs of patients at home or in hospitals.

This chapter focuses on the work of those women we call care assistants, who constitute just one of the groups of women workers in welfare-related occupations, the demand for whose labour may be expected gradually to increase as we move towards a more ageing society. Analysis will concentrate on the following questions:

1 How far back can we trace the origins of care assistants in hospitals and other such institutions, and what was their position at that time in relation to specialist workers such as nurses?
2 How did the features of these care assistants change through the Meiji, Taisho and Showa periods? Consideration of this development will include looking at their involvement with the employment agencies, whose function was to bring together the demand for, and supply of, labour.
3 What kind of working conditions (wages, hours, working practices) have these care assistants experienced? And how do these compare with those of other women workers at the same time?

4 Analysis of these three points will suggest how far problems relating to the employment of care assistants have continued into the present. One particular example will be mentioned, namely the employment as care assistants of Brazilian women of Japanese origin, who have returned to Japan to work as temporary migrant (*dekasegi*) workers.

The care assistants (*tsukisoifu*) we are talking about here are just one category of what we call 'domestic workers'. However, these kinds of non-specialized occupations have been little researched and analysed, precisely because of their non-specialist character, though some work has been done on the subject of maids, an issue which has some bearing on this one (Odaka 1989). The first aim of this paper is therefore to use the case of care assistants to paint an accurate picture of the 'domestic workers' so important in women's work. It should be noted that the 'care assistants' who are the subject of this paper are occupied with the bedside care of patients, but are not required to possess qualifications in the field of nursing or patient care.

In the second section of the paper the main features of the labour market for domestic workers will be outlined. The third section will look at how the relationship between care assistants and nurses has evolved over the course of time. The fourth section will analyse the working conditions of domestic workers using selected surveys, while the concluding section will include a look at the Brazilians of Japanese extraction working today as care assistants.

THE LABOUR MARKET FOR DOMESTIC WORKERS

Number of domestic workers

The care assistants dealt with in this chapter today come within the remit of agencies dealing with nurses and domestic staff. In a March 1988 fact-finding survey conducted by the National Association of Private Employment Agencies (Zenkoku Min'ei Shokugyō Shōkai Jigyō Kyōkai 1988),[1] the services carried out by these nurses and domestic workers were divided into four categories. Hospital care assistants accounted for 77.4 per cent of total job vacancies, household tasks 13.2 per cent, patient care in the home 8.0 per cent, and other (child care, and so on) 1.4 per cent.

Hospital care assistants thus currently account for 80 per cent of all nursing and domestic workers, and as much as 90 per cent if we include those who care for patients in their homes.

We cannot be certain of the level to which the actual number of domestic workers has risen. According to a pamphlet issued by the Japan Clinical Nursing and Domestic Management Association (Shadan Hōjin Nihon Rinshō Kango Kasei Kyōkai 1988), there were in the country as a whole 1,200 agencies with some 150,000 domestic workers on their books. It is likely, however, that only about a third at the most of those workers who are registered, that is, around 50,000 will actually be working. In the national census domestic workers are included in the category of household services as domestic servants (*kaji shiyōnin*). In 1985 the number of people engaged in household services was 31,000, less than half the 74,000 figure of ten years earlier. By comparison with the figure of 50,000 estimated from the above survey, this census figure is extremely low. If the number registered with domestic employment agencies is correct, then for every five registered only one is actually working.

Well before the appearance of domestic workers, the same kind of work was carried out by maids. According to Odaka 'maids (domestic servants) were most numerous in the 1930s, accounting in 1930 for around one out of every six women working as employees (around 700,000 workers)'. Moreover at the time only the spinning and weaving industries (860,000 workers) accounted for more female employees than did domestic service. From this it is apparent that the kinds of work discharged by domestic servants provided considerable opportunities for employment in the early years of capitalist development, particularly for unskilled girls from farming villages. Such an increase in the number of maids resulted from 'a basic condition of labour surplus in the labour market as the economy rushed headlong into the era of industrialization' (Odaka 1989: 144).

Odaka's category of 'maids' essentially comprises domestic servants, and must be regarded as including what we now term domestic workers or housekeepers (*kaseifu*). There have, however, in actual fact, been some differences between maids and domestic workers from the outset.

In volume 3 of the *Japan Labour Yearbook* (*Nihon Rōdō Nenkan*), for 1922, we read that during the course of 1918 in the city of Tokyo a succession of groups were formed whose function was to supply maids (*jochū hashutsukai*). The reason for this was a shortage of maids, as girls who would earlier have become maids were increasingly going into the rapidly-expanding commercial and industrial sectors. It was to cope with this problem that the maid associations were established as employment agencies for maids. There were two categories of maid, live-in and live-out, and an agency fee was charged. The prototype of the present day domestic worker dates from this time, 1917–18. The employment agency business can thus be said from the start to have played a major role in the employment of domestic workers, and this includes care assistants. In what way, then, did the employment agency business develop?

Employment agencies in the pre-war years

The functions discharged by contemporary private employment agencies can be traced back to the time of the old Tokugawa bakufu.[2] From about 1670 we hear of operators whose function was to try and regulate demand and supply in the labour market, and who acted as go-betweens for the hire of servants They went under various names, including *kimoiri* (sponsor), *kuchiire-dokoro*, *bangumi*, *hitoyado*, *hitoirekagyō*, and *zegen* (pimp).[3] The origin of the word *kuchiire* lies in the Genwa era (1615–24), when an individual named Zenbei, who had returned from Mikawa to Edo after finishing in the service of the Tokugawa family, was engaging to visit the houses of townspeople to negotiate for the purchase of fuel by the *daimyo* and *hatamoto* (retainer) households, and was therefore sometimes requested by the vassal families to find them maids. In every mansion where he acted as *kuchiire*, Zenbei received a fee. He subsequently made this his profession, and thus the go-between business (*kuchiiregyō*) was born.

Tokugawa regulations relating to the employment of servants dealt with matters such as restrictions on term of service, prohibition of human traffic, liabilities when a servant ran away, and payment of wages. Their purpose was to maintain order in the servant system. Well into the Meiji period employment exchanges retained many of these Tokugawa practices. Even the controlling regulations issued by Tokyo prefectural government in 1872 still used the wording *Yatoire Seishuku Kisoku* (Regulations for Hiring and Registry of Servants), and when jurisdiction afterwards passed to the Metropolitan Police Headquarters (*Keishichō*), agencies were called *yatoire kuchiire eigyō* (hiring go-between businesses). In 1917, however, they were renamed 'employment businesses' (*shokugyō eigyō*). The same trend occurred elsewhere in the country.

The methods of operation adopted by agency operators gradually improved on the practices of the Tokugawa period, and a distinction was drawn between general job offers and vacancies in women's jobs, like geisha and barmaid, where control was needed for reasons of public morality. A system of licensed operation was adopted in all parts of the country and limits imposed on agency fees, bringing these businesses under police control. Table 7.1 shows the number of individuals finding work through Tokyo city agencies over the ten-year period 1909–18.

Table 7.1 Number of Tokyo workers finding employment through agencies (1909–18) (by gender)

(to nearest 1,000)

| | Secured employment in Tokyo | | Secured employment elsewhere | | Total |
	Men	Women	Men	Women	
1909	27,000	45,000	3,000	12,000	87,000
1913	37,000	70,000	4,000	16,000	127,000
1918	48,000	52,000	3,000	–	103,000

Source: Nōshōmushō Shōkōkyoku 1919: 116

Over the first five years the increase is a sizeable one, whereas the second five years shows a decline. This was partly due to the fact that the number of agencies decreased sharply following revision of the controlling regulations in 1917. Under the revised regulations acquisition of a licence became conditional on possession of over 330 yen's worth of property (real estate). (The previous revision of 1903 had stipulated only 200 yen).[4] That women used these agencies to a far greater extent than men demonstrates how much more constrained women were in trying to find work.

Vacancies for workers such as care assistants and nurses can be found in 1913 at the Osaka hiring agencies known as *irikata sengyōsha* (go-between), and we begin to see the present format with workers either living in the agent's house and going daily to work, or else living in. The well-established existence by the start of the Taisho period of applicants seeking jobs as domestic workers and maids is likely to have stemmed from the fact that private employment agencies, typified by 'go-betweens' whose practices dated from the Tokugawa period, were already functioning in the labour market.

Let us now look at a 1918 survey of agencies in Tokyo city, which gives a comparison of public and private agencies, as well as a breakdown by kind of employment. At private agencies the largest group was male and female servants, accounting for 64 per cent out of the total of 103,000 finding employment. At the public agencies the largest group was office boys and waiters, at 90 per cent of the total 66,000, while male and female servants hardly figured at all.[5] This can be taken as evidence that the private agencies served to regulate demand and supply in the case of domestic servants.

However, there are many examples of these employment agencies, with their strong Tokugawa 'go-between' heritage, in their turn tyrannizing workers already in a weak position, and these found themselves in harsh circumstances as a result of the rake-offs demanded by the agencies. Under the Employment Security Law (*Shokugyō Antei Hō*), implemented in 1947 after the end of the Second World War, considerable consideration was given to the existence of this problem, and a firm stance was adopted that there would be a total ban on businesses dealing with the supply of and demand for labour, except in a few specified areas. This stance has been retained up to the present. The first of the small number of occupations in which fee-charging employment agencies were permitted was nursing, in 1949, followed by domestic workers, three years later in 1952.

HISTORICAL DEVELOPMENT OF CARE ASSISTANTS – THEIR RELATIONSHIP WITH NURSES

The appearance of nurses and care assistants

At the start of the Meiji period (1867–1912) many soldiers of the imperial army wounded in the fighting in the Tōhoku district were accommodated in the military hospital located on the site of the former Fujidō villa in Tokyo's Shitaya. It was at the time called the Great Hospital (*Daibyōin*), and later became the hospital affiliated to the medical faculty of Tokyo Imperial University. At the beginning nursing in this hospital was all done by men, but the hospital found it so difficult to deal with the needs of the patients that attempts were made to recruit female nurses to bring comfort to the wounded soldiers. These women can be regarded as Japan's first female nurses. In the most detailed work available on the Tokyo Imperial University Medical Faculty Affiliated Hospital we find mentioned that 'the system of authorized care nurses (*shitei tsukisoi kangonin*), adopted by the hospital, which was founded in 1868, 'was a custom carried over from the time of the Great Hospital established in the old Fujidō villa at the start of the Meiji period' (Riku 1929: 185). From this it is apparent that a system of hospital-authorized care nurses was already operating around the mid-nineteenth century, when hospitals using western medical techniques began to appear in Japan. However, the care nurses at that time worked for a contractor, and it is unclear whether or not they received any nursing training. We will assume here, however, that the care nurse system adopted by the Great Hospital, which later became affiliated to Tokyo Imperial University, may well have marked the beginning of the contemporary hospital care assistant.

When, then, did nursing first appear as an occupation? According to the *Survey of Working Women (Nurses and Midwives)*, published by the Central Employment Agency Bureau (Chūō Shokugyō Shōkai Jimukyoku 1927), the first recruitment of nurses in Japan was undertaken in 1869 by the Medical School and Hospital, the predecessor of Tokyo Imperial University, which was formally constituted in 1877.[6] Nurses did not at that time, however, receive any particular education or training, but carried out a variety of roles within the hospital, including such things as cleaning and garbage disposal.

The rise of modern nursing

The fostering of trained nurses started from around the mid–1880s, with the Tokyo Voluntary Public Hospital Nursing Education Centre (Yūshi Kyōritsu Tōkyō Byōin Kangofu Kyōikusho) at the Jikei Hospital (1884), and the Dōshisha Hospital's Kyoto Nursing School and the Nurses' Training Centre affiliated to the Sakurai Women's School, both dating from 1886. Soon after that, in the spring of 1888, lectures on topics such as first aid were given at the Medical College of Tokyo Imperial University to hospital nurses, care nurses and nursing auxiliaries (*kango kozukai*). This was the start of the golden age of the so-called 'visiting nurse', the system under which trained nurses were sent out to work in hospitals and patients' homes.

It was, of course, only wealthy families who could make use of these women's services. It was in an attempt to prevent the visiting nurse from becoming a monopoly of the privileged classes that Suzuki Masa founded the Charitable Nurses' Association (*Jizen Kangofu Kai*) in 1891. This was the real start of the 'visiting nurse' business in Japan. Suzuki Masa was one of the nurses who had trained at the Sakurai Women's School Nurses Training Centre and then completed further training at the Medical College of Tokyo Imperial University. At the Charitable Nurses' Association around ten nurses worked for pay of only 3 yen per month. By contrast the stipulated payments for visiting nurses were 80, 60 and 30 sen (0.80 yen, 0.60 yen, 0.30 yen) per day for first-class, second-class and third-class nurses respectively (Chūō Shokugyō Shōkai Jimukyoku 1927: 20), though services were sometimes given at a reduced rate or even free to those outside wealthy households. However, the association experienced a succession of management problems, and was eventually forced to change its name to the Tokyo Nurses' Association, and to call a halt to its charitable activities. The existence of nurses' associations became well established from that time.

There were two categories of women for whom patient care was an occupation: those who were employed by a hospital and nursed patients within that hospital, and those who were sent out by nurses' associations (*kangofukai*) either to hospitals or to patients' homes. The demand for nurses' associations gradually increased, but up until the time of the Sino-Japanese War (1894–5) they were still relatively few in number. After the war, however, it became increasingly common for nurses' associations and doctors to take on girls who had just completed primary school, have them carry out a variety of tasks under the name of apprentice nurses, and care for them until they reached adulthood. In 1899 in Tokyo city alone there were fifty-eight nurses' associations, with something over 900 members, and visiting nurses accounted for 80 per cent of the total number of nurses.

At that time there were no legal provisions whatsoever relating to nurses' qualifications. Some of the many nurses' association managers got as many apprentice nurses as possible to join their association, and then sought to charge improper fees by passing them off as first-class nurses (Kangoshi Kenkyūkai 1983). This kind of misuse of the term 'nurse', along with the appearance of under age nurses and exorbitant wage demands, led to a movement calling on the authorities to issue nursing regulations. In 1900 Tokyo prefectural government issued nursing regulations (ordinance no. 71), and the Greater Japan Nurses' Association (Dainihon Kangofu Kyōkai) was set up in an attempt to exclude unlicensed visiting nurses. A further 'clean-up' movement appeared in 1909, when the managers of over thirty nurses' associations came together to form the Tokyo Union (Tōkyō Kumiai), with the aim of supervising nurses' morals and cracking down on those without licences. It is worth noting that in Tokyo the nurses' associations categorized members as either regular nurses (*seikangofu*), junior (quasi-) nurses (*junkangofu*) or apprentice nurses (*minarai kangofu*), whereas in Osaka those who were not licensed were not permitted to join nurses' associations. Osaka, in fact, had separate associations for junior nurses, to which, apart from regular and junior nurses, non-qualified and unlicensed care assistants also belonged, working mainly as care assistants in hospitals (Chūō Shokugyō Shōkai Jimukyoku 1927).

One extremely interesting account which shows the use of the nurses' associations is the account of the branch hospital affiliated to Tokyo Imperial University's medical faculty, edited by Sakai Iwao (Sakai 1943). In this we find the words

> The best thing for those patients who have entered the hospital, whether at government or their own expense, is for them to be cared for directly by the hospital's own nurses, but the hospital is very short of its own nurses, and has none to spare for this purpose, so since the hospital was first set up it has made arrangements with private nurses' associations to provide visiting qualified nurses (*tsukisoi kangofu*) and care assistants (*tsukiso-ifu*) (so-called visiting care assistants).
>
> (Sakai 1943: 67)

From the time of the hospital's founding in 1917, therefore, it had private (non-governmental) nurses' associations supply it with both visiting nurses and care assistants. At that time payment for care was made by the patient directly to the nurses' association. Later on visiting nurses came from private nurses' associations specified by the hospital, and the payment for care was agreed between the hospital and the head of the nurses' association. It is also recorded in Riku's above-mentioned account of the hospital affiliated to Tokyo Imperial University's medical faculty that in order to compensate for the shortage of nurses, 'patients either had to employ visiting nurses directly from other nurses' associations, or alternatively to depend on non-qualified care nurses designated by the main hospital' (Riku 1929: 185). Moreover, these care nurses designated by the hospital originally lived in lodgings attached to the hospital and came into work from there, so incurred no travel expenses which had to be borne by those who needed their services, reducing their charges accordingly. In the Medical School and Hospital these care nurses were known as *shimafuku* (striped clothes), from the kind of dress which they wore. On top of these, over 200 qualified nurses were regularly despatched there by the city's nurses' associations. In 1928 there were 283 full-time practical nurses at the hospital affiliated to Tokyo Imperial University Medical Faculty, 241 visiting practical nurses and 48 designated, non-qualified care nurses (*shimafuku*) (Riku 1929: 187, 188). At this hospital, therefore, the number of nurses directly employed by the hospital was roughly equal to the total number of visiting qualified and care nurses who were working there.

The appearance of visiting home help associations (*hashutsufukai*)

In 1918 a visiting home help association called the Greater Japan Women's Joint Association (Dainihon Fujin Kyōritsu Kai) was established in Tokyo city by Kawaguchi Aiko of the Girls' Practical School (Joshi Jitsumu Gakkō), with the aim of alleviating the shortage of maids. This was Japan's first visiting home help association (*hashutsufukai*), and the number of individuals involved in associations of this kind increased consistently over the next few years. By 1922 associations had been set up in twenty-four or twenty-five locations within Tokyo prefecture, with a total of 2,000 members. Around 690 of these were actually working, but after the great Kanto earthquake of 1923 the number slowly increased, with 700–800 women working as visiting home helps. The third volume of the *Japan Labour Yearbook* (1923) gives the names of four visiting home help associations in Tokyo city, as well as the association rules for one of them, the Women's Co-operative Dispatch Association (Fujin Kyōdō Hashutsukai) (Ōhara Shakai Mondai Kenkyūjo 1922: 249). This provides a useful starting point for looking at the actual activities of the visiting home help associations.

The Women's Co-operative Dispatch Association was founded in October 1918. Every time a home help was provided there was a charge of 20 sen (0.20 yen), and as the function of the home help was essentially to provide emergency assistance, the stipulated period was two weeks. There were both live-in and live-out home helps. Different working hours were set for summer and winter, but were normally fixed at 7a.m. to 7p.m. The stipulated daily visiting charge was 0.70–1.20 yen for general home helps, and 1–1.50 yen for care assistants in case of illness or childbirth.

Since the fees charged by visiting practical nurses were far higher than those for visiting home helps, proportionately more households would seek to employ visiting home helps rather than visiting practical nurses. Supply did not match demand. At that time there were nearly twice as many vacancies for visiting home helps as women seeking employment in this capacity.

According to the *Survey of Working Women* published in 1924 by Tokyo City Social Bureau, the greatest demand was for general home helps (*zatsuyōfu*) (80 per cent of total visiting home helps), followed by care assistants for illness or childbirth (Tōkyō-shi Shakaikyoku 1924). Visiting home helps received a higher salary than traditional maids, and enjoyed more freedom, so the number of women wishing to take such posts also increased. There was one additional problem, in that care assistants for the sick and for childbirth were seen as encroaching on what was nurses' work. No particular restrictions were imposed as a condition for membership of a visiting home help association, except that members were required as far as possible to be single.

We should remember, then, that when these visiting home help associations first started, demand was overwhelmingly for general home helps for things such as housework, while hospital care assistants accounted for no more than 20 per cent.

The golden age of visiting nurses

In 1915 the Nursing Regulations were issued. These brought together the separate nursing regulations hitherto operative in individual prefectures and cities. The period after the First World War saw an upsurge in the number of working women, and nursing spread as an occupation. Large numbers of nurses joined nurses' associations and worked as visiting nurses. Visiting nurses were in demand from the newly rich who had benefited from the war, and visiting nurses were used on a mass scale. By 1926 there were 40,000 practical nurses, over 5,000 junior nurses and 21,000 apprentice nurses (Chūō Shokugyō Shōkai Jimukyoku 1927: 11). As the system became more widespread, the commercialism of the nursing associations became more blatant. The following, which comes from the same *Survey of Working Women* mentioned above, demonstrates how just one of these nurses' associations operated. Association members paid association dues of 2 yen per month. They gave up 20 per cent of their earnings from nursing as agency fees, and were also obliged to pay to the association more than 0.60 yen per day for food while they were in residence (Chūō Shokugyō Shōkai Jimukyoku 1927: 29).

This kind of 'exploitation by an intermediary' carried out by the nurses' associations was fiercely criticized by the socialist Yamakawa Kikue (1890–1980):

Apart from association dues, the associations rake in 20 per cent of nursing fees. Now that employment exchange has become a public function, so that things like *keiangyō* (go-between) dealing in maids and manservants are no longer permitted, if the nurses' associations too were to become public and this exploitation by intermediaries done away with, not only would this benefit patients by reducing nursing fees, but it would not in any way disadvantage the nurses themselves.

(Yamakawa 1936: 138)

The case of pre-war America

Nursing education in Japan was strongly influenced by American and British practices. If we look at hospital care assistants in America, then, what kind of conditions do we find at the outset? Some indication of the situation in pre-war America can be found in a Ministry of Labour study of practical nurses and hospital care assistants overseas, published in 1948 (Rōdōshō Fujin Shōnen-kyoku 1948). This study shows that during the 1940s the Federal Nurses' Association defined practical nurses and care assistants as 'ancillary workers hired to assist in the nursing of the sick', clearly distinguishing them from nurses. In 1940 around 190,000 practical nurses and hospital care assistants were employed, more than half

of them working as care assistants in hospitals and other institutions. However, only 15 out of the 48 states of the union had
adopted a licensing system for practical nurses and care assistants
and, according to a 1944 report, there were only 30,000 licensed
workers in 13 states. What is important here, though, is that 57
per cent of the care assistants working in hospitals and other
institutions were, in fact, men. These men worked mainly in hospitals for the war wounded, wards where all the patients were male,
or where there were male patients with particular diseases. It has
already been mentioned that records show that in Japan as well
the Great Hospital in the former Fujidō villa at the start of the
Meiji period employed men as nurses. After that, however, nursing
work switched to become 'women's work'.

Trends in post-war Japan

The end of the Second World War brought substantial changes
in Japan's political and social systems, and in its legislation. Hospitals were no exception to this. Of importance for this paper is the
implementation in 1947 of the Employment Security Law (*Shokugyō
Antei Hō*), which prohibited fee-charging employment agencies for
the hiring of nurses and domestic workers. The Law relating to
Community Nurses, Midwives and Nurses, promulgated the same
year, ordered the end of the old system, under which visiting home
helps and domestic workers had been hired to look after patients
and the sick both in hospitals and in the home, and 'stipulated
that assistance in the medical treatment of the sick should come
only from specialist nurses' (Kangoshi Kenkyūkai 1983: 213). The
result was that unskilled, visiting home helps and domestic workers
were no longer able to look after patients in hospitals.

At the same time a SCAP (Supreme Commander Allied Powers)
directive ordered that all the nurses' associations be compulsorily
disbanded by 29 February 1948. The stated reasons for this were
their 'feudal predispositions', their 'intermediary exploitation' and
their coercion of labour. At the same time private businesses, with
their strong 'rake-off' elements, were banned from operating in
the labour market, except in a few specified occupations.

The managers of the nurses' associations, face to face with the
need for survival, campaigned vigorously, and eventually succeeded in securing the continued existence of the old nurses' associations under the new name of public employment security office

commission agents (*kōkyō shokugyō anteisho itakuryō*). Under a February 1948 revision of the regulations relating to implementation of the Employment Security Law, 'fee-charging employment exchange services for nurses' were permitted.

Two years later, in 1950, following the Ministry of Health and Welfare's attempts to implement its 'total nursing' system, practical nursing again became a problem. The reason for this was that 'total nursing' meant that hospitals reaching certain nursing standards were treated under the Medical Insurance System as better hospitals, and benefited from a proportionate increase in nursing fees.[7] One of these recognized standards was that 'the patient shall not have access to individual care'. There was, however, no objection to care by families where a doctor permitted it in special cases such as chronic illness or after surgery. The result of this was that all the assistance hitherto given to patients in hospital by visiting nurses, domestic workers and patients' relatives now had to be taken over by the hospitals' own nurses, and hospitals suddenly needed far more nurses than before. This initiated an acute shortage of nurses. Demand for nurses through both private and public employment agencies shot up, while the supply of nurses remained small. This led to a situation where care assistants without any nursing qualifications whatsoever were compelled to work under the guise of being patients' relatives.

This situation led in 1951 to fee-charging employment agencies being permitted for 'domestic workers', who were effectively visiting home helps under another name. As a result the majority of fee-charging nursing agencies which already existed started to serve a dual function, as fee-charging agencies for both nurses and domestic workers. With the rapid growth of the economy which followed, the number of such agencies also increased.

At present there are some 1,200 employment agencies throughout the country, with around 150,000 domestic workers on their books. However as the economy moved into a period of less rapid growth, people became increasingly concerned with the very rapid ageing of Japan's population, and the apparent reluctance to deal with this problem. One point where response to the problem had been particularly slow was that, with the exception of nurses and doctors, there were too few qualified persons engaged in these kinds of welfare-related occupations. This trend led in 1987 to the passing of the Law on Social Welfare Workers and Nursing Welfare Workers (Shakai Fukushishi oyobi Kango Fukushishi Hō).

The purpose of this law was to lay down qualifications for professionals engaged in social welfare and nursing welfare (social workers), and to enhance general social welfare by laying down appropriate standards for their activities.

The appearance of these new social workers put the spotlight on the existence and very survival of the domestic workers who had been engaged mainly as care assistants in hospitals. Social workers came under the jurisdiction of the Ministry of Health and Welfare, domestic workers under the Ministry of Labour, and dispute arose over the spheres of jurisdiction of the two ministries. Nevertheless, it remains true that it is not just nurses and community nurses, but overall there are still far too few qualified individuals active in welfare who have received formal education and training. Now, as the result of having incorporated measures to enable domestic workers (care assistants) engaged in a variety of functions to participate in these new systems, the confrontation between the two ministries seems to have been resolved, at least superficially. It is by no means, however, a simple problem.

WORKING CONDITIONS OF CARE ASSISTANTS

This section will use four surveys selected from the limited materials available to look at how the working conditions of care assistants changed over the course of time. Visiting home helps or domestic workers are used as substitutes.

Survey by Tokyo City Social Affairs Bureau (1924)

The *Survey of Working Women*, published in 1924 by Tokyo City Social Affairs Bureau, looked at conditions among the various kinds of working women whose occupations had appeared with the rise of capitalism.

The survey included a section entitled 'Outline Survey on Visiting Home Helps'. The survey itself was carried out in July 1922, when questionnaires were distributed to twenty-two visiting home help associations in Tokyo city, responses being received from seventeen of them. With the growth of new job opportunities for young girls as industrial workers, a shortage of maids became apparent. We have already seen how in 1918 Kawaguchi Aiko, looking to the examples of America and Europe, established the first visiting home help association in response to this problem.

As far as one can judge, the Tokyo city survey seems to be the first proper survey of visiting home helps.

By the time of the survey in 1922 there were already twenty-four visiting home help associations in Tokyo prefecture, with around 2,000 members. Of these, 690 members, less than half, were actually working. More than half these visiting home help associations were run by individuals, and the majority charged two sets of fees: first, from the visiting home help herself, there was an entry fee of 1 yen and an agency fee of 15 per cent of daily earnings; second, from the employer, there was commission of 0.20–0.30 yen for every two-week time period.

Demand and supply did not match; there were more vacancies for visiting home helps than applicants, the greatest demand being for general domestic workers for tasks such as cooking and washing, which accounted for 80 per cent of the total. Hospital care assistants came next, while there were few requests for workers such as seamstresses and waitresses. Employers preferred resident to non-resident employees, so more than half ended up living in. Particular points of interest in the survey are given below:

1. *Previous employment*: many visiting home helps had previously worked as maids.
2. *Place of origin*: the largest group, 21.9 per cent, were from Tokyo itself, followed by neighbouring prefectures such as Ibaragi, Chiba and Kanagawa. Few came from Tōhoku or the Kansai area.
3. *Marital status*: out of 935 persons 24.2 per cent were married, and 70 per cent single, but the number also included a certain number of divorced and widowed women (while 226 said they were married, 307 had children).
4. *Age*: of a total of 1,242 persons 3.3 per cent were 20 years old or younger, 45.2 per cent in their twenties, 47.2 per cent in their thirties and forties, 4.2 per cent 50 or over. Whereas many maids were 20 or younger, many visiting home helps were middle aged.
5. *Education*: out of 1,242 workers, 1.3 per cent had received no education, 78.7 per cent had been through compulsory education (regular primary school graduates), and 20 per cent had started, and in some cases completed, girls' high school.
6. *Wages*: general home helps received daily wages of 0.80–1.30 yen, hospital care assistants 1.30–1.50 yen, domestic workers

1.50–2 yen, seamstresses 1.10–1.50 yen, and waitresses 3–4 yen. The range between the minimum of 0.80 yen and the maximum of 4 yen was considerable, but the average was around 1 yen. Expenses for food and return tram fares were the responsibility of the employer, whether or not a worker was resident. Assuming that a worker worked twenty-seven days a month, the average net monthly income after deducting 15 per cent for commission, would be 23 yen.

For comparison, let us now look at a survey of factory workers carried out at the same time (Ōhara Shakai Mondai Kenkyūjo 1921: 251).[8] The average monthly income calculated on the basis of the daily wage for a ten-hour working day was 25.2 yen in spinning and weaving factories, 28.5 yen in engineering factories, 22.6 yen in chemical factories and 30.7 yen in government-owned factories. The average for all factories was 26.2 yen. The 23 yen average take-home pay of the visiting home help does not seem unduly low by comparison. However, since visiting home helps were unlikely to be able to work twenty-seven days every month, and because this figure does not take into account payment for board and lodging made to the domestic worker associations, the wages of domestic workers must be regarded as rather lower than those of factory workers.

7. *Hours of work* were from six in the morning to seven at night. Demand relating to help with domestic chores accounted for over half of the total. Employers preferred workers to be resident, and over half lived in.

8. If we look at the *scale of operation* of the visiting home help associations, we find that there were two or three large ones with around 200 members, but on average 30–40 members was most common.

It is worth mentioning in this context that under 1918 regulations relating to recruitment of nurses by the War Ministry, regularly employed nursing supervisors earned a monthly salary of up to 80 yen, and nurses up to 55 yen (Ōhara Shakai Mondai Kenkyūjo 1921: 251). Nurses were therefore getting salaries which were about double those of factory workers.

Survey by Osaka City Social Affairs Bureau (1929)

The *Survey of Visiting Home Helps and Care Assistants* published by Osaka City Social Affairs Department in 1930 (Ōsaka-shi Shakaibu Chōsaka 1930) looked separately at two groups of workers – practical nurses and visiting home helps. The first group surveyed consisted of nurses or junior nurses sent to work as hospital care assistants, the so-called 'visiting nurses', while the second survey, like the Tokyo survey mentioned above, covered domestic workers belonging to visiting home help associations. The first survey was intended to cover only those with formal nursing qualifications. However, the category of junior nurses in fact includes some unqualified workers carrying out general functions similar to those discharged by domestic workers. We therefore need to look at the results of both surveys for information on the domestic care workers with whom we are concerned.

Visiting care assistants

This survey contains the results of a questionnaire relating to current conditions sent in April 1929 to Osaka city's seventy-two nurses' associations and three specialist care assistant associations for the sick. In the responses workers sent out to work in patients' homes or hospitals were categorized into two groups: nurses and junior nurses (including general domestic workers, *zatsujifu*). In the former category were 1,784, and 988 in the latter, giving a total of 2,772. However, by the end of December 1928 there were no fewer than 5,511 persons licensed as nurses by Osaka City Hygiene Section (Eiseika), as well as 640 junior nurses, a total of 6,151. If we compare these figures with the actual numbers in the survey, one thing becomes clear. Over 30 per cent of all licensed nurses were being sent to work in hospitals by nurses' associations, while in the case of junior nurses there were at least 348 workers being sent as junior nurses to perform general hospital care duties, but who were not licensed. This figure of 348 is equivalent to more than half the 640 qualified junior nurses. This demonstrates that with the increasing demand for visiting nurses resulting from a shortage of nurses employed by the hospitals themselves, the nurses' associations were starting to send out even those without qualifications under the pretence that they were junior nurses.

Visiting home helps

This survey was carried out at the end of 1928 among fifteen visiting home help associations, all with over thirty members. At that time Osaka had in all thirty-nine such associations, totalling 1,260 members.

The situation in domestic workers' associations in Osaka seems to have been similar to that in Tokyo. There were no particular restrictions in terms of qualifications for membership. The largest group, around 70 per cent, was those around thirty years of age. The largest group were again regular primary school graduates, and association fees were 10–15 per cent of earnings. One point of difference between Osaka and Tokyo was that members in Osaka were not charged a membership fee.

Wages

Let us now use the Osaka survey to assess the wages of visiting nurses (practical nurses and junior nurses) and visiting home helps (domestic workers) from the fees paid by their employers (see Table 7.2).

The upper half of Table 7.2 lists the charges made by nurses' associations for visiting nurses and junior nurses, according to the type of illness for which care was being sought. As has already been mentioned, the junior nurse category includes as hospital care assistants some unqualified general domestic workers. The daily wage of these women was in each case some 0.20 yen below that of a junior nurse. Thus, for a normal illness an unlicensed care assistant would receive a daily wage of 1 yen, which was rather low compared with the 1.20–2 yen for a sick care assistant from the domestic workers' associations, shown in the lower half of the table. However, in the more serious categories of illness, where there was added risk, this difference between the two sets of charges disappears. It can also be seen from the lower half of the table that charges for sick care assistants provided by domestic workers' associations were often relatively high compared with charges for work such as cleaning and washing.

These charges are not, of course, equivalent to the total take-home pay of the worker. Deductions by the member's boss, that is, the nurses' association or the domestic workers' association, in the form of commission, and payment for board and lodging,

Table 7.2 Charges for dispatch of domestic workers, 1928–9

	Grade	Type of illness	Daily wage	
	Grade 1	Normal illness	A Visiting nurse	¥1.80
			B Junior nurse	¥1.20
Fees charged by visiting nurses (from nursing associations) (April 1929)	Grade 2	Erysipelas, measles, mental disorders, etc.	A Visiting nurse	¥2
			B Junior nurse	¥1.40
	Grade 3	Pneumonia, scarlet fever, typhoid, etc.	A Visiting nurse	¥2.20
			B Junior nurse	¥1.50
	Grade 4	Pulmonary tuberculosis, dysentery, smallpox, etc.	A Visiting nurse	¥2.60
			B Junior nurse	¥1.90
	Grade 5	Cholera, bubonic plague, leprosy, etc.	A Visiting nurse	¥3.70
			B Junior nurse	¥2.70
Fees charged by visiting housekeepers (from housekeeper associations) (end of 1928)		Care of the sick	¥1.20–¥2.00	
		Care of pregnant women, sewing, washing, cooking	¥1.20–¥1.50	
		Preparation of banquets (celebrations and funerals)	¥1.20–¥1.70	
		Household management, child care, day nurse	¥1.20–¥2.00	
		Home tutor	¥1.50–¥2.00	

Source: Drawn from information in Ōsaka-shi Shakaibu Chōsaka 1930

Note: ¥ = yen

substantially reduced the take-home pay figure. These deductions are itemized in Table 7.3.

Table 7.3 Deductions from wages

Nature of contribution	Dispatched nurses	Dispatched domestic help (housekeeper)
Agency fee	Normally 20% (or 15%)	10–15%
Accommodation	Under general agreement ¥1.50 per month regardless of days away working	¥2 per month membership dues regardless of days away working
Meals	Places where board supplied by assoc. (46%)	Daily rate of ¥0.50 where meals taken
	¥0.45 per day (¥0.15 per meal) at 14 agencies	
	¥0.30 per day (¥0.10 per meal) at 6 agencies	
	¥0.40 per day (¥0.10 breakfast, ¥0.15 midday and evening) at 3 agencies	
	¥0.50 per day (¥0.10 breakfast, ¥0.20 midday and evening) at 5 agencies	
Entry fee	Zero	Zero

Source: Drawn from information in Ōsaka-shi Shakaibu Chōsaka 1930
Note: ¥ = yen

Let us now calculate from Tables 7.2 and 7.3 the net income accruing to a domestic worker engaged in hospital care. If one month is twenty working days, a daily wage of 1.20 yen will give an average income of 24 yen. Deduction of the association's commission (15 per cent) and 2 yen for lodging leaves 18.40 yen, but a further deduction of 0.50 yen per day for food on the ten days in the month when the worker is not sent out to work, leaves a final figure of only 13.40 yen. Where accommodation is not provided, only commission will be deducted, leaving 20.40 yen. The net income for a nurse likewise working for twenty days in the month, is around 20 yen where accommodation is provided, and about 30 yen where it is not. The respective figures for junior nurses are 15–16 yen and 25–26 yen.

The real problem is with the accommodation charge. It was standard practice for members to leave their accommodation vacant for the average twenty days per month during which they were working. Moreover, it was inappropriate to impose the constant 2 yen or 1.50 yen for lodging which on average was less than 1 tatami mat (6' by 3') per person. It was this kind of 'intermediary exploitation', which substantially reduced the worker's net income, which contributed to the tight regulation of the private employment agency business after the Pacific War.

The post-war survey by the Women's and Minors' Bureau

In the very different times after the war all private organizations involved with labour supply and demand were totally prohibited. Soon afterwards, however, under the proviso contained in clause 1 of Article 32 of the Employment Security Law, the way was reopened for private agencies for the employment of nurses and domestic workers.

Since the time of defeat, people's energies had been focused on the need for economic recovery, and there materialized a labour shortage which was a harbinger of the era of high speed economic growth. It was during this time that the Women's and Minors' Bureau of the Ministry of Labour published its *Conditions of Residential Household Servants* (Rōdōshō Fujin Shōnenkyoku 1959) and *Conditions of Non-Residential Household Servants* (Rōdōshō Fujin Shōnenkyoku 1960) The estimated number of domestic workers registered with domestic worker agencies at the end of June 1960 was 39,000 for the whole country. I want to look here at those domestic servants who were non-resident. The length of working hours and restrictions imposed on the individual's life by the job can be regarded as making these workers closer to workers in general than their colleagues who resided at their place of work.

The survey covered workers in the eleven big cities and in nine prefectures throughout the country. It consisted of interviews with 721 households who employed non-resident domestic servants, and the 701 domestic servants employed by these families, and looked only at women sent by domestic worker agencies to work as domestic servants in households, not at care assistants in hospitals.

However, hospital care assistants can be regarded as experiencing roughly similar conditions.

After the war 'domestic worker', as an occupation requiring particular skills, came under the remit of fee-charging employment agencies. Maximum levels were set to registration fees and agency commissions. By June 1961 the registration fee to potential employers was 70 yen for each time they sought an employee, while the agency commission was 8 per cent of wages paid. In the Ministry of Labour survey, more than half the domestic workers were paying the maximum 8 per cent commission. The average age of non-resident domestic servants was 42.7 years old, while resident servants were younger, with an average age of 24–26 years. There was no particular reason why workers had chosen to become non-resident domestic workers, but the desire to sustain life came first, followed by assistance to the family finances and an absence of alternative work. However, non-resident domestic workers had longer working hours. Their average working day was 10.2 hours, substantially longer than the average of eight hours for female workers in all industries (workplaces with over thirty employees only), and 8.8 hours in smaller businesses with one to four employees. As for remuneration, the prescribed charges for domestic worker agencies were set, so the basic daily wage was in almost all cases (98 per cent) 365 yen per day. Since at that time the average daily wage for women workers in all industries was around 414 yen (operations with ten or more workers), these domestic workers were receiving 88 per cent of the average female wage.[9] The amount of wages is not that much different, but the problem for non-resident domestic workers seems to be not the wages they receive, but their hours of work.

The most recent survey

Although private employment agencies have already been operating for over forty years, it remains the case that empirical data on the real state of affairs in the employment agencies run by the agency business, and on the registered applicants finding work through these agencies, are virtually non-existent.

The writer of these lines is none other than the National Association of Private Employment Agency Businesses (Zenkoku Min'ei Shokugyō Shōkai Jigyō Kyōkai). The first survey undertaken by the association to provide this 'non-existent' data was the March 1988 *Report of a Survey on Managers and Applicants in Private Employment Agency Businesses (Nurses and Domestic Workers)* (Zenkoku Min'ei Sho-kugyō Shōkai Jigyō Kyōkai 1988). Private employment agencies dealing with nurses and domestic workers, and the job-seekers themselves, were both covered in the survey. Out of 1,148 businesses 708 questionnaires were returned (a response rate of 61.7 per cent), and 3,597 job seekers out of 5,740 returned questionnaires (response rate 62.7 per cent). The survey was carried out in February 1988.

The 3,597 individual respondents can be characterized as follows:

1. Forty per cent were aged 50–59 years of age, and 34.7 per cent 60–69, so these two groups together accounted for over 70 per cent of total respondents. The average age was accordingly higher than previously, at 56 years. The average age of the non-resident domestic servants at the time of the previously mentioned survey by the Women's and Minors' Bureau, was 41.9 years. Over this thirty-year period average female life expectancy had increased by around twelve years, and domestic workers had become correspondingly older.
2. Around half, 50.4 per cent, were living with family or other individuals, 25.3 per cent had no family, 14.8 per cent were away from their families, raising the spectre of the elderly person living alone.
3. All the respondents possessed some kind of insurance against sickness and injury, most (78.8 per cent) holding national health insurance, 15.8 per cent had state health insurance, and 3.8 per cent union health insurance.[10]
4. The average years of work had increased to 7.6. Significantly, at the time of the survey (1988) the average years of continuous service for female workers as a whole was 7.1, less than the 7.6 above. One in four workers (25 per cent of the total) had been working for ten years or longer.
5. No more than 10.2 per cent of the total number of workers held any qualifications. Those who did were nurses (4.7 per cent of the total), kindergarten nurses (1.3 per cent), midwives (1.1 per cent), junior nurses (2.3 per cent) and public health nurses (*hokenfu*) (0.8 per cent). It is clear from this that although we may refer to 'nursing and domestic work' agencies, around

90 per cent of agency members are effectively domestic workers possessing no particular qualifications.

6. The most widely-expressed motive for working was a like of helping and looking after people (25.8 per cent). This was followed by good income (22.7 per cent); that the job could be made to fit in with personal circumstances (15.5 per cent); and the fact that no other suitable work was available (8.3 per cent). Given that the average age of those working was 56.0 years, these responses perhaps reflect unavoidable constraints.

7. What, then, was these workers' income, given that this was the second most widely-expressed motive for engaging in this sort of work? This depends very much on where the worker was currently employed. Of the total of 3,597 individuals, by far the largest group (77.9 per cent) was working as hospital care assistants, while a relatively small proportion, 17.7 per cent, was engaged in domestic chores in households, or home nursing. This balance was a reflection of the difference in basic daily wage paid in the two sectors (the hospital rate was higher). Moreover, in the case of hospital care work most assistants (84.5 per cent) were resident (the remainder commuted or had other arrangements), whereas the reverse obtained for household domestic helps, with 83.2 per cent non-resident. Being resident, however, can be deemed a twenty-four hour working day.

The part of the survey relating to wages requested respondents to give separate answers according to whether they were paid monthly or whether they were paid on the basis of daily rates. The vast majority (90 per cent) of the 3,597 were paid on a daily basis. Table 7.4 which looks only at those paid on a daily rate, shows the pattern of earnings distribution of hospital care assistants and household domestic workers.

The average daily amount for these workers as a whole was 8,263 yen. The daily income (inclusive of bonuses) of all female workers, calculated from the *Monthly Survey of Employment Statistics* (Ministry of Labour, 1988), is 9,450 yen for all industries, 7,804 yen for manufacturing industry and 11,992 yen for the service industries. The daily rate of 8,263 yen in the nursing and domestic work agencies is 13 per cent lower than the average female wage in all industries, 5.4 per cent higher than in manufacturing, and 31 per cent lower than that in the service sector. The fact that many workers are resident undoubtedly has an influence in that the daily rate is higher than in manufacturing.

Table 7.4 Daily wages at nursing/domestic work agencies (survey of February 1988)

	Total (%)	Up to ¥3,000	¥3,000 to ¥4,000	¥4,000 to ¥5,000	¥5,000 to ¥6,000	¥6,000 to ¥7,000	¥7,000 to ¥8,000	¥8,000 to ¥9,000	¥9,000 to ¥10,000	Over ¥10,000	Average (¥)
All workers paid daily (3,224 persons)	100	1.1	1.4	2.1	6.8	13.2	15.4	25.4	23.9	10.5	8,263
of which											
Hospital care assistants (2,542 persons)	100	0.2	0.3	1.2	4.1	8.8	15.8	29.5	28.2	11.9	8,717
Domestic workers (353 persons)	100	4.2	8.5	6.8	21.0	33.4	13.3	6.5	3.1	3.1	6,074

Source: Calculated from Zenkoku Min'ei Shokugyō Shōkai Jigyō Kyōkai 1988: 30

8. The average number of days worked during the year was 212, but one in five workers was working 300 or more days a year. This figure is just over 80 per cent of the average number of working days for women in all industries, which was about 262. It was thus the norm for these workers to work regularly. Employment agencies, with their original pattern of sending out workers to be employed on a temporary basis when it suited them to work, now seemed to be taking on a different form, with workers taking regular and continuous employment over the longer term. Certainly, more than 84 per cent of respondents, when asked how many days they wished to work, were looking for at least twenty days of more or less regular employment each month. Moreover, more than 96.2 per cent of respondents wanted to continue with similar work in the future. The reasons for this were first and foremost 'higher income than other work' (28.2 per cent), followed by 'because I like my present work' (23.4 per cent), and third, 'because I can work when I like' (22.0 per cent). These three reasons accounted together for over 70 per cent of total respondents. These preferences can be regarded as resulting from the restricted range of job choices available to older women and the relatively high daily wage paid to care assistants from the domestic work agencies.

Judging from this survey, the middle-aged and older women now working in hospital care would appear to be satisfied with the current state of their work. However, more than half of them recognized the need for education and training to improve their skills and abilities, and 70 per cent said that if courses were available they would like to participate in them. These were care assistants, who, in the pre-war tradition of unskilled labour, performed work where education and training was not a consideration. From the outset, though, these workers had been in competition with, and ancillary to nurses, who were always skilled. Now the care assistants themselves have at last become aware of the importance of skill formation, and the nature of their work has, indeed, moved into a new era where skills are essential.

CONCLUSION

Let me now summarize the main points made in my chapter. First, care assistants in hospitals and similar medical institutions have their origins in the *shimafuku* (women dressed in striped clothes) of the Great Hospital, later Tokyo Imperial University Medical Faculty, in the early Meiji period. From the very beginning they had no nursing skills and no qualifications, but were closely involved in the work of nursing. The domestic worker agencies of the kind we have today can be seen as starting as analogies or imitations of the nurses' associations, which supplied nurses, the so-called visiting nurses. At a time when nurses were in short supply, visiting home help associations modelled on the nurses' associations started in 1918 to act as domestic work agencies.

Second, the development and evolution of domestic workers took place against a background of the growing influence during the pre-war period of private employment agencies as regulators of the labour market. These agencies, however, failed to break free of the old *kuchiire* or brokerage practices dating from the Tokugawa period, and workers with nothing to sell but their labour were drawn into this fate of 'intermediary exploitation'. It was in an attempt to excise these evils from the operation of the labour market, that all private employment agency businesses were prohibited. However, in response to the argument that private employment agencies were surely essential in occupations requiring specific skills, such as modelling and the arts, agencies were then also permitted for both nurses and domestic workers. These have continued to operate up to the present. The implication is that intervention by private agencies in regulating the market for nurses and domestic workers is the most efficient method of operation. At the beginning, around 1918, more than half of all domestic workers engaged in miscellaneous household tasks, but after the war 80–90 per cent of them came to be working as hospital care assistants. As care assistants have become proportionately more important, so there has been a move towards the pursuit of a higher level of skill in their work.

Third, there was considerable dissatisfaction concerning the working conditions of these domestic workers and care assistants, particularly with the low incomes which workers were left with, a factor which had much to do with the agencies' character of 'intermediary exploitation' persisting from the pre-war years. The biggest problem after the war was not so much wages, but residence at the place of work becoming the norm, and the lengthening of the period of continuous employment. However, the surveys aimed at clarifying the circumstances of these female workers as a group are very dissimilar from each other. It is therefore dangerous to draw specific conclusions from any one of the surveys used in this paper. However, the very fact that, despite these workers now already having a post-war history of over forty years, no reliable survey has appeared, suggests that we are looking at features more characteristic of a premodern business world of former times.

On the basis of this analysis, let me now make some observations on possible future trends in the occupation of care assistants. It is undeniable that a labour shortage has developed as the number of women seeking jobs as domestic workers, a group whose average age is already high, has declined. Eventually in 1988, the Japan Clinical Nursing and Domestic Work Association took a leading role in implementing plans to bring in as temporary migrant (*dekasegi*) workers some 300 Brazilian women of Japanese extraction, to work as hospital care assistants. This trial attempt appeared to meet with some success (Itagaki 1990).

This, however, is a last measure born of desperation, when there seems to be no available alternative. This situation results from the fact that under Japanese legislation relating to immigration control and granting of refugee status, foreign workers are not at present permitted to engage in unskilled work. The Brazilian Japanese immigrants are registered as Japanese citizens, so they can just 'visit' Japan. These women of Japanese ancestry possess Japanese passports, and are not working illegally. Even so, there have been many instances where these Brazilian Japanese women working as hospital care assistants have suffered unprovoked discrimination at their place of work from fellow Japanese on the grounds of their being temporary migrant workers.

I want to draw my discussion to an end by indicating those aspects of women's work in medical care institutions which may well be problematic in the future. First, there must be a serious debate about whether or not the work now discharged by care assistants should continue to be provided through mechanisms such as private agencies. Other jobs by dispatched workers, for example, those working as computer programmers or secretaries, have a brighter outlook, but this is not true of visiting home helps, and we need to investigate the reasons for this. Second, in order to make domestic work an attractive occupation for which workers can become qualified, we need to plan for lectures and a curriculum which can lead to their qualifying as welfare nursing professionals, constituting a new system of welfare workers. Third, if care assistant is going to become an occupation requiring qualifications, it ceases to be unskilled work, for both indigenous and foreign workers. It may well be that for linguistic reasons overseas workers will not be able to take Japanese nursing examinations, but there could be a somewhat easier examination concentrating on practical skills, which would lead to a welfare nursing qualification.

As we look back from the present on the historical development of care assistants, we may think that, just as the figure of the maid has disappeared from Japanese society, domestic workers, too, will doubtless disappear from the wealthy society that Japan has now become. We have not been inconvenienced by the disappearance of maids, as various substitutes have appeared to discharge these domestic tasks. If, however, in this era of an ageing society, hospital care assistants ceased to exist, the resulting problems for patients would be immense. What we need to work for now is finding a proper place in the welfare scene for the women's occupation now categorized as 'care assistant'.

NOTES

1 This was the results of a survey carried out in 1987 of 708 agencies dealing with nurses and domestic workers, and 3,597 job seekers. The response rates were 61.7 per cent and 62.7 per cent respectively.
2 This section relies on Nōshōmushō Shōkōkyoku 1919.
3 These terms were used to describe a variety of places where maids, employees and prostitutes were exchanged. The word *kuchiire*, often translated as 'go-between', does not have a favourable meaning in Japanese.
4 The number of employment agencies in Tokyo city decreased from 916 in 1914 to 774 in 1916 and 484 in 1917 (Nōshōmushō Shōkōkyoku 1919).
5 Public agencies thus had a limited function in relation to maids and other service work. It should be noted that the male occupations of office boy and waiter had a relatively high status at this time.
6 The Medical School and Hospital (Tōkyō Teidai Igakkō ken Byōin) incorporated the old Daibyōin, and was part of a move towards the consolidation of higher education institutions in Tokyo.

7 This, of course, put pressure on hospitals to increase the number of nurses engaged in all tasks.

8 The survey of factory girls was carried out in 1921. Questionnaires were distributed to 500 factories in the Tokyo area which employed female workers, and to 2,500 workers. The response was a good one, questionnaires being returned by 317 factories and 1,964 workers.

9 According to the Labour Ministry's *Chingin Sensasu* of 1960, the monthly salary for women working in operations of ten or more people and paid a regular wage was 9,900 yen. If we take the number of days worked per month as 23.9 (Monthly Survey of Employment Statistics, for operations with thirty or more workers), that gives us a daily wage of 414 yen.

10 National health insurance was available to the self-employed, while the state insurance was a state-subsidized scheme for small firms.

APPENDIX – EVOLUTION OF CARE ASSISTANTS OVER TIME

1868 – Adoption of system of designated care nurses at the military hospital at the old Fujidō villa in Tokyo's Shitaya (later hospital attached to Tokyo Imperial University Medical Faculty). Probable beginning of hospital care assistants

1869 – Japan's first recruitment of nurses for the Medical School and Hospital (later Tokyo Imperial University)

1884 – Opening of Tokyo Co-operative Volunteer Hospital Nursing Training Centre

1886 – Opening of Kyoto Nursing School at Dōshisha Hospital. Opening of Nurses' Training Centre attached to Sakurai Women's School

1888 – Lectures start on items such as first aid for hospital nurses, practical nurses and nursing auxiliaries at Tokyo Imperial University Medical College. First visits made by modern nurses who have received training

1891 – Suzuki Masa establishes Charitable Nursing Association

1900 – Promulgation of 'Tokyo Edict no. 71 – Nursing Regulations'

1903 – Formation of Greater Japan Nursing Association, in attempt to regulate unlicensed dispatched nurses

1909 – Over thirty nursing association managers form the Tokyo Union

1915 – Issue of Nursing Regulations (Home Office Edict 9)

1918 – Kawaguchi Aiko founds a dispatched nurse association called Greater Japan Women's Co-operative Association

1930 – Dispatch of apprentice nurses prohibited under Tokyo Regulations for Control of Nursing Associations

1936 – Revision of the same regulations permits dispatch of apprentice nurses under specified conditions

1947 – Promulgation of Law Relating to Public Health Nurses, Midwives and Nurses
       Enactment of Employment Security Law. Fee-charging employment agency businesses prohibited from dealing in nurses

1948 – Revision of regulations relating to enactment of Employment

Security Law, allowing fee-charging employment agencies in the field of 'nursing'. GHQ orders dissolution of all nursing associations by 29 February

1950 – Ministry of Health and Welfare initiates 'total nursing' system
1951 – Fee-charging employment agency businesses permitted to act in the field of domestic workers. As a result most 'nursing agencies' become 'agencies for nurses and domestic workers'
1987 – Passing of Law relating to Workers in Social Welfare and Nursing Welfare (Ministry of Health and Welfare)

REFERENCES

Chūō Shokugyō Shōkai Jimukyoku (1927) *Shokugyō Fujin Chōsa (Kangofu – Sanba)*, Tokyo, Chūō Shokugyō Shōkai Jimukyoku.

Itagaki, Takayuki (1990) 'Burajiru kara yatte kita Tsukisoi Kaseifu-san no Ukeire o shite', in *Min'ei Shokugyō Shōkai-Hito*, Tokyo, National Association of Private Employment Agency Businesses, April.

Kangoshi Kenkyūkai (1983) *Hashutsu Kangofu no Rekishi*, Tokyo, Keiso Shobō.

Nōshōmushō Shōkōkyoku (1919) *Naigai Shokugyō Shōkaigyō ni Kansuru Chōsa*, Tokyo, Nōshōmushō.

Odaka, Kōnosuke (1989) ' "Nijū Kōzō" – Jochū no Jidai', in T. Nakamura and K. Odaka (eds) *Nijū Kōzō*, vol. 6 of *Nihon Keizai Shi*, Tokyo, Iwanami Shoten.

Ōhara Shakai Mondai Kenkyūjo (ed.) (1921, 1922, 1923) *Nihon Rōdō Nenkan*, vols 2, 3, 4, Tokyo, Hōsei University Publications Office.

Ōsaka-shi Shakaibu Chōsaka (1930) *Hashutsufu oyobi Tsukisoifu ni Kansuru Chōsa*, Osaka, Ōsaka-shi Shakai-bu.

Riku Sōzaburō (ed) (1929) *Tōkyō Teikoku Daigaku Igakubu Fuzoku Iin Sōran*, Tokyo, Dōin.

Rōdōshō Fujin Shōnenkyoku (1948) *Tsukisoi Kangofu to Byōin Tsukisoifu, Kaigai Fujin Rōdō Shiryō Daisangō*, Tokyo, Rōdōshō.

Rōdōshō Fujin Shōnenkyoku (1959) *Sumikomi Kaji Shiyōnin no Jitsujō*, Tokyo, Rōdōshō.

Rōdōshō Fujin Shōnenkyoku (1960) *Tsūkin Kaji Shiyōnin*, Tokyo, Rōdōshō.

Sakai, Iwao (ed.) (1943) *Tōkyō Teikoku Daigaku Igakubu Fuzoku Iin Bun'in Sōran*, Tokyo, Sakai Iwao.

Shadan Hōjin Nihon Rinshō Kango Kasei Kyōkai (1988) *Tsukisoi Kango to Kōreika Shakai no Kaigo o Ninau*, Tokyo, 12-page pamphlet.

Tōkyō-shi Shakaikyoku (1924) *Shokugyō Fujin ni Kansuru Chōsa*, Tokyo, Tōkyō-shi Shakaikyoku.

Yamakawa, Kikue (1936) 'Josei Geppyō, Kangofu no Mondai', *Fujin Kōron* 3, 138.

Zenkoku Min'ei Shokugyō Shōkai Jigyō Kyōkai (1988) *Min'ei Shokugyō Shōkai Jigyō ni okeru Jigyōsha oyobi Kyūshokusha ni Kansuru Jittai Chōsa Hōkoku – Nurses and Domestic Workers*, Tokyo, Zenkoku Min'ei Shokugyō Shōkai Jigyō Kyōkai, March.

Chapter 8

Women as bosses: perceptions of the *ama* and their work

D. P. Martinez

This article aims to tackle what seems to me to be an interesting paradox: how it is that the *ama* (Japanese diving women) have come to be perceived as independent women and remnants of an ancient matriarchy? Their work as divers is often seen to be low status labour by both themselves and outsiders, while their labour in the domestic sphere is similar to that of Japanese agricultural women who have been described as strong and independent (Embree 1936; Smith and Wiswell 1982; Bernstein 1983), but by no means as the 'bosses' in their households (Smith 1987). The case of the *ama*, I believe, raises all sorts of interesting questions of interpretation both for the Japanese situation and in a wider, more theoretical framework. The central issue is: is it possible for women to behave independently (whatever that means), to have some economic power, and still be considered to be of low status and subordinate to men?

What I want here is not to argue for some symbolic or structural analysis of the *ama*'s position in society, but to examine how folklorists, physiologists, geographers, ethnographers and others have interpreted the *ama*'s life and position in a manner totally at odds with the reality of the life the *ama* themselves say they lead. For all of the former academic specialists, the *ama* are the 'bosses' in their households and it is said that they have higher status than other Japanese women (Maraini 1962; Linhardt 1988), while the *ama* see themselves as being very like all other Japanese women. They feel that their position in the household is dependent on a myriad of factors which includes their relationships with their mothers-in-law, their ability to be good wives and mothers *as well as* skilful divers. In short, a young diver is still the *uchi no yome-san* (the household's bride), who aspires to the authority and power of her mother-in-law, yet who will always keep in mind that she must obey the men of the household: a situation not uncommon in any multigenerational household in Japan.

Perhaps this would not be such a confusing issue if the ethnographic work on Japan had taken into account more mainstream anthropological theory on the position of women in society. However, as Ben-Ari (1990) and Moeran (1990) have recently pointed out, rarely do Japanologists take on board wider theoretical debates. In this case I believe that *ama* communities have been mythologized into that elusive beast, the matriarchal society. This might not have occurred if *ama* marriage and work patterns had been analysed in the light of theories on women, production and exchange (see Meillassoux 1975) or, more recently, in the light of ways in which feminist anthropologists have looked at class, status, domestic spheres and women's productive work (see Beneria 1979; Harris *et al.* 1981; Weiner 1980). What I propose to do below is to argue for a reassessment of the *ama* and who they really are. To do this I propose to look at the material written by others in the light of my own field-work experience. I will also rely on the seminal work of Segawa Kiyoko (1956), who pointed out that the *ama* were not really so free and independent, but whose work is always being cited as proof of precisely the opposite.

PRODUCTION, STATUS, CLASS AND MARRIAGE: INTERPRETING THE *AMA*

The *ama* are women who dive for various shellfish – of which the most important is abalone (*awabi*) – as well as for sea snail, sea slug and various seaweeds. They do not, nor did they ever, dive for pearls. The work consists of either wading out from the shore and diving to a depth of about five metres (in the case of young, inexperienced or less skilled divers); or of diving from boats to ten or more metres (generally done by the older, most experienced women).[1] A diver can hold her breath for up to three minutes (although averages generally vary from thirty seconds to one minute) while she cuts seaweed, collects the shellfish, or pries free the abalone.

Divers now wear masks, wetsuits and weight belts to aid in their descent; boat divers also carry a heavy weight which the boatman (often the woman's husband) hauls into the boat once the diver has reached the sea bottom. The man also pulls the diver up at the end of each dive and keeps track of the boat's location, diving times, and any potential problems for the woman. The work for both is exhausting and the men claim that women cannot do the boat work because hauling the *ama* up takes the upper body strength of a man. Men, however, can wade out from the shore and dive; in the warmer southern parts of Japan, men have always dived. Recently, in the few remaining diving villages of the main island (Honshū), fishermen have taken to diving for abalone only, to add to the income of their households.

The stereotypic representation of the *ama* by outsiders is: 'in that village women are the bosses' (Iwata 1931:81; 1961:1). As I found during my field-work, there are various ways in which people explain their perceptions. The first which I heard was somewhat naively Marxist in its assumption that consumption was a marker of status, that is, since diving for abalone was so lucrative, the divers made lots of money which was considered *theirs*; they did not have to share it with the household. This money they would then spend on luxury items such as expensive dresses and jewellery. 'See all these expensive shops?', one informant told me. 'Only the *ama* in this village can afford to shop here'. This was in Tateyama in Chiba prefecture, where the husbands of divers had long since given up fishing and worked in various other jobs. The few divers whom I interviewed in the area gave the lie to this depiction of *ama* as rich shoppers. Abalone had been over-harvested in the past and now there were restrictions on the size of the shellfish which could be harvested and on the amount of time spent diving. Although abalone was still an expensive seafood on the market, divers brought in less abalone than they had in the past and so made less money. Moreover, with their husbands working as agriculturalists, construction workers, in tourist inns, and, in a very few cases, in white-collar jobs, the money divers made was needed in the household. Many divers both dived and worked part-time at other jobs in order to make ends meet. The only women who had time to spend all day in the diving hut before and after diving were the *ama* in their sixties, who spent hours chatting nostalgically about life, the past and daughters-in-law who didn't work nearly hard enough.[2] The expensive shops, they claimed, were there for the tourists, for that was how the villages along the coast continued to thrive: on money earned from domestic tourism.[3]

Another standard description, used as an argument for the *ama*'s higher status at home, was that the men had to do little work, they could live off the earnings of their wives and were often relegated to female domestic work. I do not think it is necessary to go into much detail here in order to make clear that *if* men really did nothing but live off female labour, we would have a classic case of exploitation, not necessarily one of low male status. As far as I could determine, the men in diving villages, like the women, did numerous jobs: fishing and farming were only two of the traditional male domains. As for being delegated to female domestic work, the only proof offered of this was a photograph of a man, baby strapped to his back, seeing his wife off to dive. The fact that in many rural areas (Hendry 1981) the oldest and least useful member of the household, often the grandfather, was left to care for the baby is ignored. Suddenly it is only in diving villages that this phenomenon is seen.

A corollary of the above argument appears in the work of Japanese folklorists and is summed up by Maraini (1962) in his book on Hegura divers, with the statement that since in the ancient past Japan was a matriarchy, the *ama* must be remnants of that time when women had higher status. I will not argue here about the problems of this rather nineteenth-century assumption about social evolution,[4] but this assumption conflicts with solid evidence that at least some divers migrated to Japan from Cheju Island in Korea.[5] Moreover, Segawa (1956), who did extensive research on *ama*, noted that this essentially male perception of the divers was incorrect; like so many other women in Japan, a diver was subject to the authority of her mother-in-law. Her hard-earned money was turned over to the household coffers and the mother-in-law was quite capable of indulging *her* son's desires when it came to spending the money. This description of household relations does not conflict with various descriptions of relationships in rural and urban households throughout Japan.

We have come to the final and most frequent manner in which it is 'proved' that divers have higher status than the men in their households: this is the claim that the proportion of adopted sons-in-law (*yōshi*) is higher in diving villages than elsewhere in Japan. It is here that we come to a knotty issue which involves production, reproduction and female status, the central issue which I believe has not been resolved by the material on divers.[6]

There are two points which are important to make in relation to the tension between production and ideal reproductive strategies (that is, marriage) among the *ama*. The first, more complex, point is that all of the assumptions about the divers which have been outlined above are the sort of mirror-image stereotypes which are often made about marginal people.[7] In the case of the *ama*, academic assumptions range from postulating that certain modes of production, such as diving and fishing, are more primitive than others and therefore the social structure of the people who live in this way must also be 'primitive', to asserting that the *ama* lived in isolation from the rest of the Japanese society, and so just did things differently. As I will show below this is just not true. Granted that the mode of production of divers was very much at variance with the main agricultural work of all of Japan, but, as Kalland (1990) has argued, no one is sure how to classify the work of fishermen. Is it really just a form of hunting and gathering? And if we do classify diving and fishing in this manner, I would agree with Meillassoux (1981:9), who points out that it is poor anthropology and worse theory to take for granted the fact that certain modes of production must give rise to very specific forms of social organization.

The second point is briefer: to argue that *ama* communities adopted more sons-in-law than other sorts of communities is to ignore the very important point that before the Meiji Restoration marriage strategies throughout Japan were just that: strategies. As Bachnik (1983) has so persuasively shown, the *ie* (family) was seen as an economic and corporate unit whose various positions had to be filled and were filled by a variety of means. The patrilineal, eldest son inheriting, ideal of post-Meiji Japan is but an ideal. Even in modern Tokyo where the *ie* is supposedly on the decline, Hamabata (1990) is able to describe how elite internationally-minded Japanese business families still rely on a variety of marriage strategies to fill the main positions in their *ie*. Temporary matrilocal residence, husband service, or the formal adoption of a daughter and/or son are not unique to diving communities. Moreover, just as in the rest of Japan, these practices also have declined in the last eighty or so years in *ama* villages.[8] At this point it is best to turn to some empirical data to make the point more clearly.

KUZAKI *AMA*

Once a village near Toba City in Mie prefecture, the 'village' of Kuzaki is now a ward of that city. Field-work was conducted there from 1984–6 and the first thing I was taught about the village was that it has a long history, portions of which are well documented. The villagers claim that Kuzaki is 2,000 years old and prove this by saying that they have been supplying Ise Shrine with dried abalone (*noshi awabi*) for all that time. Documents record the relationship between the village and the shrine as far back as A.D. 1111 (Aichi Daigaku 1965) and this date can be taken as a start for Kuzaki history.

I begin with this short historical overview because it is important to demonstrate that, despite their work patterns, the people of Kuzaki always had some contact with the rest of Japan. In this case, it was during the Tokugawa era that Kuzaki came most to the notice of the feudal lord (*daimyō*); the divers and fishermen were always protesting about the fact that the *daimyō* controlled the prices of the abalone which was sold as far abroad as China. Kuzaki's relationship with the *daimyō* was unusual only in that, unlike other diving villages, the villagers did not pay tax to the ruler (see Kalland 1984). The relationship with Ise allowed for this freedom.[9] As well as controlling the money which fishermen and divers could earn from the sale of their goods, each *daimyō* imposed his own Buddhist sect on the village. In the eighteenth century a Sōtō-Zen priest came to Kuzaki and his temple has been there ever since.[10] The point here is simply that Kuzaki was seen as very much part of Japan; it was a place to be governed and monitored (there was suspicion that the government-imposed priests might be spies). The men of Kuzaki fulfilled some of the village obligations to the *daimyō* by serving in the Coast Guard of that area, and so had wide contacts outside of their village.

More interesting to note is the fact that Kuzaki has long been a *han-nō han-gyo* (literally half farming, half fishing) village. As well as living by fishing and diving, the villagers harvest their own vegetables and rice. This conflicts with any theory one might try to construct about the different social structures necessitated by different modes of production such as rice irrigation and fishing.[11] The people of Kuzaki have long had to juggle the inheritance of land with the passing down of knowledge about good fishing and diving areas.

Village marriage patterns are also interesting. The preferred marriage has always been with villagers from the nearby villages of Anori and Ijika. From interviews with Kuzaki grandmothers, a clear pattern emerged: if a daughter was a good diver her family might try to hold on to her until a good diver could be found to marry the household's son. If there was no son, or if the sons of the household seemed destined to be poor fishermen, there would be an attempt to find a *yōshi* for the diving daughter. However, the marriages among the women who were between 60 and 70 in 1986 had been mostly patrilocal, exogamous and, as a result of their parents waiting to marry them off, with younger men. Many of the husbands of the women in this group were two to three years younger than their wives. The divers who had married Kuzaki men would always point out their natal households to me; Anori and Ijika brides were often pleased that their sisters had also married into Kuzaki. Whenever a sister still living in one of these two villages was ill, or some kin died, Kuzaki grandmothers would pack a small travel bag and 'go home'. In this age group there seemed to be only one *yōshi* marriage;[12] the other three *yōshi* marriages in the village of 116 households occurred in the age group of 30-year-olds, whose *ie* ran inns and could, in the villagers' words, afford to attract a young man. Thus, while not denying the strength of matrilineal ties, it was clear that Kuzaki women lived within a traditionally patrilineal structure.

What may have confused previous researchers is the fact that passing on information about diving techniques and the secret best places to dive is very much the business of mother and daughter for information about techniques, and mother and daughter-in-law for knowledge about locations. That is, teaching one's daughter to dive is often done within the realm of a woman's *nakama* (group), a sphere represented by the diving hut (*koya*), which no man may enter without permission. The passing on of knowledge about the best places to dive is a matter left until quite late; in the past it often had to be taught to one's daughter-in-law *after* she and her husband returned to live in the village. Traditionally young couples and their children would live on boats and spend a large part of the year travelling up and down the coast fishing and diving.[13] If the Kuzaki *ama* was ever independent it was from the household and mother-in-law until about the age of 40, when she and her husband would return to the village to take over local diving, fishing and the household agricultural work.

The modern diver is a young *yome* (daughter-in-law) who avoids diving until after she has had two or three children and begins to feel the need of extra household money as well as the social pressure of the *fujinkai* (wives' club) which is dominated by divers and their needs. What is interesting about Kuzaki is that, while fishing is no longer a way of life for the men (only twenty-five households fished full-time), there were, even in 1991, still one hundred women diving in the village. With modern restrictions on the length of time spent diving and the amount which can be harvested, and with the end of migrant diving, the modern Kuzaki *ama* also combines diving with part-time work in the fields, in the tourist inns and in Toba City shops. The money from all this labour, of course, goes to the *ie* to support the building of large new houses and the children's education, among other things. The last description one would give of these women is that they are the bosses in their households. They are strong, independent and resourceful, but they are also the first up in the mornings, the last to eat, the last to bathe and the last to bed. In short, in terms of status, they are still subordinate to the men in the household. How, then, have they been so misrepresented as to be seen as the opposite of the agricultural and urban ideal housewife and mother?

CONCLUSION

Gluck (1985) and Harootunian (1988) have examined the historical sources of modern Japanese discourse and ideology. Despite the great changes during the Meiji Restoration and after the Second World War, the roots of what Gluck calls 'modern myths'[14] still exist in the past. It is here that I think one can search for the origin of the *'ama* as bosses' theory. Both during the Tokugawa era and in the early years of this century (Taishō and Shōwa), there was a type of discourse which sought the sources of the real Japan: a mythical place where Shinto was a coherent, organized religion and the customs of ordinary people were the true customs of the country. For Harootunian, Ōkuni Takamasa was one of the leading proponents of a model which based the origins of the country on agricultural work and kin linkages; he argued for the closeness of the folk custom to the primal acts of the deities. In this century, it is clear that Yanagita Kunio was one of the most important figures in a similar movement and it was Yanagita who insisted, in a work entitled *Shima* (Yamagita and Hika 1931), that fishing and diving traditions had been too long ignored in favour of Japan's agricultural traditions. For Yanagita, it was among these folk that researchers would learn what Japan had been like before its various foreign invasions.

In the work on the *ama*, which often ignores the women's possible Korean origins, strands of both these approaches can be seen. The divers are remnants of the original Japanese and, like the original Queen country, the women must be (must have been) important. The divers of Kuzaki are quite capable of arguing that the term *ama* indicates their closeness to the deities. In their folk etymology, *ama* comes from Amaterasu, the village tutelary deity and the mythical ancestress of all Japan. The people of Kuzaki clearly took on board the Meiji notion that all Japanese were kin, with the Imperial Family at the head of a complex hierarchy. Thus their village customs are true Japanese customs. This theory has served them well in the era of domestic tourism which searches for the lost Japan (see Moeran 1983; Martinez 1990). Any worries about Korean origins are answered with the comment that, although there are Koreans in the area, they all live in the village next door. Yet, in their insistence on being as Japanese as anyone else in Japan, the villagers emphasize the very 'traditional' structure of their households as proof that they are exactly like all Japanese. When I asked women if they were different from other Japanese women I was told 'of course not, don't we have to care for our children and obey our men as do other Japanese women?'

In order to understand how outsiders have mistakenly taken the *ama* for women of high status, one must turn to current anthropological theories of production and reproduction, as well as to class theory in the Marxist sense. As Beneria (1979) has pointed out, women forced to work by their position in the social hierarchy are often seen to be more independent than their middle-class counterparts because they break the rules of accepted behaviour for women. In Muslim societies this means that women do not keep purdah, but are out in the fields, half-naked and working. This perceived 'boldness' leads outsiders to assume that the women must have great power within their households. So too with the *ama*. I was frequently told how loud, brash and rough these women were and that such bold behaviour must come from some sort of freedom which other (more upper-class) women did not have. There was a tacit implication that such women could not be controlled by their men and that the poor men must be henpecked by these large, sun-tanned and loud women. The truth is far more complex than this simplistic picture drawn by outsiders, just as the reality of male and female relationships in all of Japan is far too complex to be reduced to an *uchi* (domestic/interior) and *soto* (public/exterior) dichotomy (Kondo 1989).

A woman diver's work year in Kuzaki is still divided into seasons of backbreaking, gruelling labour. The *nori* seaweed diving which once began in February is no longer done, but in March the divers begin to dive for *wakame* seaweed as well as to prepare the fields for cultivation; for women with fishermen husbands, evening fishing is the work of the couple and not just the men. Seaweed diving goes on until May, when the abalone season begins, as does intensive rice cultivation and shrimp fishing. From May until September, the women divers have but an hour or two free to sit in the diving huts before tackling the next task at hand. In September things ease up a bit, but there is still sea slug diving as well as a short spate of sea snail and sea-urchin collecting to be done, various harvests have to be got in from the fields and the octopus season precedes the lobster fishing season. There is no real break in the work until late December. Throughout all this the women still clean house, cook meals, prepare baths, do the laundry and supervise the children. Many women have added part-time work in the tourist inns, so that in the summer and autumn they may spend their evenings serving meals in village inns.

With all this hard labour, the women considered it unnecessary to 'waste time' on village politics or to be involved in the village fishing and farming co-operative (*gyogyō kyōdō kumiai*). Thus, women had little power of any sort outside the household. Inside the household, their power depended on their relationship with their in-laws, and their husbands. Some women were seen to be extremely 'bossy', but they were the exception; a diver's power inside the *ie* had to be exercised as covertly as that of the average housewife (Lebra 1984). While it was clear that it was the women in Kuzaki who kept track of kinship ties and worked to keep the relationships between both the living and the dead functioning, it was the men who represented the household at all family gatherings or important ritual observances. In short, high status was always accorded to the men, no matter what outsider observers thought of the women's 'free and easy' behaviour.

The more academic argument for *ama* high status has its roots, not only in the ideological discourse of writers such as Ōkuni and Yanagita, but in the simple fact that the researchers who have worked on the *ama* have not been able to ignore the importance of women's productive activity for the fishing and diving households. It took the feminist revolution in the west to convince anthropologists that in hunting and gathering societies it was women's gathering which was the most important to the food supply of the group. For Japanese researchers it was clear, without feminism, that in terms of the cash economy, the female divers earned more than the male fishermen. Thus, an interesting thing occurred: because the focus was on the importance of women's production, researchers assumed that this must correlate with better status for women. In contrast to the western material, which ignored women's crucial role in both production and reproduction, Japanese researchers (among others) could not ignore the former, but failed to consider the latter. If they had done so, they would have found that the divers not only worked hard and earned lots of cash, but had to exist within the same network of marriage and kinship relationships as did other Japanese women.

There is one final but very telling point to make about the status of women and diving. In the third century A.D., according to the Chinese chronicles, all Japanese loved diving.[15] The introduction of rice cultivation obviously changed this. Fishing and diving became marginalized, especially after the introduction of Buddhism, with its strictures on the killing of animals. On the main islands of Japan the diving was left to women, for reasons which the available material on *ama* does not make entirely clear, but which – I suspect – included the fact that it was easy to combine diving with child care, especially the breastfeeding of young children. It is interesting to note that abalone diving, the lucrative crop for the *ama*, does include male divers. In Kuzaki, as well as in a few other villages in Mie, however, this has only happened as a last resort; fishermen take to diving only when the fishing is not profitable (Plath, private communication). Divers and their men have taken up the argument that only women dive because they have a thick layer of subcutaneous fat to protect them from the cold, but the truth appears to be that women dive because it is low-status work and men do not want to do it unless they have to. The true history of the *ama* – if such a thing is possible – seems to be that, in the past, all the Japanese dived, but in the present only those of the lowest *class* status do so and, within that class, it is mostly the work of those with the lowest status of all: the women.

NOTES

1 There are various terms for the different classes of divers, which differ from region to region. These include: *nakaisodo, kachiama, kachido* and *oyogioo* for shore divers and *funedo, funado, okazuki, okiama, funekazuki, ooisodo, ooama, oakazuki, funa-ama* and *okedo* (Nukada 1965; Kita 1965; Plath personal communication).

2 One Chiba *ama* Tanaka Noyo, kept from diving by illness, has written two beautifully simple and nostalgic books about a diver's life and the importance of the women's groups (*nakama*) which form the core of various diving huts (*koya*). Although these books have earned her some fame, in 1985 she still lived in an old wooden farm house with no great signs of wealth either from diving or her writing.

3 See Martinez 1990 for a description of the relationship among the household, divers and part-time work in the tourism trade.

4 Various feminist anthropologists have pointed out the flaws in this argument, first put forth by Engels and elaborated in various ways. A good summary of the problems with this can be found in Webster 1975. The issue of Japan as an ancient matriarchy rests on its ancient description as Queen country, as it was called in the Chinese chronicles of the Wei dynasty, A.D. 220–265 (Tsunoda 1951). The question here is whether the mythical shamaness rulers had anything more than religious power (Blacker 1975: 131).

5 Of course, it could be argued that many of the inhabitants of the Japan archipelago migrated through Korea, so the divers are no less Japanese than the Imperial Family, but that is not the point. The point is simply that archaeological evidence demonstrates that *ama* are probably not remnants of some lost original inhabitants (see Birukawa: 1965). Interesting to note is that Korean divers are also seen to have high status by outsiders, but Cho's work on Korean divers (Cho 1979) demonstrates how the men of the community manipulate religion in order to maintain high male status.

6 Kalland (1988) has written an important article examining some of the tensions generated by the conflict between work and marriage patterns among Kyūshū *ama*; tensions which he believes led to the end of diving in that area. However, as far as I am aware, the connection between work, marriage and status has not been fully examined.

7 In the case of the *ama* the stereotypic suppositions also include notions about the greater sexual availability of divers. As I have noted elsewhere (Martinez 1990), the men of diving communities assume that sexually-available women live in the cities, because they know they do not dwell in their villages. It seems clear that Maraini, who points out that the *ama* are rather like 'our' gipsies, is stepping into a similar trap (Maraini 1962:17). As Okely (1983) has pointed out, gipsy ideas of purity, sexual restraint and proper behaviour are much stricter than in the wider society; people just assume that travellers who live on the edges of society are freer – the same principle seems to be at work with suppositions about the *ama*.

8 In Kalland's examination of the material on Kanegaseki, he notes that historically there existed a situation in which 'the prized abalone, the technology involving female divers, marriage and residential patterns including migration, and the interests of the feudal authorities were interwoven into a delicate fabric' (Kalland 1988:2).

9 Kuzaki's relationship to Ise was that of a sacred guild or *kanbe*; in return for a yearly supply of dried abalone which was offered to the deities, and fresh abalone for the Ise priests, the village was free from paying taxes to the *daimyō*.

10 Although the village Sōtō Zen temple is an important part of every household's cycle of caring for the dead, many villagers also continue to practise the Shingon Buddhism which seems to have been strong in the Mie prefectural area, making pilgrimages to Asama Temple where they keep memorial *sotōba* (stupas) to their dead.

11 One of the arguments for the 'unique' structure of the Japanese household is that it has grown out of the needs of rice production (Nakane 1967). The argument for the *ama* being different implies that since they do not need land for rice-growing, they do not need to emphasize the continuance of the patrilineal household. While the villagers of Kuzaki told me that the *dōzoku* system in which the main household set up a branch household for a younger son made no sense in a place where there was so little land to divide, it was clear that rights to fishing areas and the right of caring for the household ancestors were inherited in the same way as in agricultural villages.

12 One household in Kuzaki has claimed to be different from the others in that it always took in *yōshi* (Kurata 1974:86–90). According to one version of the beginning of the village-Ise relationship, the ancestress of this household was the woman who initially promised that she and her descendents would always supply the Shrine with abalone. Thus, in order to preserve the knowledge and skills which the *ama* of this household had, they and only they took in husbands rather than marrying out. I was not told this version while doing field-work. In fact, when I asked about village women preferring *yōshi* marriages, I was told that either only rich families such as those who owned inns could do this; or was met with confusion and the information that village-preferred marriages were always with Anori and Ijika.

13 Some Kuzaki families made it as far away as Korea. One 65-year-old woman in 1986 could still recall summers spent diving there in her childhood.

14 See Martinez 1992 for a discussion of Gluck's use of the word 'myth', which is closer to the traditional sense of upholding ideology through origin stories than to the more modern sense of an untrue story.

15 'The people are fond of fishing; regardless of the depth of the water, they dive to capture fish' from Tsunoda's translation of the Wei dynasty histories (Tsunoda 1951:10).

REFERENCES

Aichi Daigaku (1965) *Ama no mura – Toba shi, Kuzaki chō* (An *Ama* village, Toba City, Kuzaki Ward), special issue of the memories [sic] of the Community Research Institute of Aichi University, Toyohashi City, Aichi University.

Bachnik, Jane (1983) 'Recruitment strategies for household succession: rethinking Japanese household organisation' *Man* 18(1), 160–82.

Ben-Ari, Eyal (1990) 'Wrapping up: some general implications', in Eyal Ben-Ari, Brian Moeran and James Valentine (eds) *Unwrapping Japan*, Manchester, Manchester University Press.

Beneria, L. (1979) 'Reproduction, production and the sexual division of labour', *Cambridge Journal of Economics* 3, 203–5.

Bernstein, Gail Lee (1983) *Haruko's World: a Japanese Farm Woman and her Community*, Stanford, CA, Stanford University Press.

Birukawa, Shōhei (1965) 'Geographic distribution of *ama* in Japan', in Rahn and Yokoyama (eds) 57–70.

Blacker, Carmen (1975) *The Catalpa Bow, a Study of Shamanistic Practices in Japan*, London, Allen & Unwin.

Cho, Haejoang (1979) *An Ethnographic Study of a Female Diver's Village in Korea: Focused on the Sexual Division of Labor*, unpublished PhD dissertation submitted to the University of California.

Embree, John F. (1936) *A Japanese Village, Suye Mura*, London, Kegan Paul, Trench, Trubner & Co.

Gluck, Carol (1985) *Japan's Modern Myths, Ideology in the Late Meiji Period*, Princeton, NJ, Princeton University Press.

Hamabata, Matthews Masayuki (1990) *Crested Kimono: Power and Love in the Japanese Business Family*, Ithaca, NY, and London, Cornell University Press.

Harootunian, H. D. (1988) *Things Seen and Unseen, Discourse and Ideology in Tokugawa Nativisim*, Chicago, University of Chicago Press.

Harris, Olivia *et al.* (1981) 'Engendered structures: some problems in the analysis of reproduction', in J. Kahn and J. Llobera (eds) *The Anthropology of Pre-capitalist Societies*, London, Macmillan.

Hendry, Joy (1981) *Marriage in Changing Japan: Community and Society*, London, Croom Helm.

Iwata, Junichi (1931) '*Mie no ama sagyō no konseki*' ('Mie diving women's past and present') in Yanagita and Hika (eds) 60–122.

Iwata, Junichi (1961) *Shima no Ama: fu Shima no gyofu no mukashigatari* (The *Ama* of Shima, with Reference to the Folktales of Shima Fishermen), Toba City, Shinto Insatsu Kabushiki Kaisha.

Kalland, Arne (1984) 'Sea tenure in Tokugawa Japan: the case of Fukuoka domain', in Kenneth Ruddle and Tomoya Akimichi (eds) *Maritime Institutions in the Western Pacific*, Osaka, Japan, National Museum of Ethnology, Senri Ethnological Studies 17.

Kalland, Arne (1988) 'In search of the abalone, the history of the *ama* in northern Kyūshū, Japan', reprint from *Seinan Chi-iki no Shiteki Tenkai*.

Kalland, Arne (1990) 'Sea tenure and the Japanese experience: resource management in coastal fisheries', in E. Ben-Ari, B. Moeran and J.

Valentine (eds) *Unwrapping Japan*, Manchester, Manchester University Press.

Kita, Hiromasa (1965) 'Review of activities: harvest, seasons and diving patterns,' in Rahn and Yokoyama (eds) 41–55.

Kondo, Dorinne K. (1989) *Crafting Selves: Power, Gender, and Discourses of Identity in a Japanese Workplace*, Chicago and London, University of Chicago Press.

Kurata, Masakuni (1974) '*Noshi awabi no yurai*' ('The origin of *noshi awabi*') *Ise-shima, vol. 13 of Nihon no minwa*, Tokyo, Rengō Insatsu Kabushiki Kaisha.

Lebra, Takie Sugiyama (1984) *Japanese Women: Constraint and Fulfillment*, Honolulu, University of Hawaii Press.

Linhardt, Ruth (1988) 'Modern times for *ama*-divers', in Ian Nish (ed.) *Contemporary European Writing on Japan. Scholarly Views from Eastern and Western Europe*' Woodchurch, Ashford, Kent, England, Paul Norbury Publications.

Maraini, Fosco (1962) *Hekura: the Diving Girls' Island*, trans. from the Italian by Eric Mosbacher, London, Hamish Hamilton.

Martinez, D. P. (1990) 'Tourism and the *ama*: the search for a real Japan', in Eyal Ben-Ari, Brian Moeran and James Valentine (eds) *Unwrapping Japan*, Manchester, Manchester University Press.

Martinez, D. P. (1992) 'NHK comes to Kuzaki: ideology, mythology and documentary filmmaking', in Goodman and Refsing (eds) *Ideology and Practice in Japan*, London, Routledge.

Meillassoux, Claude (1975) *Maidens, Meal and Money: Capitalism and the Domestic Community*, Cambridge, Cambridge University Press.

Moeran, Brian (1983) 'The language of Japanese tourism', *Annals of Tourism Research* 10(1), 92–108.

Moeran, Brian (1990) 'Rapt discourses: anthropology, Japanism and Japan', in Eyal Ben-Ari, Brian Moeran and James Valentine (eds) *Unwrapping Japan*, Manchester, Manchester University Press.

Nakane, Chie (1967) *Kinship and Economic Organization in Rural Japan*, University of London, Athlone Press.

Nukada, Minoru (1965) 'Historical development of the *ama*'s diving activities', in Rahn and Yokoyama (eds): 25–39.

Okely, Judith (1983) *The Traveller-Gypsies*, Cambridge, Cambridge University Press.

Rahn, Herman and Yokoyama, Tetsurō (editors) (1965) *Physiology of Breath-Hold Diving and the Ama of Japan: Papers Presented at a Symposium August 31 to September 1, 1965 Tokyo, Japan*, Washington DC, publication 1341, National Academy of Sciences National Research Council.

Segawa, Kiyoko (1956) *Ama*, Tokyo, Koken Shorin.

Smith, Robert J. (1987) 'Gender inequality in contemporary Japan', *Journal of Japanese Studies* 13(1) 1–25.

Smith, Robert J. and Wiswell, Ella (1982) *The Women of Suye Mura*, Chicago, University of Chicago Press.

Tanaka, Noyo (1983) *Amatachi no shiki* (*Amas*' four seasons), Tokyo, Katō Masaki.

Tsunoda, Ryūsaku (translator) (1951) *Japan in the Chinese Dynastic Histories:*

Later Han Through Ming Dynasties, L. Carrington Goodrich (ed.), South Pasadena, P. D. and Ione Perkins.

Webster, Paula (1975) 'Matriarchy: a vision of power', in Rayna R. Reiter (ed.) *Toward an Anthropology of Women*, New York and London, Monthly Review Press.

Weiner, Annette (1980) 'Reproduction: a replacement for reciprocity', *American Ethnologist* 7 (1), 71–85.

Yanagita, Kunio and Hika, H. (eds) (1931) *Shima, Shōwa go nen zenki* (Islands, the five years preceding Shōwa), Tokyo, Takase Sueyoshi.

Chapter 9

Equal employment opportunities for Japanese women: changing company practice

Alice Lam

INTRODUCTION

In many western industrialized countries women's labour market position has improved markedly in the 1970s and 1980s as a result of labour market pressures and equal opportunity legislation. Many of the labour market pressures are also present in Japan, and in 1985 the Japanese government passed the Equal Employment Opportunity (EEO) Law. In addition, Japan has come under increasing pressure from the international community to improve the position and status of women in all aspects of society. The EEO Law was partly a product of these external pressures. Indeed, labour market pressures and the EEO legislation appear to have brought about many changes in Japanese companies' policies on women in recent years.

The aim of this paper is to examine the extent to which Japanese companies have modified and adapted their employment and personnel management practices towards more egalitarian treatment of women. We shall first look at how labour market changes and commercial pressures have pushed major companies to introduce policies to utilize better the abilities of women before the introduction of the EEO Law. Then we look at the impact of the EEO Law itself on company policies, notably how the law has affected their policies on women and whether the model of equal opportunities pursued by Japanese companies will have a positive impact on women's careers. In practice, one can never isolate the effects of the law from changes that are caused by a combination of other social and economic changes prior to the introduction of the law. Our primary objective is not to 'measure' the effects of the law as such, but to see how much further action companies have taken since the law was introduced. The final part of the paper analyses the major obstacles and constraints which limit equal opportunities for women in the Japanese employment system.

ECONOMIC AND MARKET PRESSURES FOR CHANGE

Traditionally, Japanese companies were rather indifferent to women's career development issues. The well-known lifetime employment, internal company training and *nenkō* (seniority)-based wage and promotion systems applied exclusively to men. Women were excluded from the core career jobs and they were treated as a single group of short-term temporary work-force. The personnel management practices carried out by the majority of Japanese companies present strong barriers to women's participation in the workplace on an equal basis to men (Lam 1992).

However, from the mid-1970s many companies started to talk about 'utilization of women power' (*josei no katsuyō*) or 'revitalization of the female workforce' (*joshi rōdōryoku no kasseika*). Some companies began to introduce new personnel practices and design career development programmes for their women employees. Several changes in the economy and labour markets have pushed Japanese companies to pay more attention to their female work-force.

First, the rapid expansion of the service economy since the mid–1970s has greatly transformed the employment structure and led to increased demand for more female labour. Between 1975 and 1985 the total employed labour force increased by 18 per cent; male employment increased by 12 per cent and female employment increased by 33 per cent. Of the 3.8 million increase in the number of female employees between 1975 and 1985, service industries contributed 40 per cent, and wholesale and retail industries contributed 30 per cent of the increase. These are all traditionally female-intensive sectors, and their rapid expansion has led to growing demand for more female labour. The sectoral shift of the economy has also altered the occupational distribution of the labour force. In particular, there has been an expansion of white-collar jobs and knowledge-intensive occupations into which more women have entered. The proportion of women engaged in clerical, professional and managerial occupations increased from 11.0 per cent in 1955 to 24 per cent in 1970 and 35 per cent in 1980 (Mizuno 1984: 24). The increase has been most remarkable in the tertiary sector.

The rapid growth of the services, finance, banking and retail distribution industries has prompted companies to recruit more highly-educated women and train them as specialists and experts in various fields. There has been not only a demand for more female labour but, more importantly, there has been a demand for better quality female labour. Many companies which had previously closed their doors to female university graduates changed their recruitment policies after the mid–1970s.[1]

A second factor, not unrelated to the first, has been the growing shortage of skilled labour, particularly in the rapidly-expanding high-technology industries, which has caused companies to look for ways of using more women. The shortage of skilled labour has been particularly acute in information technology, especially software engineers. Major electronics firms such as Fujitsu, Nihon Electrical Company (NEC), Toshiba and Matsushita started to recruit female university graduates and train them as software engineers in the early 1980s. Labour market pressures have prompted these companies to look towards women as an untapped human resource.

A third factor motivating Japanese companies to utilize women better has been the growing importance of women in the consumer market. Paradoxically, the extreme sex role segregation in Japanese society, which is often deemed the source of sexual discrimination in the workplace, has led to expanding job opportunities for women. Japanese women are almost in total control of the consumer market because they control the family budget. Increased market competition has made more companies realize that in order to remain competitive, they need to bring in more women and use their ideas in product development, marketing and sales. This phenomenon is not limited to the retail distribution and financial sectors, but is also present in manufacturing companies such as electrical appliance makers, automobile and office automation machinery manufacturers. Many companies in these sectors set up special women project teams to plan and develop products to suit 'women's tastes' and to market the products to women consumers.

Changes on the demand side explain only part of the shift in companies' policies on women. The rapid rise in the educational level of women has been one of the most important changes on the supply side which has brought about changes in companies' policies after the mid–1970s. In 1965 only 6.0 per cent of women entering the job market were graduates (including junior college and four-year university graduates), the figure rose to 27 per cent in 1975 and crept further up to over 40 per cent after the mid-1980s (MOE). The increased entry of the highly-educated women has prompted companies to adopt more positive personnel policies.

WOMEN UTILIZATION PROGRAMMES[2]

Changes in the industrial structure and the shifting characteristics of the economy implied that a growing number of Japanese companies could no longer afford to treat all their women employees as a single group of marginal or temporary work-force. Some companies began to introduce new policies in an attempt to open up promotion opportunities for women and to improve their morale, particularly for those who have stayed with the companies for a reasonable number of years. The average length of service of women workers increased from 4.5 years in 1970 to 6.8 years in 1985, according to the Ministry of Labour. Companies employing a large number of women began to show concern about the low morale of their female work-forces. Special career development programmes were introduced to 'revitalize' the female work-force.

In the following we shall look at some of the most significant 'women utilization programmes' introduced by major Japanese companies after the mid–1970s, before the introduction of the EEO Law. There appear to have been no statistical surveys of the extent of the new practices. My survey of secondary literature and management journals shows that the following three types of policies were most frequently described as companies' 'pioneering attempts' in giving women better opportunities to use their abilities.[3]

Women's project teams

The most common approach adopted by some major companies as a first step to 'revitalize' the female work-force has been to set up women's project teams. They have been most widely adopted by department stores and supermarkets since the mid–1970s where women are organized into small groups to improve productivity and customer services and to make suggestions to management regarding improvement of working environment and welfare for women. Since the early 1980s, similar project teams have been taken up by manufacturers of consumer electronics to promote product development and marketing by utilizing 'women's ideas'. Some well-known examples include electrical appliance manufacturers such as Sony, Matsushita Electric and Hitachi, where women were specially assigned to project teams to plan and develop electrical appliances. These companies believed that products made using men's ideas were failing to penetrate the market (*The Japan Times*, 25 July 1985). Another example is Toshiba, where a 'women's marketing group' was set up in 1984 to promote the sales, development and marketing of household appliances. The company also established a 'Toshiba Lady Headquarters' in 1986 to promote the sales of word processors. According to the company, the major reason for organizing women in project teams was increased market competition in office automation machinery (*Koyō Shinkō Kyōkai* 1986: 92–6; *Nikkei Shinbun*, 1 March 1986).

These are some typical examples of how some companies have been integrating their policies of 'revitalization of women' with their productivity improvement activities and marketing strategies. They are often dramatically taken up by the mass media to portray an image of 'progressive' company policies on women. However, the original purpose had little to do with promoting equal opportunities. Some companies started to organize women's project teams in response to business needs, and in others, they were designed to enhance women's sense of participation through involvement in team work. The project teams were often established on an *ad hoc* and informal basis and they were normally not part of the formal organization structure. Thus, there was no formal link between these project teams and formal career progression in the company. However, in some cases these special project teams have led to a second stage in women's career development programmes with the training of 'female group leaders'.

'Female group leaders'

The creation of the role of 'female group leader' has been most commonly found in the female-intensive industries such as banking, insurance and retail distribution. Surveys carried out by Inagei Noriko (1983: 15), an expert on female leadership training in Japan, found that the group leader system was quite widely practised and had been gaining popularity since the 1970s.

The group leader role has been created in order to provide a training ground for women with supervisory potential. This is partly because some women are staying longer with the companies, which start to feel that there is a need to provide a career for them to avoid demoralization. It also stems from the belief that women are better qualified to train women. In most cases the female group leader system has been introduced in sections or departments with a high concentration of women. Generally the first line supervisor (*kakarichō*) will be a man and a female group leader will be appointed to play the role of 'go-between' between the *kakarichō* and the female members of the work group. The 'female group leader' system is a unique Japanese adaptation in two respects. First, it manifests extreme sex role segregation in Japanese companies – the belief that women are better at training women and that a woman is needed to play the role of 'go-between' between the male supervisor and the female group members. Second, the 'female group leader' is a specially-created work role outside the formal organizational chart: it is not a formal supervisory role. It provides an opportunity for women to demonstrate their supervisory abilities but it does not threaten the role of the male supervisor.

As the system involves very low training costs and causes little disruption to the formal organization, companies are quite willing to 'try it out'. However, the female group leader system is usually not uniformly applied throughout the company but mainly introduced in sections where there is a high proportion of women or where the nature of the tasks requires a female group leader. Inagei's study (1983) showed that in the majority of cases, the role of the female group leader was an informal one and its position within the organization was ambiguous. According to Inagei, it was only under exceptional circumstances that the female group leader would formally become a supervisor (*kakarichō*). In the majority of cases the supervisor was still a man. Many companies simply stopped at the stage of training women as group leaders on an informal basis; no further step was taken to provide these women with promotion opportunities.

The career conversion system

In the early 1980s some major companies in the banking and financial sectors took new steps to open up formal promotion chances for women by introducing a 'career conversion system' (*shokumu tenkan seido*). The main objective was to improve the morale of women. The financial sector has become increasingly competitive since the late 1970s; many companies saw the motivation of their women employees as an important factor in enhancing their competitive edge.

The conversion system allows women in clerical positions to apply for conversion to the managerial career route at a certain stage in their careers. Previously, women employed in the banking and securities fields were assigned to clerical positions where they remained throughout their careers. Men, on the other hand, joined the companies as prospective managers, gained work experience in different sections, to eventually assume managerial positions (Figure 9.1). Jobs in the clerical stream involve mostly routine work which does not need widespread training or job rotation. There is no requirement for job transfer involving geographical mobility. Promotion is only limited to a lower managerial grade. The managerial stream involves broad training in different kinds of jobs and experience. There is frequent job rotation which may

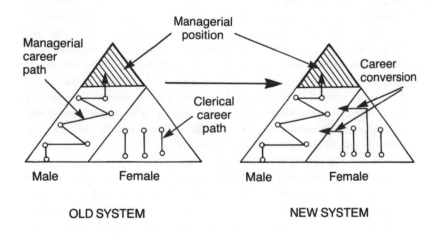

Figure 9.1 Career conversion system
Source: Adapted from Yashiro (1986: 230)

involve geographical mobility. Promotion up to top management is possible. Women who apply for conversion to the managerial career route need to make a commitment to the mobility requirement.

From the viewpoint of the company, the 'career conversion system', as a way of utilizing women, has a double advantage. First, by providing a chance for the career-oriented women to join the mainstream career route, the system improves the morale of the female work-force and they work better during their earlier years. Second, it permits better screening by giving the company a chance to 'screen out' those women who are capable of pursuing the male career pattern and are prepared to commit themselves to the company long term. This explains why most companies set the minimum conversion age at around 30 – the risk of women leaving to establish a family is much reduced. That means the chance of not being able to recoup the training cost is much reduced, so companies are more willing to offer them promotion to more responsible positions.

In practice, only a minority of women have succeeded in converting to the mainstream career jobs. The mobility requirement presents the greatest barrier. Moreover, it is hardly a means of providing women with equal opportunities, because those women who succeeded in converting to the male career route did not previously receive the same amount of training and experience as their male colleagues, and it is very unlikely that they would be able to compete with their male colleagues on an equal basis.

Yashiro's study (1986: 226–8) of the career conversion system in a major bank illustrates the limitations. The bank introduced a 'two-track personnel system' in 1982. All the jobs in the company were divided into two streams: the clerical stream and the managerial stream. Each stream has its own grading and promotion system as shown in Figure 9.2. As a general principle, women started their careers by joining the clerical stream and all the men are expected to join the managerial stream. The career conversion system enabled women who had reached clerical grade 1 and were above 30 years of age to apply for conversion to the generalist stream. As can be seen in Figure 9.2, the conversion would take a woman of clerical grade 1, grade 2 or grade 3 to manager grade 2, which would normally take a male university graduate 8 years to reach that grade (about 30 years of age). That is to say, no matter how many years of work experience the woman has with

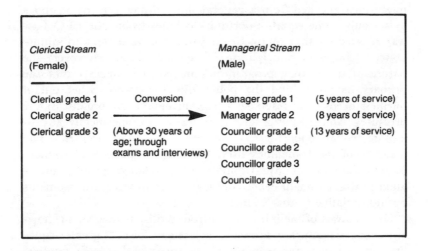

Figure 9.2 Career conversion in company A
Source: Adapted from Yashiro (1986: 227)
Note: The minimum ages for women to enter clerical grades 1, 2, 3 are 25,
35 and 40 respectively.

the company, success in coversion implies that she has to start
again at the junior supervisory level. From the company's point
of view this is rational, because former clerical job experience does
not offer women any training in supervisory skills. Within three
years of the introduction of the conversion system, thirteen women
in the bank succeeded in converting from the clerical to the generalist career route. This was a small minority taking into consideration that the bank employed several thousand women. However,
the crux of the problem is not just that only a small number of
women can comply with the company's requirements, but that
men and women still started their careers on an entirely unequal
basis. Yashiro argues that this type of 'post-entry correction of
discrimination' hardly offers women true equal opportunities. The
majority of women were still trapped in secondary jobs (Yashiro
1986: 229).

The limits of 'women utilization programmes'

Companies' moves to adopt more positive utilization policies on
women started before the introduction of the EEO Law. One
cannot eliminate the possibility that some of the policy initiatives

might have resulted from a general shift in management attitudes as a result of the equal opportunity debates before the EEO Law was enacted, or that companies might have taken steps to initiate policy changes in anticipation of the legislation. However, the nature of the change programmes introduced suggests that the primary motive behind the policy initiatives were either out of business needs or in response to labour market and organizational pressures. None of the programmes was aimed specifically at promoting equal opportunities between men and women. The majority of the companies used the term 'utilization of women' (*josei no katsuyō*) not 'equal opportunity', although positive utilization of women might eventually lead to improvement of women's position relative to that of men.

Our analysis of the initiatives introduced by management, however, suggests only very limited development towards greater equality between men and women. There are several reasons for this. First, most of the special 'career development programmes' for women were introduced on an *ad hoc* basis and their implementation was often restricted to certain sections or departments rather than on a company-wide basis. Second, project teams or special work roles created for women were mostly informal, lying outside the formal organizational structure, and there was very little formal link between these special work roles and the formal career structure. The informality of these policies means that disruption to the formal organization and career structure was only minimal. Third, in the case of formally opening up promotion chances for women through career conversion, a screening procedure was introduced to ensure that only those women who could comply with all the requirements imposed by the company, which virtually meant adopting the 'male career pattern', would be offered some chances. The 'career conversion system' actually justified promotion practices which were both directly and indirectly discriminatory against women.

To summarize, commercial considerations and labour market changes have not caused companies to alter the fundamental personnel management rules and practices which allocate men and women in separate career tracks. A survey by the Ministry of Labour in 1981 showed persistent discrimination against women in all stages of employment, especially in recruitment, job assignment and promotion (MOL 1981). According to the survey, 71 per cent of the firms restricted their recruitment of graduates to

men only, 83 per cent of the firms had positions that were not
open to women and 43 per cent gave women no opportunity for
promotion.

THE EQUAL EMPLOYMENT OPPORTUNITY LAW

In May 1985 the Japanese government passed the EEO Law
which took effect from April 1986.[4] How much have further
changes occurred since the law was introduced? Before answering
this question, here is a brief examination of the nature of the
legislation.

From the western perspective, the Japanese EEO Law may
appear rather peculiar. It has granted women very few new rights
and imposed only limited legal obligations on employers. The
legislation makes a distinction between 'prohibition' (*kinshi kitei*)
and 'exhortation' (*doryoku-gimu kitei*) in its provisions for ensuring
equal treatment between men and women. Prohibition against
discrimination applies to basic vocational training, fringe benefits,
retirement and dismissal – areas in which substantial changes had
already taken place before the law was introduced. These are
also areas where equal opportunities for women will cause least
disruption to the core personnel management system. With regard
to the most important stages in employment including recruitment,
job assignment and promotion, sections 7 and 8 of the law merely
'exhort' (morally oblige) employers to treat women equally as
men: 'employers shall endeavour to give women equal opportunity
with men'. These are the areas governing entry to the company
and job allocation within the company over which employers
resisted strongly any form of legal intervention during the bill's
drafting stage. The basis of management's argument centred on
the difference in the average length of service between men and
women, and the 'logic' of the lifetime employment practice (MOL
1986: 52–3; Ōwaki 1987: 11–14). Management argued that legal
enforcement of equal opportunities in recruitment, job assignment
and promotion would cause chaos in companies' personnel management systems and eventually destroy the vitality of the Japanese
economy (Honda 1984: 119; *The Japan Times*, 25 March 1984).
The hortatory provisions clearly represent an adaptation to, and
compromise within, the existing employment system.

The hortatory provisions appear to be highly ambiguous and
their enforcement is dependent upon the administrative guidance

(*gyōsei-shidō*) of the Ministry of Labour. An analysis of the contents of the law and the guidelines set by the Ministry of Labour suggests that the standard of equality as required by the Japanese legislation falls far short of the 'western norm'. The way 'equal opportunity' is being defined appears to be rather narrow and limited. According to the interpretation of the Ministry of Labour, 'to give women equal opportunity' means 'not to exclude women and not to treat women unfavourably'. 'To exclude women' means not offering women any opportunity; 'not to exclude women' means offering women some opportunity. For instance, in recruitment employers are not allowed to advertise jobs for men only, although they can specify the number of employees they intend to recruit by sex, such as '70 males required' and '30 females required'. This is not against the requirements of the guidelines because the employers do not exclude women. Similarly, with regard to assignment and promotion, employers are asked 'not to exclude women'; for instance, companies which do not offer women any job rotation or promotion chances will be required to 'make efforts' to offer women some opportunity. However, in the case where the frequency of job rotation for women is less than for men or where assignment of certain jobs is limited to women workers with certain qualifications – these do not constitute exclusion of women.

A second meaning of 'equal opportunity' means 'not to treat women unfavourably'. According to the guidelines, to treat women unfavourably means to set different qualifications or conditions of employment for men and women. Discrimination in this sense means unequal treatment; non-discrimination means equal treatment. The guidelines specify that if as a result less women than men are able to comply with such terms and conditions, it does not constitute 'unfavourable treatment'. For example, according to the guidelines, in the case of promotion tests 'unfavourable treatment' means not to offer women the opportunity to take the test or to impose qualification requirements on women different from those of men, such as requiring longer years of service. If the results of the tests turn out to be that less women than men are qualified for promotion, this does not constitute 'unfavourable treatment'. Clearly, the Ministry of Labour's interpretation does not embody the concept of 'indirect discrimination'.

Taking the above interpretation literally, one can say that the guidelines are aimed at no more than removing the most blatant forms of direct discrimination against women. 'Equal opportunity' is interpreted as 'equal treatment of women to that of men'. On the whole, the Ministry of Labour seems to have compromised with the status quo and makes little attempt to tackle the problem of institutional discrimination.

The Japanese Ministry of Labour, however, points out that the EEO Law is a developing piece of legislation and that the requirements stipulated in the law represent no more than temporary minimum standards aimed at raising the average norm of equal opportunities in the Japanese enterprise community by reducing the number of bad practice companies. According to the ministry, the spirit of the law goes beyond the requirements stipulated in the law. Good practice employers, that is those who have already satisfied the minimum requirements, are expected to fulfil their 'moral obligations' by making 'further efforts' in providing equal opportunities for women, in respect of the spirit of the law (MOL 1986: 44). The EEO Law has two objectives. The first is to use the prohibitory provisions to remove the most blatant forms of direct discrimination; this first objective in effect aims at formally ratifying changes that have mostly occurred in the past and also to enforce changes in the worst practice companies. Its second, more important, objective is to use the hortatory provisions to exert 'moral pressure' on the good practice employers to move beyond the minimum requirements enshrined in the law, and set the new norms and standards of equality. Thus, the real significance of the law lies not only in the extent to which companies in general are prepared to comply with the stipulated requirements but, more importantly, in the extent to which it can act as a symbol of a new moral standard to stimulate the good practice employers to set the pace for further change, particularly in the areas of recruitment, job assignment and promotion.

The effectiveness of the model of change underlying the EEO Law will have to be evaluated, not only in terms of whether companies have responded to the legislation, but also the extent to which the policy changes will actually benefit women in terms of their job status and career opportunities. Moreover, the attitudes and responses of women to the new situation will also be a crucial factor in determining the future outcome. The rest of this paper looks at how companies have responded to the legislation and the reaction of women to the new situation.

CHANGING COMPANY PRACTICE IN RESPONSE TO THE EEO LAW

Recruitment and conditions of employment for new entrants

So far, survey evidence shows that the law has been quite effective in reducing the most obvious forms of direct discrimination against women, particularly in the areas of recruitment and conditions of employment for new entrants. It is in job advertising that the most remarkable changes have taken place. The proportion of companies which excluded female job applicants (specifying that jobs were open to male graduates only) declined from 41 per cent in 1986 to 17 per cent in 1987; those which offered jobs to graduates without specifying the sex requirements rose from 36 per cent in 1986 to 77 per cent in 1987 (JIWE 1986, 1987).

An increasing number of companies have also taken steps to remove the unfavourable terms and conditions applied specifically to female job applicants such as requiring women to have special qualifications or skills or restrictions that women should be commuting to work from their parents' homes, and so on. A more remarkable change has been the move towards equalization of starting wages for new recruits. The proportion of companies offering equal starting wages for male and female graduates rose from 36 per cent in 1980 to 79 per cent in 1987, according to surveys by the Rōmu Gyōsei Kenkyūsho (*Rōsei Jihō* 1987). The EEO Law has made it difficult for companies to specify the sex requirements in job advertisements and to impose obviously unequal terms and conditions on women at the point of entry.

Nevertheless, some of the changes in recruitment policies are more in form than in substance. Staff at the universities' employment information office reported that even when they received job offers for both sexes, firms often revealed preference for men in the screening process (JIL 1987). There were also widespread complaints from female graduates that the changes in job advertising had only created false expectations and caused confusion in their job-hunting activities as they only discovered that companies had no real intention of recruiting female graduates or offering them equal career opportunities when they approached the companies (*Asahi Shinbun*, 9 September, 1987). In practice, 50 per cent of the firms still restricted recruitment for technical-related jobs to men, and over a quarter did not seek to recruit female graduates for administrative or sales jobs, according to the latest survey by the Ministry of Labour (MOL 1990: 4).

The EEO Law does not seem to have had much effect on eliminating many traditional Japanese recruitment practices which, although not in direct violation of the requirements stipulated in the guidelines, discriminate against women. Many companies still conduct their recruitment and screening activities for men and women separately. One common practice is to set aside different dates for accepting applications from men and women. Companies would normally finish the interviews for male job applicants first before they start interviewing female applicants. This could mean that companies only offer job opportunities to women after they have failed to recruit a sufficient number of men. In the case where recruitment activities for both men and women are conducted on the same day, it is still a common practice for companies to organize separate meetings for male and female job applicants. These practices do not constitute discrimination against women, as defined by the Ministry of Labour, because companies have not 'excluded women' in the recruitment procedures.

Sex is still one of the most important criteria on which many companies base their annual recruitment plans and make their manpower decisions. In 1986, three out of four companies still decided in advance the number of men and women they intended to recruit each year (Rōsei Jihō 1986). Out of these, more than half indicated that they did not plan to change this practice in the near future. The main reason for this, as pointed out by the companies, being that 'the type of jobs' for men and women were different. This raises a crucial question of how far the present legislation has helped to remove the traditional practice of recruiting men for core career jobs and women for clerical support jobs. Equal opportunities for women will not come about unless companies are prepared to eliminate the practice of making a clear distinction between 'men's jobs' and 'women's jobs'.

In the areas of job assignment and promotion, the majority of women are still facing insurmountable barriers. Changes over the last few years seem to indicate that companies are moving towards more indirect, yet institutionalized, ways of segregating the majority of women into inferior career tracks.

The career-tracking system

Since the promulgation of the EEO Law, an increasing number of major firms have introduced a new selection system – the 'career-tracking system' (*kōsubetsu koyō-seido*). Over 20 per cent of the firms which had no formal distinction for regular employees' career tracks adopted such a system after the EEO Law was introduced (JIWE 1986). Among those firms which had introduced the system, half of them indicated that the main objective was to cope with the law. The number of companies adopting the system has been rising in recent years. Career tracking is primarily a 'big firm phenomenon'; 42.3 per cent of firms with 5,000 or more employees have introduced the system as compared to 11.4 per cent for firms with 300 – 900 employees (MOL 1990).

The system offers employees a choice of career tracks at the point of entry: usually the managerial stream and the clerical stream. The one common criterion used by all the firms adopting the new system is the mobility requirements for jobs in the managerial track. Some companies have simply used instead the commitment to mobility, calling the two career tracks the 'mobile' and the 'non-mobile'. The managerial track (usually called '*sōgōshoku*') includes jobs which require complex judgement, such as business negotiations, personnel management, designing or developing products, planning of company policies or strategies. Employees in this track are subject to comprehensive job rotation and transfers for career development and business necessities, and there is no limit to promotion; employees can eventually become top-level managers or executives. In contrast, jobs in the clerical track (usually called '*ippanshoku*') are considered less complicated and more manual; job rotation and transfers are carried out within a limited scope (notably employees are not required to move to other localities). Promotion for those in the clerical track is limited to only lower-level or local management positions. In some firms, an additional track is organized between these two tracks for 'specialist employees' (*senmonshoku*), who specialize in jobs requiring high-level skills or knowledge.

According to the Kantō Management Association (1986), the career tracking system is designed to clarify each individual's career choice at the early stage of their careers so as to facilitate career planning. It also points out that selection for entry to the different career tracks is based solely on 'merit' and that all career options will be open to both sexes. As the same standards and criteria for selection will be applied equally to both sexes, the new system is therefore, according to the association, intended to eliminate the past informal practice of discrimination against women at the point of entry. The association also claims that the new system, in which individuals are recruited for specific 'jobs' based on 'merit' and in accordance with individual 'choice', signifies a fundamental shift from the traditional sex-based personnel management system to one that is based on merit. This new form of employment system is strongly recommended by the Kantō Management Association as an appropriate way to fulfil the equal treatment requirement of the EEO Law:

> treating women equally with men as required by the new legislation can be met if firms fully implement the merit-based personnel management system. In such cases, the differential treatment for those in different career tracks is not based on sex but solely based on individual merit or abilities.
>
> (Kantō Management Association 1986: 6)

The crucial issue here is the meaning of the concepts of 'job', 'merit' and 'choice' and the way the system is being implemented in practice.

First, one needs to look at the criteria used for classifying the different job categories or career streams. How far are they job-related and how far are they behavioural requirements? In the majority of the cases, the job classification is no more than a broad distinction between the 'managerial' and the 'clerical' jobs. It is often not clear what precisely the job specifications are and what type of requirements and qualifications companies are looking for.

Second, job specifications are often very broad and general. The job abilities and qualifications required for the different career streams are often no more than a set of behavioural expectations, such as a commitment to be geographically mobile. At those companies which had adopted the new system, there were complaints from women that they were doing the same kind of work as men but were classified into the inferior 'clerical career track' simply because they did not make a commitment to the mobility requirement (JERC 1987: 125–7). This is clearly a form of indirect discrimination against women.

Third, implementation of the new system raises serious doubts about the fairness of the selection and screening procedures.

Formally, the management career track is open to both men and women (in most cases restricted to graduates only), but in practice men are almost assigned to it *automatically*, whereas women are selected for it only *exceptionally*. During selection interviews with management, women often appeared to be challenged with tough questions about mobility and potential sacrifices of family life.

Some good practice companies implement the career tracking system with goodwill and genuinely hope to select a small number of women to be put on the elite career course. However, companies are only prepared to offer such 'special favour' to women providing that they are willing to make a full commitment to work like their male colleagues. Despite the formal offer of opportunities, in reality very few women managed to pass the selection procedures. Table 9.1 gives some examples of firms which have introduced the new employment system and have recruited women for the managerial track in the spring of 1987. The number of female graduates who managed to enter the main stream managerial track was extremely small.

A survey by the Japan Institute of Women's Employment (JIWE 1990) on forty firms in the finance, insurance and banking sector, which had adopted the career tracking system, found that only 1.3 per cent of the women employees were in the managerial

Table 9.1 Examples of companies which have recruited female graduates for managerial career track (*sōgōshoku*) in the spring of 1987

Name of company	Total no. of male graduates recruited (all 'managerial career track')	Total no. of female graduates recruited*	No. of females selected for 'managerial career track'
Orientorisu	56	152	2
Sumitomo Bank	420	60	20
Taishō Kaijō Kasai Insurance	120	43	3
Tokyo Gas	108	12	12
Daiwa Security	300	(Approx.) 130	3
Nikkō Security	396	(Approx.) 160	3
Mitsubishi Bank	385	30	(Approx.) 10
Mitsubishi Trading	138	125	3

Source: *Nikkei Shimbun* (Evening), 14 April, 1987

Note: * Figures inclusive of those selected for 'managerial career track'

track, as compared with 99.0 per cent of the men (Table 9.2). In contrast with the managerial track, the clerical track has remained exclusively a female domain. Under the present EEO Law, it is considered acceptable for companies to restrict certain jobs to women only.

Table 9.2 Distribution of male and female employees by career tracks (survey on forty firms with career tracking system)

	Male (%)	Female (%)
Managerial (*Sōgōshoku*)	99.0	1.3
Clerical (*Ippanshoku*)	0.8	96.2
'Mid-way' (*Chūkanshoku*)*	0.0	2.4
Specialist (*Senmonshoku*)	0.2	0.1
Total	100.0	100.0
(No. of employees)	(82,049)	(55,615)

Source: JIWE (1990: 26)

Note: * This is a kind of 'middle-of-the-road' career track recently introduced by some companies to enable some selected women to take up more responsible jobs, but unlike those in the managerial track, there is no requirement for geographical mobility.

The formal classification of employees into different career tracks is in effect the institutionalization of past informal practices which segregated women in the inferior dead-end jobs. The present system is more of a classification of employees by status rather than by type of work. It would seem that, from management's viewpoint, the offer of a 'choice' to the individuals at the point of entry not only fulfils the equal treatment requirement of the EEO Law, but also automatically justifies the differential wage systems, training and promotion opportunities accorded for the different 'class' of employees in different career tracks. Employers thus could justify paying a woman lower wages, and offering her less training and fewer promotion opportunities because she has made a 'choice' to enter the clerical career track.

The career tracking system preserves the 'male-oriented' core personnel system even better and ensures that equal opportunities will be only offered to a limited number of 'male women': those with the 'right ability and motivation' (*nōryoku to iyoku aru josei*) – meaning those who can conform to the existing organizational rules and work practices like their male counterparts. It is therefore not surprising that so few women are able to enter the managerial track.

HAS THE EEO LAW RAISED WOMEN'S CAREER CONSCIOUSNESS?

As pointed out earlier, the future of equal opportunities for women will depend, not only on changes in company policies, but also on how far Japanese women themselves start to perceive the possibilities of improvement and begin to make more demands on their employers.

My own detailed study of women's career attitudes at a major store (a company with a reputation for its innovative equal opportunities policies), *before* (1984) and *after* (1988) the introduction of the EEO Law, shows no evidence that women's career aspirations and expectations have risen over time (Lam 1992). This is rather surprising as one would expect the equality debates since the early 1980s and the EEO legislation itself to have raised women's career consciousness. On the contrary, my study shows that a much greater proportion of young women (aged under 24) and graduates – women who are most likely to be affected by the law – displayed a greater degree of 'uncertainty' and 'ambivalence' about their career future. The career tracking policies adopted by the company appeared to have made women more aware of the 'price of equality' and put them under greater pressure to make their career choices through formal screening at the early stages of their careers. As compared with 1984, fewer women in 1988 intended to pursue a continuous career without interruption and more of them would prefer to retire from work when they have children. The intensive demands on employees in career jobs to work excessively long hours and to make a commitment to relocation appear to have driven a growing number of women to become more 'home-oriented'. The majority of the women interviewed pointed out that if equal opportunities meant that they had to forego having a family and work like men, they would rather seek a compromise by adopting a 'two-phase work profile.' Indeed, government surveys show a decline in the proportion of women intending to pursue a continuous career, from 20 per cent in 1979 to 14.4 per cent in 1989. In contrast, the proportion of women who prefer to adopt a two-phase work profile, retire from work when they have families and re-enter the labour market when their children have grown up, has increased from 39 per cent in 1979 to 64.2 per cent in 1989 (PMO 1979 and 1989). For the majority of Japanese women this is probably a pragmatic choice in a system which does not allow career jobs to be compatible with family life, and in a society which expects women to take up sole responsibility for raising children.

An increasing number of good practice companies might have allowed and even encouraged more women to compete with their male colleagues on an equal basis, but the intensive demand of the core career jobs, and the lack of flexibility in career planning, mean that such opportunities are seen as irrelevant by the majority of women. In the case company there was some evidence that women were actually turning down promotion. Some women interviewed in 1987 pointed out that the company appeared to be more willing to appoint women to senior management positions than before, but such efforts often turned out to be futile because women appointed to management positions tended to resign afterwards. If the incidents mentioned were representative, then the 'equal opportunity efforts' made by the company might not have much effect on women's positions.

WHY SO LITTLE IMPROVEMENT?

Commercial pressures and the EEO legislation have pushed Japanese companies to improve the job prospects and employment conditions of women, especially the graduates. Some companies are more willing to give a selected few women more responsible jobs and to train them as specialists in areas where female consumers dominate. Despite all these changes, Japanese companies are reluctant to offer women equal job assignment and promotion opportunities. Women's career tracks are still entirely separated from those of men and they are still treated as a special category of work-force. For many Japanese companies 'equal opportunities' simply means to 'use women's abilities to the full', but it does not necessarily mean equality between women and men.

Why are Japanese companies so reluctant to introduce more liberal equal opportunities for women? Many companies are well aware of the dilemma they are facing. In order to attract and retain more able women in top jobs, companies would need to change the promotion rules and the work practices governing the core career jobs, for example, allowing for greater flexibility in career planning, enabling women to retain their seniority after a period of career break, reducing the intensity of work and allowing for the mobility rules to be applied in more flexible ways. However, altering these rules too radically could have two 'undesirable' consequences from the viewpoint of management.

First, offering women true equal opportunities would imply redistribution of the promotion chances between men and women. This would disrupt the job security and long-service promotion expectations of the male employees which are part of the long-standing implicit understanding between management and the male employees. This customary expectation has been the major force generating high commitment, high output effort and willingness to co-operate in furthering the aims of the company. The benefits that management derives from these long-standing practices are considerable, and it is not at all clear that Japanese companies are willing to give them up. As long as 'good employers' in the Japanese enterprise community are still expected to be able to offer long-term job security and stable career progression for their (male) regular employees, giving up the benefits of the traditional system too rapidly might jeopardize the status of companies in the enterprise community and their ability to attract good quality male graduates. Management's continued attachment to the traditional employment practices imposes a severe constraint on their willingness to introduce more liberal equal opportunities for women.

Second, introducing fundamental changes in the career rules to allow more women to retain their seniority and career continuity would not only imply an absolute increase in labour costs, but would also lead to an expansion of the number of employees under the guarantee of lifetime employment with its associated career expectations. The guarantee of lifetime employment under the *nenkō* wage and career progression system is extremely costly and rigid. The smooth operation of the core employment system depends on the existence of a large number of women willing to work as low-cost 'peripheral' employees to provide the necessary flexibility. Full equal opportunities for women would not only destabilize the male career hierarchy and the established work practices, but would also upset the flexibility of the employment system.

In the 1980s and 1990s the increased pressure for greater equality for women has pushed Japanese companies to adopt more cautious policies in maintaining a delicate balance between the need to give some selected women equal opportunities and at the same time ensuring that the long-standing employment practices governing the internal career jobs will not be disrupted. The career tracking system has been designed to co-opt a small number of highly-educated women with strong career aspirations and, at the same time, to prevent the EEO Law from inflating the expectations of all women. Indeed, since the introduction of the EEO Law, Japanese companies have introduced more clear-cut formal policies of segmentation by employment status. An increasing number of women are now employed as contract or part-time workers who are outside the scope of the EEO Law.[5] This segmentation policy helps to dilute the potential destabilizing effects of equal opportunity pressures.

The EEO Law does not have enough power to prevent employers' sex-based personnel policies. The equal treatment approach has clearly failed to tackle the problem of indirect discrimination. Although the law has helped to reduce many of the formal written rules which discriminate against women directly, many substitute rules are written with sexual differentiation in mind and continue to discriminate indirectly against women. By defining 'equal opportunity' as 'equal treatment of women to men' but not the other way round, the law has created a loophole for employers to earmark jobs for women only. The present EEO Law is clearly a product of political compromise with management power. By appealing to the voluntary 'moral obligation' of the employer to provide women with equality in the most important stages of employment, the EEO Law has done no more than reasserted management control over the agenda of change.

One final question the readers might raise: Why is it that Japanese women appear to continue to accept their conditions? There has been little evidence that Japanese women have become more career conscious and begun to make more demands on their employers. Does this indicate that equal opportunities are not desired by the majority of Japanese women? Or is it that there is a lack of awareness of the need for change?

Opponents of equal opportunities for women in Japan often use the following observations to argue against the introduction of more drastic policy changes: (1) improved career opportunities do not always seem attractive to women and (2) Japanese women themselves endorse the sex role ideology and their psychological identity with the traditional feminine role renders external action ineffective. These observations are not entirely inaccurate but they should not necessarily be used as a guide for policy.

What deserves more consideration is why the majority of Japanese women are not prepared to accept the type of 'equal opportunities' offered by their employers. Under the present employment system, women who desire equal opportunities are asked to accept and conform to the male working norm which requires them to work continuously without interruption, to accept the mobility requirements in a very rigid way, to work excessively long hours as a sign of commitment to the company, and to ensure that the occupational sphere remains aloof from the domestic sphere. All these practical constraints have made any expectation for career advancement unrealistic for the majority of women.

Nevertheless, it is true that compared to their counterparts in western countries, Japanese women have been slow in developing their equality consciousness. Experience in the United States and the United Kingdom suggests that active intervention by the government in the provision of equal opportunities policies for women was largely a result of political campaigns and lobbying by women's pressure groups (Meehan 1985). In Japan, women's pressure groups have not consolidated as a major social force to exert pressures on the government to intervene more actively in equal opportunity issues. The women's voice was almost unheard in the process of drafting the EEO Law. The present legislation is a manifestation of the dominance of management power in Japanese society.

One major lesson that Japanese women can learn from their counterparts in the west is that grassroots lobbying and political campaigns from women themselves are important means for propelling equal opportunities issues to the top of the political agenda (Meehan 1985). Unless there are stronger political pressures from Japanese women themselves to campaign for more active state intervention in both the economic and social spheres, the future of equal employment for Japanese women is unlikely to progress beyond its present limit. If Japanese women are to achieve full and real equality, it cannot be on men's terms. The male work norm will have to be changed and the Japanese management system will need to be challenged.

NOTES

1 According to annual surveys by the *Monbushō* (Ministry of Education), the job placement ratio of female university graduates increased by

10.6 percentage points between 1975 and 1985, rising from 62.8 per cent in 1975 to 73.4 per cent in 1985; whereas the job placement ratio of male graduates increased only slightly from 77.5 per cent to 79.8 per cent during the same period. Women graduates not only have been entering the job market in greater numbers, but the type of occupations they enter has also changed significantly. The most significant change in recent years has been the increase in the number and proportion of those engaged in specialist and technical jobs other than the traditional field of teaching. In 1965 over half of female university graduates went into teaching. At that time job opportunities for female graduates in the corporate sector were extremely limited. However, by 1989 only 20 per cent of them became teachers; the majority went into specialist, technical and clerical jobs in the corporate sector. The expansion of specialist and technical jobs has been particularly dramatic after the mid-1970s. In 1975 14.6 per cent of women graduates went into specialist and technical jobs, this increased to 25.1 per cent in 1989. The increasing need for more specialists and technical experts has prompted companies to open their doors to female university graduates.

2 I have referred a great deal to the following journals which contain useful up-to-date information on companies' personnel policies: *Rōsei Jihō*, *Gekkan Rikuruto*, *Rōdō Jihō*, *Kantokusha Kunren*, *Keieisha*, *Shokugyō Kunren*.

3 The 'specialist career system' (*senmonshoku seido*), which has been widely referred to as one of the new attempts among major companies to provide a career path for women, is not dealt with in this section. This is because in many companies, the system was not designed specifically for women. A complex variety of other factors, including the shortage of positions for middle-aged male employees and the need to move towards a merit-based personnel system, have prompted companies to introduce the specialist career route. Some companies, particularly those in the department store industry, have also used the specialist career route as a means for expanding women's career chances. For a detailed analysis of the specialist career system and its effects on women, see Lam (1992: Ch. 8).

4 For a more detailed analysis of the historical background leading to the introduction of the law, see Lam (1992: Ch. 5).

5 While the majority of women continue to be excluded from the framework of 'lifetime' employment, their role as non-regular workers, including those employed as part-time, *arbeit* and contract workers, is becoming increasingly important. The proportion of women employees classified as part-time, *arbeit* and contract workers increased from 26 per cent in 1981 to 36 per cent in 1990. In comparison, male non-regular workers showed only a slight increase from 6 per cent to 8 per cent over the same period (Sōmuchō 1981, 1990).

REFERENCES

Honda, J. (1984) *Danjo Koyō Kintō Towa Nanika* (What Equal Employment Opportunity Law is all about), Tokyo, Daiyamonda-sha.

Inagei, N. (1983) *Josei to Riidashippu* (Woman and Leadership), Tokyo Yūhikaku Sensho.

Ishida, H. (ed.) (1986) *Josei no Jidai: Nihon Kigyō to Koyō Byōdō* (Woman's Era: Japanese Companies and Equal Employment Opportunity), Tokyo, Kōbundo.

Japan Economic Research Centre (JERC) (1987) *Koyō Kintō Hō no Eikyō to Kigyō no Taiō* (The Impact of the Equal Employment Opportunity Law and Company Responses), Nihon Keizai Kenkyū Sentaa (Japan Economic Research Centre), no. 58, May.

Japan Institute of Labour (JIL) (1987) 'The impact of the Equal Employment Opportunity Law at its first stage of enforcement', *Japan Labour Bulletin* (Japan Institute of Labour) 26 (10), 5–8.

Japan Institute of Women's Employment (JIWE) (1986, 1987) *Shinki Daigaku Sotsugyō-Sha Saiyō Keikaku Chōsa* (Survey on Recruitment Plans for University Graduates), Josei Shokugyō Zaidan (Japan Institute of Women's Employment).

Japan Institute of Women's Employment (JIWE) (1990) *Kōsubetsu Koyō-kanri ni kansuru Kenkyū-kai Hōkokusho* (A Survey Report on Career Tracking), Josei Shokugyō Zaidan (Japan Institute of Women's Employment).

Kantō Management Association (1986) *Danjo Koyō Kikai Kintō Hō to kore-kara no Koyōkanri no Hōkō* (The Equal Employment Opportunity Law and the Future Direction of Personnel Management), Tokyo.

Koyō Shinkō Kyōkai (1986) *Koyō Kikai Kintō no Genjō to Kadai* (Equal Employment Opportunity: The Present Situation and Issues), Tokyo, Sangyō Rōdō Chōsa-sho.

Lam, A. (1992) *Women and Japanese Management: Discrimination and Reform*, London, Routledge.

Meehan, E. (1985) *Women's Rights at Work: Campaigns and Policy in Britain and the United States*, London, Macmillan.

Mizuno, A. (1984) *Keizai Sofutoka Jidai no Josei Rōdō: Nichi Bei Ō no Keiken* (The Service Economy and Women's Employment: Japanese, American and European Experience), Tokyo, Yūhikaku Sensho.

Ministry of Education (MOE) (various years) *Gakkō Kihon Chōsa* (Basic Survey on Education), Monbushō (Ministry of Education).

Ministry of Labour (MOL) (1981) *Joshi Rōdōsha no Koyō Kanri ni kansuru Chōsa* (Survey on Employment and Management of Women Workers), Rōdōshō Fujin-kyoku (Women's Bureau, Ministry of Labour).

Ministry of Labour (MOL) (1986) *Danjo Koyō Kikai Kintō Hō Kaisei Rōdō Kijun Hō no Jitsumu Kaisetsu* (A Practical Guide and Explanation of the Equal Opportunity Law and the Amended Labour Standards Law), Rōdōshō Fujin-kyoku (Women's Bureau, Ministry of Labour), Tokyo, Rōmu Gyōsei Kenkyū-sho.

Ministry of Labour (MOL) (1990) *Joshi Koyō Kanri Kihon Chōsa* (Basic

Survey on Women's Employment and Management), Rōdōshō Fujin-kyoku (Women's Bureau, Ministry of Labour).

Ōwaki, M. (1987) *Kintō Hō Jidai ni Ikiru* (Living in the Age of Equal Opportunity Law), Tokyo, Yūhikaku Sensho.

Prime Minister's Office (PMO) (1979) *Fujin ni kansuru Ishiki Chōsa* (Attitude Survey on Women), Sōrifu (Japan Prime Minister's Office).

Prime Minister's Office (PMO) (1989) *Josei no Shūgyō ni kansuru Seron Chōsa* (Public Opinion Survey on Women's Employment), Sōrifu (Japan Prime Minister's Office).

Rōsei Jihō (1986) 'Koyō kintō hō e no kigyō no taiō' (Company responses to the Equal Employment Opportunity Law), *Rōsei Jihō* 2789, 3–31.

Rōsei Jihō (1987) 'Kettei shonin-kyū no dōkō' (Trends in starting wages), *Rōsei Jihō*, 2834, 2–7.

Sōmuchō (1981 and 1990) *Rōdōryoku Chōsa Tokubetsu Chōsa* (Report on the Special Survey of the Labour Force Survey), Sōmuchō Tōkei-kyoku (Statistics Bureau, Management and Co-ordination Agency).

Chapter 10

The role of the professional housewife

Joy Hendry

Housework and the care of children has undoubtedly always been a part of the working life of Japanese women, as it is part of the lives of most women, but in few parts of the world have these roles been granted the importance and status they have acquired in Japan. Although more than half of Japan's married women are to be found in the labour force, there is a very noticeable *M*-curve when participation is plotted against age,[1] and many women try to give all their attention to the home during at least the early years of the lives of their children. A substantial number of women[2] continue to devote their energies, full time, to the home, and these have succeeded in carving out, or perhaps having carved out for them, a role which is widely regarded as a professional occupation.

During the period of industrialization, when women in the workforce were putting up with low status occupations, and a real struggle to combine these with their increasingly separated domestic tasks, a class of women whose husbands were economically able to support them began to develop an alternative niche for themselves. Building on an ideology partly inspired by the European notion of a 'better half', and advocated by the Ministry of Education (Monbushō) using an existing Japanese idea of *ryōsai-kenbo* (good wife and wise mother), these women have not only made a highly-regarded occupation out of household activities,[3] but in recent years have even been promoting an alternative economy.

This chapter will examine the role of these so-called professional housewives. It will look at their chief activities, and the social value attached to them. It will try to identify the ideology which supports their continued existence, in the public view, as part of governmental policy, and in the opinions of the housewives themselves. It will attempt to locate the role of professional housewife

in the Japanese economy more widely, both from the perspective
of an outside observer, and within the specific circles they most
affect. Finally, it will turn to look at the efforts of some Japanese
housewives to promote alternatives to an economy they resent,
and to some extent, reject.

This chapter takes a social anthropological approach, which
draws heavily on implicit and explicit knowledge gained through
long-term participant observation with the people under study.
Based largely on field-work carried out at various times during
the 1980s, it also aims to find voices for these people themselves.
There were two extended periods of participant observation, of six
and nine months duration, in the lives of housewives living mostly
in a provincial town some two hours by train from Tokyo, and
shorter periods following up a previous year's residence in a rural
area of Kyūshū. A further period of research was carried out with
Japanese housewives living abroad, in the UK. The specific topics
of research were childrearing in the first instance (see Hendry 1986
for further details) and the use of politeness in the second.

In each case, however, the data was collected largely by spending as much time as possible in the usual lives of the housewives
under study. In the first case, this involved mostly mothers of
small children. In the second the net was spread more widely, but
the most intensive interaction was with some of the same inform-
ants from the first study, five years further into the life cycle.
Comparative material has been gleaned from other anthropological
studies, with similar research methods carried out by different
researchers, both foreign and Japanese. Unfortunately most of the
reports are from the Kanto region, so there may be discrepancies
elsewhere. Only minimal reference is made to surveys, statistics
and the results of questionnaires, since the aim is to uncover
opinions and attitudes which exist at a deeper level than these
usually reveal.

THE ACTIVITIES OF HOUSEWIVES AND THEIR SOCIAL VALUE

What then are the activities of these Japanese housewives which
may be described as so 'professional'? Like housewives anywhere,
they spend a substantial part of their time engaged in keeping
their homes clean and tidy, shopping, cooking and washing for
the family, and taking care of their children. They also try to

maintain good relations with their neighbours and relatives, and with other people whose goodwill may be of benefit to their husbands and their careers. The tasks are not in themselves unusual, but they have been 'crafted'[4] in ways which allow considerable pride and responsibility to accrue to their successful accomplishment. Let us consider some examples.

First of all, it is widely reported that Japanese men hand over their salaries to their wives to distribute between the various demands the house may make on it. The wife will then allocate a certain sum to her spouse for his own personal use, and retain the rest for the household expenses. In theory, then, the wife is *de facto* head of the house in terms of decision-making about its upkeep and decoration, and many of the activities of its members. In practice, the degree of power a man retains over decisions about the spending of large sums must vary from house to house, but this principle makes it more likely that a fair measure of responsibility will be transferred from the wage-earner to his partner.

This responsibility is fine when there is plenty in the pay packet, but draws on considerable skill of juggling and manipulation when it is stretched. During the years following the Second World War, housewives struggling to feed their families in times of scarcity and rocketing prices, co-operated to form consumer groups, together to mount campaigns against black-market profiteering and other fraudulent business practices. The Japan Housewives Association (Shufuren) is one such group, which exemplifies the serious and active way in which women have approached their role as consumers. As the country grew more prosperous, such groups developed an interest in a wider range of concerns, such as the quality of the products they were buying, the degree of environmental contamination, and the dangers of deceptive advertising.

These issues have been tackled in various ways by groups of Japanese housewives, as we shall see, but it is interesting that very often the groups themselves remain rather localized. There are *fujinkai*, literally women's groups, in most regions of Japan, and these form a loose federation.[5] Further groups of housewives have been established in cities, notably to order goods in bulk to keep prices down, and, more recently, to seek organically-produced food. For the vast majority of the women involved, however, their prime interest is in matters related directly to their own house and family, rather than to wider political issues leading from these interests. Imamura's study of Japanese housewives, for example, reported that neighbours would not even sign petitions unless the problem affected their families directly (Imamura 1987, 109–10).

This self-interested activity reflects again the responsibility that housewives attach to their role. It is their first duty to take care of their own home and family, if necessary by banding together with other housewives to fight for their needs and preferences for that home. Unlike the case of such women elsewhere, however, part of the role is not necessarily to carry out voluntary work for the wider community, nor, indeed, to develop a political career for themselves. Some women do, of course, follow just these paths in Japan as elsewhere, but the chances are quite high that they will be criticized for neglecting their housewifely duties if such a route takes up too much time (see Imamura 1987, 124–9).

Taking care of husbands is, of course, one important role. In fact, for many full-time housewives, a husband is only rarely in the home because he will leave early to commute away to his place of employment, sometimes a journey of as much as two hours, and return only after spending the evening in bars and night-clubs with his colleagues. Even for these husbands, however, and probably more so for those who work locally, it has become a wife's responsibility to take care, not only of his physical needs, such as food, clothes and rest, but also to look after the social side of his personal and professional relationships.

In general, this task is accomplished in a large part through the movement of gifts, particularly at the two main seasons of *seibo*, at the year end, and *chūgen*, in the middle of the summer. These occasions provide opportunities to confirm the continuing existence of valued relationships, and allow the expression of debt and gratitude for favours, and other forms of benevolence, from one party to another. They are very often non-reciprocal, and therefore also express and maintain differences of status and hierarchy.[6] Other gifts, which may in the long term be reciprocal, acknowledge the life-stages of members of related families and, in long-standing communities, surrounding houses.

Sometimes the maintenance of good relations between families and neighbours may play a vital part in the professional life of a man and his household. Hamabata's recent book *Crested Kimono* (1990) examines the importance of the roles of marriages and the women they involve, in the affairs of big business families in Japan. This rather unpretentious book offers a remarkable insight into the possibilities so-called housewives may have to influence and, indeed, to exercise quite some power in the running of some of the largest and most succesful of Japan's family enterprises. This example actually illustrates a rather common expectation that a man's concern may well involve the help of his wife, or any other member of his family.[7]

This principle is still particularly evident in rural Japan, where most of the households are continuing ones, with three or even four generations sharing one roof. This situation allows the numerous obligations between houses to be shared amongst a number of people. Here it is likely that the life-stages of neighbours as well as relatives will be marked, but there are also community obligations which exist in urban and provincial neighbourhoods as well. It is common practice, for example, for each house in a neighbourhood to participate in regular communal cleaning and weeding of the paths and streams[8] which run through the area. Somebody is expected to attend meetings of local residents, and in most areas, there is a circulating notice board, a *kairanban*, which must be handed on to the next house in the circle as quickly as possible. In the nuclear families which have proliferated in the post-war years, there is usually only one person to carry out all these tasks: the housewife.

Undoubtedly the most pressing reason why, in a Japanese view, women should remain in or near their own home, however, is to care for the children they are automatically expected to have (see Lebra 1984:158). The task of rearing children is taken extremely seriously, particularly in the early years, and it is not thought to be a good idea to employ substitutes from outside the family to help out. Thus, where possible, a young woman with small children will try to devote herself full-time to this end. There are day nurseries in Japan. In fact, they are rather readily available, but this reflects the importance attached to the nurture of small children, and the recognition that not all families are able to afford a member to stay at home all day, and only incidentally the needs of the mothers who might prefer to go out to work.

In a popular view, the child is said to be a 'gift of the gods', and another oft-cited piece of popular wisdom is that 'the soul of the 3-year-old lasts till a hundred'. Thus all efforts made during these early years will pay off as the child grows up. Even before she gives birth, a pregnant woman should take particular care of the new being she carries, and a baby's needs should where possible be anticipated before it becomes distressed. Small children are taught how to accomplish the various tasks they must learn through patient demonstration and repetition, a principle which applies even to the most basic activities such as eating, washing and eliminating, elsewhere often left to children to pick up by themselves. The aim is to inculcate habits for life in the child's body, and these should be passed on as early as possible.

This task is taken so seriously that mothers with the time available will spend a good deal of it acquiring and reading all the available literature on the subject of childrearing, as well as watching television programmes and attending lectures. In a three-generation household, experience as well as physical help is always at hand, but for the housewife in a nuclear family, her mother and mother-in-law can usually only occasionally be called upon in this way. Here is another reason for housewives to consult one another, then, and informal groups tend to cluster around the local park, or shopping precinct.

Later, when the children start to attend kindergarten, as the vast majority do, mothers with the time available very often find themselves called upon to participate in PTA activities, as well as attending open days, called *sankanbi*, when they are invited to observe the progress of their children. They may also be called in from time to time to help with the care and upkeep of the kindergarten grounds, and this role is carried through to the primary school. It is customary for children daily to clean their classrooms, but mothers will be called in regularly to clean the areas they are unable to reach. The primary schools also tend to send home particularly the youngest children at varying times, sometimes as early as 1p.m., so that mothers find it difficult to be working away from home, and those who do must make special arrangements.

Many professional housewives become much more involved in the education of their children than this minimum participation, however, and the term 'education mama' has not been idly applied to them. The education system in Japan is the one chance for social mobility, and the main chance for the children of professional people to follow in the footsteps of their parents. Entry into a good university[9] is the main criterion for future employment, and entry into a good academic high school the best way to prepare for this. Until that point the education system is comprehensive, with school entry based on the catchment area, but there are various ways to gain an advantage, and this is where the 'education mama' may have a role to play.

In most cases Japanese children attend the state schools which are provided in the area where they live, and their mothers may at first help them to accomplish the homework which they are assigned right from the start, in their seventh year. In fact, the majority of children are able to read at least the phonetic script before they even enter school, although mothers of my acquaintance would sometimes brush off this ability by claiming that their children had learned 'naturally'. When pressed, however, they do admit to providing games which help the children to become familiar with the characters, and seeing that their children watch the television programmes which have the same aim.

Another way in which parents are able to help their children with their academic development is by enrolling them in classes after school, and a substantial number of children actually start these private classes before they even attend school. The availability of such classes, particularly in cities, is such that mothers may need to spend a good deal of time researching and investigating them, in order to choose the best course they feel their child should follow. Those who are most serious will ensure that their children have a good grasp, not only of the Japanese script, but also of mathematics, and possibly English and music, before they even enter the educational system proper.

In some areas there are private regular schools, too, and in others, certain of the state schools will have a particularly good reputation, so strategies may be devised to help a child even further. A popular example is for a child to be entered for one of the schools attached to the famous private universities. These are sometimes described as 'escalator' schools, because once entry is gained, there is a high chance that the child will move on through the system with little trouble, entering either the attached university or another of a similar standard. The problem then becomes gaining entry, in practice through the attached kindergarten, and each system has devised ways of selecting such young children.

Some places are simply allocated by lottery, others by testing the mothers themselves, but yet another group actually tests 3- and 4-year-old children, a system which spawns yet another series of classes to prepare children for the entrance test. Mothers who wish to adopt this strategy find themselves taking children as young as 1 year of age to classes to develop the skills they will need. A university graduate who had come through the system this way reported that her mother had felt the investment of time and money at this early stage would be well worth it in the long run, because once a place was secured, the school would take over much of the responsibility, and she would not need to work so hard.

This is a good argument, for much of the work of the 'education mama' is later concerned with finding out about good high schools and universities, helping the child to decide where best to apply, and generally being supportive in the years of study that the child will need to spend in order to fulfil the hopes and ambitions their parents project on them. Families with mothers who can help out in this way probably do allow a child greater chance of success in the educational rat race,[10] although there are also cases of over enthusiasm, where the child simply rebels altogether.

SOME SUPPORTING IDEOLOGY

In general, the nuclear family with a good income is the kind of family for whom education is particularly important in modern Japan. Continuing families, which pass a house through successive generations who share the family home,[11] are more likely to have their own occupation or business to pass on to their children, and this will usually occupy the women of the family as well as the men. Part of the duty of a mother may then be to pass on the skills required to her children, and the educational role of the wife of a man who works for a big company, or perhaps in a university or government office, may be seen as parallel to this more traditional role. An occupational group which is particularly noted for industry in this respect is the medical profession, for the investment in a small hospital or private clinic in one generation only pays off in the next, and entry to medical school in Japan is one of the toughest to gain.

Viewed in this way, the role of the 'professional' housewife nicely parallels the role of her very often 'professional' husband. In the ideology of the *ie*, the continuing Japanese household, each member is expected to share the tasks which need to be done for the overall benefit of the whole unit, putting its well-being before his or her own personal desires. In continuing families, most wives are still expected to contribute in whatever way they can. For families where the future of the next generation requires educational success, it is only logical that the mother should help out in whatever way she can, and, in practice, this is precisely what she does.

With this principle established, then, the role of the full-time housewife actually looks rather more traditional and Japanese than might at first have been thought, especially since the model appeared to have been influenced from Europe. Industrialization has required many more people than before to work away from home, and the problem of the consequent separation of work and domestic life has simply been solved in some cases by a division of labour along gender lines. In many ways the full-time housewife is carrying on single-handedly roles which are shared by two or three generations of both sexes in the continuing *ie*.

From a more official point of view, the role of the professional housewife has also suited government ideology at various times during the modern period. Reasons have varied depending on specific political issues, but the importance of the rearing of the next generation has never been in doubt. There is thus often an underlying assumption in public documents that there will be a mother (or other relative) in the home where there are children to be taken care of. As mentioned above, there are day nurseries, but these are for the sake of the children, and even their own headteachers will lament the fate of their charges, whom they think may be unable later to be successful parents themselves (Hendry 1986:31).

The government even helps out with the childrearing roles which are seen as so important. Under a programme designed by the Ministry of Health and Welfare, there are free check-ups for pregnant mothers, who are required to register with their local health centres. They receive a 'pocket-book' with advice about pregnancy, childbirth and upbringing, in which a record is kept of their own health, the birth, and the health of the child once it is born. Public health nurses and midwives carry out home visits during pregnancy and after the baby is born, persisting if the families are experiencing problems, when they may also be entitled to free milk. This governmental concern is not limited to those with special needs, however.

It also involves a nation-wide programme of Parent Education Guidance, subsidized by the Ministry of Education, comprising the distribution of information, lectures and classes. In Chiba prefecture, for example, the prefectural government issued postcards to mothers, timed to arrive at various stages of the child's development, which offered advice about the specific stage the child had reached. Checks on health and general progress were here also made at eighteen months and three years, apparently attended by 97–8 per cent of the families concerned. Others would be visited.

In Kyūshū, in the area of Fukuoka where I worked, talks and classes were arranged from time to time, and a lecture given by a visiting child psychologist was extremely well attended. These events were timed for the middle of the day, when working women would usually be otherwise engaged, but several of the young farming women of my own community were encouraged to take a day off to hear the lecture. The senior generations were available to help with children, and full of advice, but they did not deny the possible benefits of new information, and they felt the youngsters more suited than they to glean from this opportunity.

Large companies also implicitly support the idea of full-time housewives, expecting their female employees to leave work on marriage, or at least when they become pregnant. They may well be prepared to provide family housing for their male employees, but most provide only single accommodation for women. This also often differs from the same accommodation for men in that women are expected to work harder on domestic tasks such as washing and cleaning. Lo, for example, reports that dormitory accommodation at Brother Industries offers automatic washing machines, driers and janitorial cleaners for men, whereas the women are expected to do all these chores themselves (Lo 1990:57).

Furthermore, until recently, the expectations of availability of men in large companies, often until quite late in the evening, with regular more-or-less compulsory jaunts to local hostelries after that, precludes the possibility that they be much involved in domestic life. It is said that some men are beginning to rebel against this in recent years, and women who do manage to work on through marriage and childrearing may also be concerned to leave work at a more reasonable hour, so the system may be less severe than it used to be, but it has by no means disappeared.

In practice, there are still many housewives who themselves share an ideology in favour of their full-time employment in the home. Despite the complaints of feminists, who advocate an equal sharing of domestic tasks between men and women to allow the latter to go out to work on an equal footing with the former, there are many women who prefer to preserve the domestic sphere for themselves. There are also women who are happy to help out with the business of their husband and his family, perhaps where this is a family concern, but who claim they would hate the responsibility of running it themselves.

CONTROL AND STATUS

A glance at the everyday lives of some full-time housewives could give us a clue to this apparent tenacity of role. First of all, these women actually have a good deal of control over their lives.[12] Even, or perhaps especially, when their husbands work far away and therefore spend very little time in the home, their activities are often quite rewarding. The small children will, of course, take up most of the day in their early years, although their care is itself described as rewarding, and may anyway be shared with friends in a similar situation. As they move off into kindergarten, and subsequently school, mothers find they have more and more time to spend in other ways.

There are many possibilities, of course, and it is difficult to generalize, but the housewives I worked with in Chiba prefecture spent quite a large part of their lives attending classes. Some were related to housewifely roles, such as cooking, sewing and knitting, but another popular one at that time was tennis. The coaching took up a couple of hours a week, and there were other occasions when they would go out and practice, as well as the odd social occasion attached to the tennis milieu. The kindergarten many of the children attended, for example, held a tournament one Sunday. Since it included the participation of the headteacher, who had never played before, and the head of the PTA, who had only played once or twice, the emphasis was evidently on the social aspects of the afternoon.

Older women with time available may have activities which they take more seriously than this. Many of them may have moved by means of various classes to qualify to teach the same skills they were previously studying, and this will, of course, bring some income into the home. The traditional skills of flower arranging, the tea ceremony and the donning of kimono are still *de rigeur* for young girls preparing for marriage, who form a plentiful supply of regular pupils, and the best students will pursue their studies further.[13] Annual cultural festivals (*bunkazai*) provide opportunities for these afficionados to display their skills to one another, and to the world at large, and some become well known in a wider arena.

Similar opportunities are available for the development of a wide variety of other skills, including art forms and musical instruments, and most full-time housewives will find time for one or more of these activities. They are thus able to pursue personal skills and accomplishments to provide challenge and personal satisfaction beyond the more immediate roles of attending to the family, whether these roles add to the family income or not. These activities also offer opportunities for personal status within their own worlds, and as members of those worlds, to others in their neighbourly circles.

In fact, the status of full-time housewives is gained through several channels. First of all there is a general status accorded a family able to afford to keep a full-time housewife, made more specific depending on the actual occupation of the husband. This is particularly important in housing belonging to a company or other enterprise, such as the self-defence corps or the police. In this case, women will know very clearly which of their neighbours is married to a superior of their husbands, thereby requiring respect, and which are approximately equal or inferior, allowing less care. In outside accommodation, this kind of status may be associated with a company name, or the professional role of the husband.

Further status may be acquired through the achievements of children, another reason for the efforts made on their behalf. A generally-accepted idea that children are born rather malleable, and their behaviour and success determined in a large part by the way they are treated, puts a huge responsibility on the full-time mother and housewife, who can lay blame for shortcomings nowhere else but with herself. The progress of local children is a popular subject of conversation, in venues as public as the supermarket, so this kind of status – good or bad – is something which cannot easily be avoided.

Nevertheless, in the end, women who spend most of their time within the neighbourhood where they live have plenty of other opportunities to curry favour and status with their counterparts from other families. Their own personal skills have been mentioned, and their contribution to neighbourhood ventures may reflect these skills, but in the circles where I carried out my research, there was a wealth of other possibilities in the everyday life of these professional housewives. Just as people who work together come to know one another, women who have children close in age find themselves working together for the kindergarten bazaar, preparing together for the neighbourhood sports day, weeding the school garden. They share the tasks which form part of the duty of childrearing, and they learn to assess one another in the way any co-workers will.

THE HOUSEWIFE AND THE ECONOMY

From the perspective of an outsider, it is plain that a highly-valued housewifely role will have an effect on the wider economy of the society where it is found. It will, of course, keep the personnel of the housewives themselves out of the labour force, and, in providing someone to take complete care of domestic life, it allows the men who can afford these wives to spend as long at work as they are required. In the case of Japan, this is no nominal support, for men are so often expected to stay late at work that their wives worry if they fail to do so. From the point of view of an employer, then, this kind of availability is probably well worth the salary which can support a whole family. Such employees are evidently of higher value than those who need to rush home at 5p.m.

Small wonder, then, that companies have found ways to resist the principles of equal opportunity which are being advocated, by law, in the media, and undoubtedly amongst their female employees. In fact, many of the women in the Japanese work-force accept 'part-time' employment to ensure that they will be able to leave work at a fixed hour, and many of them work as long a day as their full-time counterparts in other countries.[14] As noted above, there is growing pressure for more reasonable expectations about working hours, and more time available to spend at home. A labour shortage current at the time of writing may help to improve conditions, but families with professional housewives are not doing very much to help this cause. Their contribution to the changing economy lies in a different sphere.

At the beginning of this paper it was mentioned that housewives often band together to form co-operative consumer groups which resist pressure to buy goods produced in ways harmful to the environment. One in particular achieved international recognition in 1989 when it was awarded the Right Livelihood Award, an alternative to the Nobel prize awarded in the Swedish parliament, 'to support those working on practical and exemplary solutions to the real problems facing us today'.[15] The Seikatsu Club Consumers' Co-operative was granted the award 'for creating an alternative economy based on co-operation, human contact and ecological sustainability'.[16]

This club grew out of a bulk purchase of milk in 1965, which was an effort, initially on the part of one housewife, to counteract continually rising prices over which the consumer seemed to have little control. The Seikatsu Club proper was formed in 1968, and since that time it has developed a list of some 400 products, but always with only one variety, selected to conform to its high standards. Where suitable goods were not available, the club has commissioned them, even on some occasions setting up its own means of production employing its own members. An example of this was the organization of facilities for producing organic milk, run with local dairy farmers, and agreements with organic agricultural co-operatives in Yamagata prefecture. The latter started with rice in 1972, expanded to vegetables and fruit, and now accounts for 30 per cent of the Club's total purchases.

The Seikatsu Club always emphasizes the direct link between consumer and producer. An advance ordering system operates to ensure freshness and eliminate waste. Members meet regularly in groups called *han* of six to thirteen families to order goods in bulk. Once a month they receive literature, pay for the previous month's supplies, and put in an order for the next month. A few deliveries are weekly, milk comes twice a week, but rice and other long-lasting goods arrive once a month. Club members see themselves not as customers, but as participants and joint owners of their own Co-op.

The underlying principles which support these activities include the creation of a self-managed life-style to replace the wasteful one they see as characterizing the capitalist market-oriented society. They advocate that the way to improve the quality of life is to have a 'simple but meaningful existence' and refuse the 'having-it-all illusion created by commercial products'.[17] To change the image of consumers as the 'mere target of sales activity', they seek to use their purchasing power (or non-purchasing power) to gain more control over production processes and their possibly harmful effects.

Apart from the supply of safe foods, their more specific ventures include the preservation of clean water by promoting the use of natural soap to replace the chemical variety, the active support of recycling programmes, and the development of workers' collectives to stimulate citizen participation in economic activities. With this last venture, members are able to invest and work in projects they support, rather than selling their 'part-time' services to larger enterprises of which they fundamentally disapprove. These include services such as the preparation of packed lunches, a home-help business, and a Mutual Benefit Fund which replaces the need for insurance as a product.

All these projects have been supported, and some made possible, by the substantial investments made in the club by members. Each household is expected to pay a smallish sum monthly, and their contribution is retrievable if they should pull out. These investments, in 1990 totalling nearly 10 billion yen, are used solely to further the aims of the club and no dividends are paid because profit is not the purpose of the investment. In fact, these principles are by no means new, they are the tried and tested ones of mutual benefit organizations which have existed all over Japan (and elsewhere) since the pre-modern period. The innovation is the application of the power of such a co-operative group within a complex society.

Finally, members of the Seikatsu Club have begun to enter active politics in order to extend their spheres of influence. The ups and downs of the movement to oppose the use of harmful detergents provided an experience which brought home the need for more active participation in the political process, and networks were formed to contest local elections. In 1990 there were thirty-three such councillors in the Chiba, Tokyo and Yokohama councils, all of them women, and all of them emphasizing the value of local participatory economics. In the future, the Seikatsu Club aims to contact every household in Japan with its slogan 'From Collective Buying to All of Life'.[18]

CONCLUSION

This chapter has tried to present a little of the flavour of the lives of Japan's 'professional' housewives, and to demonstrate the seriousness with which those women approach their role. This role is a far cry from the downtrodden image sometimes associated with housewives elsewhere. Indeed, they are in my experience rather privileged, and proud of the position they occupy. Most of them would, I think, be most reluctant to change places with their husbands. They enjoy the freedom they have to plan, organize and carry out their lives in their own time, a freedom many of their husbands lack.

The chapter has also touched on the direct implications for the wider economy of maintaining a profession of housewifely support, a profession which is seen to bring less tangible benefits to the economy in the high quality training such mothers are able to impart to their children. I have not been in a position to assess the extent of the impact that the environmentally-conscious consumer co-operative groups might be having – this would be an interesting subject for a future research project. Ironically, it is quite possible that many of the women who feel so strongly about the disadvantages of the capitalist world of big business may actually be married to men who make their living (and, of course, that of their wives) in precisely this way.

Another issue which has been touched on, although only in passing, is the relationship between the views and ideals of the women described here and those who are fighting for equality in the labour force. A common cry in recent years is that men should participate equally in the home so that women can go out to work on an equal footing with them. This would hardly seem to be compatible with the role of professional housewife, and co-operative consumer groups are a bone of particular contention since most of them appear to rely on women being at home with time to organize themselves for ordering, taking deliveries and so on. However, the ideals of at least the Seikatsu Club, which include 'the empowerment of women', equality with men, notably in political spheres, and the aim of employing its own members in the workers' collectives, does to some extent seem to counter the feminist objections.

It is important to bear in mind that equality is different from sameness, and women who are satisfied with their different spheres may still seek to be regarded as 'equal' to men. This I think is the important factor to remember in considering the place of the professional housewife in Japan. She is not regarded, by herself or by her family, as a second-rate citizen. She is regarded as playing a vital role in several ways, just as has been described above, and it seems that this is a role many women are, for the time being, happy to play. It must, however, be remembered that women who are able to play these roles are usually of a social class which is higher than average, and another important factor is that much of their role is simply that of helping to maintain this class distinction. This is an aspect of their role that Japanese 'professional housewives' share with women in many parts of the world.

NOTES

1 A good source for this graph, showing changes in Japan over the last thirty years, and making comparisons with western countries, is the *Josei no Dētabukku* (Inoue and Ehara 1991:91).

2 According to the *Japan Statistical Handbook* (1990) nearly 30 per cent of all women were classified in 1989 as 'mainly doing housework' (Table 3–1:71).

3 See also Uno's paper in this volume, especially references to the subject of *ryōsaikenbo*. The development of this ideology, and subsequent modifications, such as the suggestion of Masuda Giichi that the notion be replaced by *kensaijibo* (wise wife and affectionate mother) is summarized in Kamishima (1976).

4 For the use of this word in the context of the lives of Japanese women, I must acknowledge a debt to Dorinne Kondo (1990).

5 The full title for this federation of regional women's groups is *Zenkoku Chiiki Fujin Dantai Renraku Kyōgikai*, usually abbreviated to *Chifuren*.

6 For a detailed consideration of some aspects of this role, see my paper entitled 'The ritual of the revolving towel', in Jan van Bremen and D. P. Martinez (eds) *Ritual in Japan*, Routledge, forthcoming.

7 Lebra (1984:34) describes this expectation that women participate in the tasks of the household enterprise as 'an extension of her domestic assignment'.

8 Streams abound throughout most parts of Japan to carry away waste water, and in rural areas, to irrigate the paddy fields. The care of these streams in built-up areas is usually the responsibility of the surrounding residents, as is the care of minor roads and thoroughfares.

9 It is a feature of the Japanese education system that attendance at a university is enough to secure a place of employment. The degree result is usually of little importance, and the granting of a degree very often a formality. The university years are in fact regarded as a time of freedom and personal development.

10 Rohlen's research on high schools in Kobe found a very high correlation between educational achievement and socio-economic background, even to the extent of arguing that educational achievement was as good a measure as any of socio-economic class (Rohlen 1983:xx).

11 This arrangement of passing a house through successive generations who share the family home was the norm in Japan until the modern period, and continues to be practised in rural areas, especially where land is owned, and in family businesses. The concept of the *ie*, as

such a household is termed, includes a notion of continuity through time.

12 It is true that this control is often subject to men working away from home, and it would be severely restricted if those men spent more time in the home. Japanese women realize this, and some report that the divorce rate has recently increased among groups above the male retirement age.

13 Lebra (1984:234) suggests that if 'bridal training' becomes a profession, it is often because of circumstantial pressure, such as economic need, but she also describes a wealthy woman who taught such classes for years, feeling guilty 'about pursuing her own pleasure through teaching'.

14 See Kondo (1990), for example, for details.

15 This quotation is taken from the pamphlet issued by the Right Livelihood Award association in Great Britain.

16 Ibid.

17 Quotations from the English language literature distributed by the Seikatsu Club.

18 Figures and quotations from the Seikatsu Club English language literature.

REFERENCES

Hamabata, Matthews Masayuki (1990) *Crested Kimono: Power and Love in the Japanese Business Family*, Ithaca, NY and London, Cornell University Press.

Hendry, Joy (1986) *Becoming Japanese*, Manchester, Manchester University Press.

Hendry, Joy (forthcoming) 'The ritual of the revolving towel', in Jan van Bremen and D. P. Martinez (eds) *Ritual in Japan*, London, Routledge.

Imamura, Anne E. (1987) *Urban Japanese Housewives*, Honolulu, University of Hawaii Press.

Inoue, Teruko and Ehara Yumiko (1991) *Josei no Dētabukku*, Tokyo, Yūhikaku.

Kamishima Jirō (1976) *Ryōsaikenboshugi*, in Emori Itsuo, *Gendai no Esupuri: Nihon no Kekkon*, Tokyo, Shibundō.

Kondo, Dorinne (1990) *Crafting Selves: Power, Gender, and Discourses of Identity in a Japanese Workplace*, Chicago and London, University of Chicago Press.

Lebra, T. S. (1984) *Japanese Women: Constraint and Fulfilment*, Honolulu, Hawaii University Press.

Lo, Jeannie (1990) *Office Ladies, Factory Women: Life and Work at a Japanese Company*, Armonk, New York and London, Sharpe.

Rohlen, Thomas P. (1983) *Japan's High Schools*, Berkeley, CA, University of California Press.

Index